# Wine and Economics
## Transacting the Elixir of Life

Denton Marks

*Professor of Economics, University of Wisconsin-Whitewater, USA*

Edward **Elgar**
PUBLISHING

Cheltenham, UK • Northampton, MA, USA

Published by
Edward Elgar Publishing Limited
The Lypiatts
15 Lansdown Road
Cheltenham
Glos GL50 2JA
UK

Edward Elgar Publishing, Inc.
William Pratt House
9 Dewey Court
Northampton
Massachusetts 01060
USA

A catalogue record for this book
is available from the British Library

Library of Congress Control Number: 2014950743

This book is available electronically in the **Elgar**online
Economics subject collection
DOI 10.4337/9781849805971

ISBN 978 1 84980 294 9 (cased)
ISBN 978 1 84980 597 1 (eBook)

Typeset by Servis Filmsetting Ltd, Stockport, Cheshire
Printed and bound in Great Britain by T.J. International Ltd, Padstow

# Contents

# Figures

# Tables

# Preface and acknowledgments

A reasonable motivation for writing a book is answering the question to oneself and selected colleagues over time: "Why has no one written a book about that?" After asking for years, I started this book. Since the literature seems young (note the dates on most of the items in the Bibliography section) and somewhat unsettled, I have not been looking for a research survey directed at scholars entering or in the field. I also wanted something more cohesive than an edited volume of papers. My interest has been a discussion of some of the connections between wine and basic economics directed primarily at serious students of wine and economics, both formal and informal, and, to a lesser extent, economists seeing if something interesting is happening.

I came at this subject from unusual origins. Food was important, but wine culture was not in my background. Aside from recalling the rumor that our neighbor drank too much Four Roses, my clearest childhood memory of adults and alcohol is from an annual visit to a locally famous Italian restaurant: once I outgrew babysitters, my mother, sister, and I would join our best family friends, and the three parents would share one *fiasco* of Chianti with their wonderfully fragrant pasta while the four children watched with mild curiosity. The bottle was more interesting than its contents. Compared with some of my school friends, I was not interested in alcohol; and, while it was forbidden, I never thought of it as "forbidden fruit".

When I think of wine books that started in the author's childhood, Sergio Esposito's *Passion on the Vine* (2008) comes to mind. Mine does not.

My interest in wine economics arose from a variety of other sources. I grew up in a region with a strong culinary tradition that excluded wine—except perhaps dandelion wine—but mealtimes were important as was good cooking. The first time I heard someone say that "you eat with those you love", it was an epiphany. Mealtimes were the most consistently enjoyable events in my upbringing. The vision of the possibilities expanded many years later when a Banfi sales representative hosting a tasting noted how good wine could transfigure a meal of hamburgers.

My earliest memory of truly enjoying wine is sharing it during college with the parents of a friend. They seemed to love good food and wine and life. I had never eaten and drank so well in a family setting and seen older people seem to savor a meal so much.

Another early influence emerged as I left graduate school for my first faculty position in Vancouver. Knowing his interest in wine from sharing meals with visiting speakers in some of Trenton's good Italian restaurants, I asked my advisor Orley Ashenfelter if I should stock up on wine before moving to Canada: in addition to providing much of my technical training, Orley added some practical details for good living that my formal education had missed (e.g., warning me about the Canadian system of provincial beverage monopolies). He directed me to a wine shop outside Chicago that was both on my AAA Triptik and one of his favorites. I stocked up on deeply discounted '73 Bordeaux—a poor recent vintage at the time but still worth $5 a bottle for Classified Growths. Orley encouraged my interest (and subscribing to *Liquid Assets*) during my years in Vancouver and beyond. Collecting and studying wine were completely beyond my money and time budgets, but I had other sources and serious influences.

That was primarily my father-in-law. Bernard Hoeter was the wine columnist for the *Vancouver Sun* for several years when I was there. Through various means—primarily by investing heavily in relationships with other local wine aficionados that ranged from other postwar European immigrants to early Okanagan Valley wine pioneers—Bernard had developed a deep network of contacts, extensive access to wine sources, a respectable cellar for the time and place, and a strong local reputation. He had a wealth of wine knowledge from his hundreds of books, numerous magazine subscriptions, and extensive travels, many of which resulted from his wine journalism. While he rarely invited discussion of wine with me, he frequently shared knowledge, complete with pop quizzes after dinner. He patiently answered some of my naïve questions but, more importantly, helped me see how an interest in wine fed so many other interests such as travel, culture, and history.

Orley's advice was instrumental when we moved to Wisconsin and lived just up the Lake Michigan shoreline from two major wine auction operations in Chicago that Orley knew (Michael Davis and Chicago Wine). He also connected me to Bruce Kaiser of Butterfield and Butterfield wine auctions in San Francisco: having left Canada, it was now legal to fax bids to wine auctions and actually take delivery without paying punitive duties. Primarily through *Liquid Assets*, Orley taught the appeal of buying fine wine at auction during the 1990s. Through Orley, I learned that fine wine could be more affordable than I thought (at least in the early years of the US consignment auctions)—one of his themes not lost on economists. Aside from learning some of the technicalities of auctions and bidding, I learned many powerful lessons from my experience with wine auctions—for example: (1) when you are bidding with real money, do your homework; (2) doing your homework and seeing the results increases knowledge; (3) government regulation permeates wine markets (and alcoholic beverage markets more generally); and (4) the correlation between wine enjoyment and price is positive but weak, in part because quality is subjective.

Also, fine wine opens doors. After a successful bid at a Michael Davis auction in 1995, I took a bottle of '75 Ch. Ducru Beaucaillou to a fine dining restaurant in Madison, Wisconsin, for an anniversary dinner. For the first time in my life, a server and a maître'd served our table all evening—and I saw the connection that sharing a glass with a knowledgeable aficionado could create. More generally, wine can serve as a remarkable entrée. It seems that everyone wants to talk about wine, especially in international settings. Usually more exciting to discuss than the weather, it can provide a deep well of common interest, especially if one respects the varieties of past experience, information, and knowledge.

Wine economics was emerging as an area of research in the 1990s. After presenting a paper on wine auctions at a Vineyard Data Quantification Society (VDQS) conference in Macerata in 2005, I began to see numerous opportunities. While papers on wine economics had appeared in various journals earlier, the introduction of the _Journal of Wine Economics_ (JWE) in 2006 increased considerably both the opportunity to publish in and the visibility of the field.

One appeal of writing a book is that one has the opportunity to write a formal Acknowledgment, think about past influences and pivotal events, and thank at least some of those who have contributed to my interest. As my most durable influences, I would first thank Orley and Bernard. While providing different kinds of technical knowledge and encouragement that stoked my interest, I also saw through them a common influence of wine research and shared experience that is more difficult to measure or even identify—perhaps wine's mellowing influence and encouragement of conviviality.

While Orley is very much alive, Bernard died while I was writing this book. He knew I was writing it and encouraged it, and I think he would have been interested in seeing it.

More recently, I have others to thank. Karl Storchmann has been a leader in the development of the field and a good colleague for many years. He has been a tireless colleague as the chief organizer and cat herder of the American Association of Wine Economists (AAWE) and the Managing Editor of the JWE. He was the reason I had a fruitful visit to the University of Trier and the Mosel Valley during a sabbatical in 2009.

The other participants in the AAWE and VDQS conferences and, more recently, the Association of Wine Business Research (AWBR) over the last decade have contributed immeasurably to my intellectual development. If I start naming the stalwarts, then this section gets long, and I risk omitting someone important. The repeat attendees know who they are and can now know that the shared experience has enriched my professional and personal life.

My neighbor historian Philip Naylor of Marquette University has been particularly encouraging through his innate interest in good scholarship and finding and answering important questions. Another neighbor, economist Dennis Jesmok, has also been encouraging and invigorating during our animated conversations about everyday wine economics and the consumer's problem whether on the sidewalk or sharing a delicious feast (with complementary wine) from Janet Jesmok's *cuisine*. Though I have never met Professor James Thornton from Eastern Michigan University, it was helpful to learn of the publication of *his American Wine Economics* (2013) as the most comprehensive discussion of wine economics that I have seen. I learned much from his approach to the subject as well as the reviews of his book. I wonder why these first books on wine economics are coming from authors working in the vineyard-challenged Upper Midwest of the US. Perhaps, like the best vines, we do our best work when challenged by the environment.

I have enjoyed access to affordable housing near St. Emilion for the past dozen years through Professor Edward Clark, Emeritus of Royal Holloway, University of London. Ed and I met at conferences in the Czech Republic on the future of Central and Eastern Europe after the end of the Soviet era. A new chapter in our relationship opened when he and Mary-Anne invited Tessa and me to visit their new property in southwest France. Annual access to that *terroir* has had an unmistakable influence upon my interest in wine. Ed's neighbors, Philippe and Mylène Poivey, owners of Ch. Tour Montbrun, have provided invaluable knowledge and wisdom to me as they have shared their experience of operating a small French winery and allowed me on occasion to work with them in harvesting the grapes and making the wine, especially "Cuvée Denton (moelleux)" in 2009.

Various industry people have encouraged or inspired this work, perhaps without knowing it or inviting it—Rick Laev from Ray's Wines and Spirits in Milwaukee, Ray Denton from Binny's (Ivanhoe Castle—Chicago), Bruce Kaiser from Butterfield and Butterfield, and Michael Davis and John Hart from Michael Davis and Co.

The Department of Economics and the College of Business and Economics, especially fellow wine lover Dean Emeritus Chris Clements,

*Wine and economics*

at the University of Wisconsin-Whitewater have supported me by approving my course on the Economics of Alcoholic Beverages, various leaves of absence for writing, and travel to wine economics conferences. Conversations with beverage licensees and colleagues Professors David Bashaw and Russell Kashian have been helpful. I appreciate the cooperation from my home department, college, and university.

Moving this work from an idea to a published book has involved a number of important people from Edward Elgar Publishing Ltd. This would never have happened without the initial interest from Edward Elgar at the AAWE meetings in Reims and subsequent discussions with him, Joanne Betteridge and Alex Pettifer. Of those, Alex, Editorial Director and, for this volume, Commissioning Editor, has stayed with the project throughout, even allowing extra time for the initial submission when my employment and family responsibilities slowed my progress. After the initial submission, a number of professionals employed by or associated with Edward Elgar have gently but firmly held my hand as we walked (and sometimes sprinted) through the process of revising, editing, and polishing the text to get it into its current form. I am grateful for the help of Managing Editor Caroline Phillips, Copy Editor Sarah Cook, Deputy Managing Editor Jane Bayliss, Marketing Executive Sue Sharp, and especially Editorial Assistant Harry Fabian and Desk Editor Chloe Mitchell. I cannot know who was doing what behind the scenes on the other side—any omissions are certainly unintended—but most of the everyday handholding seemed to come from Chloe and Harry.

My wife Tessa has been a patient partner and a wonderful companion through a vast range of tastings, travels, blending and tasting experiments, and other wine adventures. She has been a constructive critic and constant supporter all along the way. While my mother Frances Marks shaped the almost-wineless childhood environment described earlier, her contributions include a lifelong dedication to education, critical thinking and communication, and the spirit that, I hope, shapes this work.

## ABOUT THE AUTHOR

Denton Marks has taught at the University of British Columbia, Simon Fraser University, and the University of Wisconsin-Whitewater with sabbatical teaching at the Technical University of Brno (Czech Republic), Umeå University (Sweden), and the University of Trier (Germany). He has published journal articles beyond wine economics in a variety of fields including labor economics, urban and housing economics, law and economics, transition economies, and the economics of higher education.

# 1. Introduction

A 2006 article in *Time* reported on the findings of a Harvard Medical School/National Institute on Aging research study of the effects of consuming resveratrol, a natural substance found in grape skins (Sayre 2006). While they gained weight, mice fed a high-calorie diet along with large doses of the substance lived longer and suffered fewer of the effects of overeating such as liver damage and diabetes. This led some wine lovers to conclude that, sure enough, wine could be the "elixir of life". The designation "elixir" here is particularly fitting as it captures both the potentially genuine health benefits of wine and the historic tendency to impute alchemic, even mystical properties to it.[1]

Consistent with the long tradition of such elixirs, subsequent investigation cast some doubt upon the designation (Semba et al. 2014).

The finding of life-enhancing qualities of wine is simply another in a long line of stories connecting wine and the human experience. The quip that "like a fine wine, I get more complex with age" might contain more wisdom than humor. More than one observer has noticed the remarkable similarities between the life of a wine and human life. The themes—and language—of conception, "pre-natal care", birth (and concern about infanticide), nurture, maturity, environmental quality, aging, decline, and death are prominent in both. The variety of outcomes that reflect origins, culture, chance occurrences, and different values is common to both. Both worlds are populated by a large variety of inhabitants reflecting hierarchies with large and densely populated lower rungs and increasingly rare and remarkable characteristics as we rise through them. Some of these hierarchies have many levels, some very few. They are typically culture-specific so that comparisons across cultures are challenging: we find differences at both the tops and the bottoms, but we cannot say that one hierarchy is superior to another. Tendencies toward homogeneity clash with determination to preserve differences.

Popular discussion of wine often involves economics: the aphorism "Life is too short to drink bad wine" is a statement about both time horizon and opportunity cost.

Also, just as economics strives to provide a comprehensive understanding of behavior, the seemingly timeless search for narcotics—something that provides "the power to banish care"—is full of economic content.

If we find enough similarity, then it should not be surprising that looking at the story of wine—past, present, and future—as economists provides a rich journey just as the analysis of human behavior from the economic perspective is rich and rewarding. Few products in the world enjoy such wide distribution and rich history and interest as wine. When one finds other examples such as cheese or bread, they are among the necessities of life at the core of various cultures' sustenance.

In this book, we examine various dimensions of transacting wine. As we shall see, economics provides a rich literature with many insightful—and sometimes surprising—applications to the market for wine. We touch upon the primary fields of economics from agricultural economics and international trade to public choice and econometrics and discuss their relevance to the market for wine. We emphasize how the basic principles of economics help us to understand better the market for wine, the variety of institutions that have arisen in that market, and the international differences in that market.

The organization of the material resembles that of many introductory economics books. We start with a discussion of the meaning of economics and the ubiquity of choice—the central theme of economics—in the world of wine. While our focus is market transactions, we note some alternative allocation mechanisms. We then present a discussion of the motivation to transact and review the economics of both the buying and selling decisions, including a note about the importance of models in economics. We then discuss markets in which wine-related trade occurs and the motivations of participants to adapt to and sometimes modify "free market" activities. Introduction of the political nature of these markets leads to a discussion of the varieties of government involvement in them. We then turn to two particularly challenging characteristics of wine markets—the challenge of knowing what is in the bottle and the wider importance of wine as a cultural good—and provide some concluding remarks.

In every chapter we provide not only a discussion of the basic economics of the topic but also reference to related recent research. The more technical material is based upon basic economics so the book should be accessible to anyone with even a limited background in the subject. The discussion draws upon basic microeconomic principles and develops these selectively. Those without that background can turn to one of many elementary texts to learn it, although they might find the thrust of much of the discussion accessible even without it.

The book is directed to those with a general interest in the topic but has applications to management. The managerial content appears in the topics we choose to emphasize, the illustrations, and the applications. One goal is to illuminate the relevance of sound economic reasoning to management rather than to provide a prescription for making money from wine. The breadth of coverage here should be useful not only to those in the industry looking for the guidance in critical thinking and problem solving that "thinking like an economist" can offer but also to those seeking an overview of the insights and issues economics highlights in this remarkable marketplace.

## A NOTE ON THE EVOLUTION OF WINE WRITING

As with any market, communication and education are central to understanding wine markets. Consider the evolution of wine writing. As Storchmann notes (2012), wine writing goes back thousands of years. As happens when we start recording information in any area, the early writings are descriptive—perhaps general tasting notes, reports of "wine tastings", and descriptions of winemaking that seemed successful and worth sharing. Wine reports and books have existed for at least centuries and probably proliferated apace with the invention of the printing press in the fifteenth century. By the time of the Third Edition of his popular *Wine Buyer's Guide* (1993), Robert M. Parker was including a discussion of wine writing in his introductory material and characterized popular wine writing prior to his introduction of his *Wine Advocate* newsletter in the late 1970s as largely romantic and promotional and lacking contributions that aimed for objective product analysis. Along with other publications like the *Wine Spectator* that began publishing about the same time, the publication of the *Wine Advocate* newsletter attempted to provide that, much in the spirit of consumer empowerment that was a movement of that era. Not surprisingly, the emergence of consumer-oriented journalism brought along the beginnings of the analysis of wine value: rather than simply discuss wine characteristics, we began to evaluate something akin to pleasure per dollar (like the "marginal utility per dollar" or additional enjoyment per dollar examined in the theory of the consumer). Rather than say simply that Wine A is good or Wine A is better than Wine B, we might say that Wine A is better value than Wine B in some sense: Wine B is not worth the extra money if what you want is enjoyment (versus status, rarity, etc.).

Technical material on wine production has existed for centuries, growing along with the fields of viticulture and enology—a literature on growing grapes and making wine that might parallel any horticultural literature on plant science and food processing. With their focus upon topics such as agronomy and production methods, these aspects of winemaking

are relatively scientific and amenable to rigorous analysis in the laboratory and field. One can argue that this technical expertise is generally
necessary but not sufficient for producing the best wine—which might be
closer to producing great art than the best strain of wheat. Studies of the
wine market beyond that have, until recently, tended to be less academic
because they were less amenable to rigorous analysis—sales, marketing,
consumer psychology.

The early work in wine economics attempted to apply rigorous analysis
to some of those later steps—although collecting data and applying sophisticated econometric techniques does not necessarily amount to rigorous
analysis of the wine market. In order to accomplish that—and actually
to define a field of wine economics distinct from consumer behavior or
agricultural economics or the economics of monopolistic competition—
requires that we identify unique characteristics of the market that set it
apart (e.g., like labor economics or public economics).

The discussion attempts to push the edges of what we know into what
we do not and would like to; later in the book, we concentrate upon topics
that we are only beginning to appreciate. For example, we consider the
question of whether it is possible to evaluate wine quality the way one
might evaluate the relative quality and value of automobiles—a question
related to neuroeconomics and philosophy. While the emergence of a
market for consumer information about wine has likely led to an overall
improvement in wine quality and value, it does not mean that consumers
are able to understand fully what they are buying.

Also, if wine has cultural content beyond the pleasure enjoyed by the
buyer, then markets might fail to value it appropriately and we ask what
more is needed to assess that cultural value and preserve enough of it—
something not thoroughly considered in the literature.

## NOTE

1. The print shown on the cover of this book comes from *Dell' elixir vitae* ("On the elixir
   of life" (1624)) whose subject is a beverage of distilled alcohol better known as "aqua
   vitae" (http://www.chemheritage.org/discover/collections/collection-items/rare-books/
   dell-elixir-vitae.aspx?image=2). Distilled beverages may have a longer life than many
   wines, but wine may be better for prolonging the good life—thus, the alteration found
   on the cover. Another more recent reference to wine as an elixir comes from the introductory narration to the "Vintage: Napa Valley 2012" television series from the Public
   Broadcasting Service (PBS) in the US: "It allows viewers to join the winemakers in the
   vineyards and on the crush pad as they coax from the earth one of life's true elixirs"
   (http://vintagetvseries.com/about-vintage).

# 2. The relevance of economics

## INTRODUCTION: THE UBIQUITY OF CHOICE

When most of us think of wine, our minds do not immediately jump to economics, especially if we have little or no background in the field. However, as the "science of choice", economic behavior permeates the world of wine. A variety of decision makers populate that sector of the global economy, and decision making is "choice making".

Why is the idea of choice integral to economics? All forms of life must deal with scarcity: they typically lack enough of many things to satisfy completely all that they want or to "make the most" of their opportunities, either now or in the future. Most of economics addresses this challenge from the perspective of humans—how we allocate our spending and our time, how we choose between spending and saving, how we allocate current spending for immediate versus future gratification—but the challenge is pervasive in nature. Animals act as if they make choices—for example, where to settle to economize on their costs of raising a family and finding food and water (see, for example, Alcock 2009). Plants act as if they make choices such as seeking maximum sunlight by turning their leaves toward the sun and developing roots in the direction of moisture (e.g., Chamovitz 2012). Even human instinctive behavior represents economic choice: if we decide to change our direction of movement by 90 degrees, we turn and walk forward in that direction rather than walking sideways so that we decrease our "metabolic cost" of movement in that direction by more than two-thirds (Handford and Srinivasan 2014). Of course, the underlying body of research here builds on Darwin's work—not only the classic *On the Origin of Species* (Darwin 1964) but also less known but important work such as *The Power of Movement in Plants* (Darwin and Darwin 2013). Nineteenth-century scholar Herbert Spencer—originator of the phrase "survival of the fittest"—was among the first to move Darwin's ideas into the realm of economics (e.g., *The Principles of Ethics*, Vol. 2, 1978).

If we face scarcity, then we must make choices. We cannot have everything. For example, most of us realize the importance of earning a living at some point and proceed to learn how to produce something that others will value. A popular approach to this historically has been to follow in the footsteps of one's parents or family and either learn "the family business" or learn a parent's trade: for centuries throughout the world, young people either failed to perceive a choice or, if they perceived it, felt that any alternative was not feasible. That model of finding a livelihood still dominates some traditional communities. More recently, especially in more industrialized economies with more developed educational systems, young people can choose among a variety of livelihoods and have used formal education as a path to a chosen line of work. That process invariably involves choosing one career path to the likely exclusion of many others: we cannot do everything.

A variety of decision makers—choice makers—populate the world of wine, and all of their decisions represent a potential topic to be discussed in wine economics. We illustrate this in what follows.

## PRODUCERS' CHOICES

In today's marketplace, we have wine because someone has chosen to become a farmer and, among the various crops s/he can grow, has chosen to be a vigneron—that is, to grow grapes and wine grapes in particular. Some farmers grow a wide variety of grapes, but the environment affects significantly the suitability of certain grapes to certain places. While wine grapes are grown in remarkably diverse environments and it is possible to make wine out of "common household items" (http://www.warpbreach. com/6/6.html), traditionally wine exists because farmers choose to grow wine grapes—and the best wines start with farmers growing wine grapes where they are best suited. One cannot grow everything profitably just anywhere.

Given the grapes most suited to their location, winemakers must choose the kind of wine to make. If local conditions allow a choice, do they choose grapes whose wine requires relatively immediate consumption (e.g., the gamay used to produce Beaujolais Nouveau or one of several such as azal for a Portuguese Vinho Verde), or do they choose grapes whose wine is potentially ageworthy (e.g., a cabernet sauvignon)? If they choose the latter, do they vinify to make the wine approachable early, or do they try to make a more ageworthy wine that might be less pleasant when young? Often, they cannot do both, given the local conditions, but sometimes they have a choice—or they might choose to re-locate to satisfy their grape-growing or winemaking objectives. If they produce an ageworthy wine, do they release the production all at once, or do they release tranches of it (often done with the Classified Growths of Bordeaux) since, unlike fresh produce, the wine will not suffer—and might benefit—from being stored properly and released in the future? A variety of conditions beyond the farmer's control can affect crop size and quality—weather in particular. The farmer might need to decide how much of a crop to allow to mature (versus "green harvest") and, once mature, how much to provide to different producers (including perhaps or certainly herself) and even how much to channel into non-wine use (e.g., brandy, industrial alcohol).

One of the more subtle choices in grape growing and wine production— the amount of water provided—determines the degree of "water stress" which affects grape characteristics and wine quality. Relative to many crops, the amount of water available to a grape vine can affect the quality of the fruit produced for wine in subtle ways (Robinson 1994: 1059). For example, up to a point, more water might increase the size of the crop and the corresponding yield of must and grape juice from a given set of vines but can dilute the color, tannins, and aroma extracted from the grape that are important for wine complexity and overall quality. Too little interferes with proper ripening and, of course, can kill the vine (des Gachons et al. 2005). Given the option, the farmer wants to choose an amount of moisture consistent with the market s/he hopes to serve—a larger quantity of lower quality wine or a smaller quantity of higher quality wine, though the link between stress and quality is not well understood—and, of course, would not choose a level of watering either way that would damage the vineyard.

In contrast, some communities outlaw this farmer's choice: some governments do not allow artificial watering (e.g., France). The farmer lives not in isolation but in several communities, perhaps by choice, perhaps not. For example, if we think of community in a legal sense like a jurisdiction, then s/he is nested in several communities—a commune within a département within a région within the country France within the European Union (EU) or a village within a county within a state within the United States. S/he might also be a member of a commercial community (e.g., the Conseil des Vins de Saint-Emilion or the Napa Valley Vintners community of winemakers making similar wines) or an ethnic community—in the case of wine, one with a strong tradition of producing a certain wine a certain way (e.g., Hungarian Tokaji). A persistent theme in the interface between the farmer and the community, often represented by a regulatory agency or a producers' association, is the extent to which the farmer is free to produce as s/he chooses or must instead abide by restrictions imposed by the various communities of which s/he is a part, either by law or by custom.

After harvest, the winemaker must choose the extent to which s/he sorts the grapes into potentially different quality wines or creates blends (if allowed) or chooses instead to produce a single vinification or even sells some of the grapes, or their juice, to other producers or for other uses (perhaps other producers' wines). S/he wants to avoid "diluting a brand", and sometimes regulations require this (e.g., France): they limit wine production per unit of land so any surplus must be sold (Mariani 2014) or somehow "declassified". Given the "laws" of demand and supply discussed in Chapters 4 and 5, simply producing and selling all that one can of a given crop or cuvée likely lowers prices which may both lower revenue and profit and tarnish the perceived quality of a wine to the extent that naïve consumers assume a direct correlation between quality and price and believe that "you get what you pay for" (more on this in Chapters 4 and 7). For marketing purposes, a producer may actually choose to process "too little" of a crop to reinforce the cachet of a rare wine (e.g., Smith 2014).

Intermediaries such as Cameron Hughes Wines in the US and From Vineyards Direct (FVD) in England have developed successful businesses from purchasing such surplus fine wine and discounting it significantly under another label (of course, hiding the identity of the original producer is crucial to avoid any hint to the consumer that they are perfect substitutes). The "mystery wine" series from Jon Rimmerman's Garagiste operation in Seattle is another example of a channel for disposing of surplus production.

In some appellations, the winemaker's choices are limited in a number of ways if s/he wants the wine to bear a certain name such as the name of the appellation in many "Old World" regions (e.g., Champagne)—for example, the grapes allowed, the minimum content of particular grapes in a blend, the origin of the grapes, the yields, the time required between vinification and release. The producer must choose whether to adhere to those rules because of the value of that designation or to disregard the rules and lose the designation because some alternative production seems likely to be more rewarding—or even risk prosecution for noncompliance. For example, with the expansion of the international wine market, producers are more aware of the choice between producing a traditional wine that adheres to the rules of its production and producing a wine that might be more appealing to the tastes of the global market but lacks traditional characteristics and composition and the corresponding designation. Tuscan winemakers have become more creative in producing "super Tuscans" which might contain a significant proportion of their traditional sangiovese along with other grapes but cannot be called "Chianti" or "Brunello" because they are not produced according to those sangiovese-based wines' appellations.

A more subtle problem might be deciding what to do with small quantities. Theoretically, every grape tastes different. More practically, one might have small batches of distinctively different wines, and one must choose how many different wines to bottle. If they are truly distinctive, then it might be worth the additional cost (e.g., different labels, extra advertising and promotion, cost of cleaning and re-setting equipment) to produce different bottlings: some wine consumers might value small batches of closely related but different wines highly, and claims of limited production ("only 100 cases produced!") appear regularly in advertisements for "collectable" wines. Data on small bottlings are difficult to find, at least in part because their production and sale are often accomplished through word of mouth and casual communication instead of conventional publicity (unless the producer feels that the benefit of increased demand justifies the cost of the related advertising and perhaps small-batch distribution).

One producer whose operation provides a glimpse of the idea is David Coffaro of Geyserville (Dry Creek Valley, Sonoma County), California. Coffaro produces potentially dozens of bottlings annually (primarily but not entirely from estate grapes). For example, he offers 36 bottlings for the 2012 vintage with production ranging from 23 to 343 cases. His production ranges from varietals to blends and, in this vintage, adds choices by offering wines that are the same except that part of a vinification was aged 10 months and part was aged 16 months (https://coffaro.com/shop/orderform.html).

Once a wine is ready, the producer must decide how much of the production to sell in bulk, if any, and how much to package. For the latter, s/he faces a range of packaging choices. Bottles? Boxes? Novelty (e.g., pottery, wineskin, the Volére "purse")? What sizes? How many of each size? One of the surprisingly complex choices that emerged in recent years is the choice of closure for bottles. While producers have closed wine bottles with corks for centuries, cork can introduce impurities into a wine—most notoriously, 2,4,6-trichloroanisole (TCA)—which can neutralize the desirable aroma and flavor of wine and leave it "corked", smelling and tasting musty and "dead". Taber (2007) has told the remarkable story of the development of wine corks and the effort to improve upon it with closures such as screwcaps and synthetic plugs. All the alternatives involve other disadvantages (e.g., cost, consumer acceptance), and the choice is probably not obvious—but the producer must choose.

The evolution and varieties of capsules (the covering usually found over the top of the wine bottle and closure) have not received the same scrutiny, but they represent another choice: use or not, metal or plastic or other synthetic, standardized or personalized to the producer or even the bottling.

Once packaged, how is it sold? At this point, the producer must have some idea of her target markets—the market for the traditional wines of her region if one exists, some new market that seems to appreciate a nontraditional wine if s/he has produced one, the domestic market, the international market. The prospect of selling outside one's own jurisdiction introduces a number of special concerns. A different jurisdiction means a different government. Exporting a product typically involves adjusting one or more characteristics of the product because another government is likely to view one's product differently from one's own, often for purely political reasons, and require modifications accordingly—often the disclosures on the label, perhaps other parts of packaging, perhaps the components or ingredients of the product, perhaps the amount of domestic content, and so forth.

If the product is a narcotic—in the pharmacological if not in the legal sense—then the government's interest increases considerably. First, narcotics have a potential impact upon public health which is inherently a concern of government. Second, the market conditions for narcotics are special—perhaps on the supply side but certainly on the demand side. The demand for narcotics tends to be relatively insensitive to price so these goods are particularly good sources of tax revenue because governments can impose taxes which tend to push up the price, but consumers are relatively willing to absorb the tax burden in order to purchase the good. Producers can expect that governments will tax their product, though the tax rate can differ considerably among jurisdictions.

Aside from the potential for different treatment of a product by two different governments within their jurisdictions, the fact of being a good exported from one jurisdiction to another attracts governments' attention per se. Some governments impose export controls, for example, hoping to capture domestic supply and decrease domestic price. More often, governments of importing jurisdictions raise the concern that the imported product may threaten the viability of a competing domestic industry in the importing country, and/or they see imports as a source of tax revenue since they can impose a special tax upon imports (tariff). The government in the importing country might want to protect its domestic industry with various barriers to entering the country—tariffs, limits on the quantity allowed to enter (quotas), and assorted non-tariff and non-quota barriers (e.g., inspections, quarantines, various adjustments in the product, supply channel requirements) whose intention is not to ensure the quality of the incoming product but to make it more difficult for the exporting producer(s) to compete with domestic producers.

Beyond the challenges of gaining access to the markets one targets, the producer faces other more standard commercial choices. Is it worth advertising and, if so, how? This begs the definition of advertising since it is self-evident that, if a producer wants to sell—to engage in transactions—then s/he must tell people. For wine, one might not even decide to become a "producer" until reactions from family and friends suggest that one's production might actually be commercially viable. Then advertising ranges from a posting on social media to a full, carefully planned long-term campaign through various media. Even strategies as basic as "word of mouth" require choices such as the strategic selection of which mouths to target.

One of the most challenging sets of choices is the determination of an advertising budget and, within that, the allocation to various advertising media. Given that the content of a wine bottle—particularly premium brands and fine wines—is largely unknown to the consumer, is it worth trying to earn recognition for the wine by entering it in competitions or submitting it to tastings by experts who write about wine? Otherwise, the consumer is left to believe the producer's own opinion which might appear less than objective. To what extent does one choose to advertise the wine in other ways—from inviting the public to "the factory" (often a particularly enjoyable experience among wine producers, but a costly one) to travelling with the wine among the various target markets to introduce it to vendors and consumers directly or at least sending free samples to potential buyers?

The rules of nature are largely beyond the control of vignerons and winemakers, and at any time technology and production choices are set. However, looking across the global wine industry, they might not take the market environment as given. They might want to create rules governing their businesses and can become involved in the public policies governing their industry. They appreciate the interdependence of their profitability with the profitability of their neighbors and competitors. For example, rather than simply choosing grapes and output targets as individual farmers, vignerons might seek government intervention to support industry profitability. A number of national governments set rules governing various aspects of local wine production and sales (e.g., output limits) whose focus is the economic performance of the industry, and various groups in the industry want to affect the choices of rules. Since wine is traded internationally, the health of the national industry depends also upon international competition, and governments seek to regulate that—sometimes through provisions in trade agreements and treaties, sometimes through super-national governments like the European Union (EU). Recognizing the policy environment that governs the market and the possibility of affecting that adds significantly to the choices facing market participants.

Beyond the local governments affecting one's production more directly, one may also want to influence the governments in one's target markets to make those markets more welcoming of the product—seeking to weaken or avoid any of the barriers to trade just described.

## CONSUMERS' CHOICES

Beyond producers' involvement in production choices and perhaps trying to influence public policy, consumers face choices, starting with the decision to choose wine as a beverage in the first place. Beyond that, we ask: Whether to buy a wine for immediate consumption or one worth laying down? For an ageworthy wine, whether to buy a case now or wait and see if the wine's price falls in the future? Of course, once the consumer focuses upon a particular type of wine, there are often scores of alternatives available within type. For example, in a major US city, one might find wine shops listing thousands of wines on sale in one location and thousands more available by special order. For example, Ray's Wine and Spirits, a small independent shop in Milwaukee, Wisconsin—a US metropolitan area of fewer than two million residents—carries "over 8,000 wines" and can order tens of thousands more at any given time. Its two major local competitors—who, unlike Ray's, have multiple locations—advertise similarly large selections.

Like producers, consumers might realize that the nature of their wine market is not limited to their current purchasing opportunities. Because of the particularly significant role government plays in the operation of this market, many consumers realize how government affects their choices— from the particularly high taxes imposed on alcoholic beverages to the number of vendors allowed to sell to consumers in various settings (e.g., wine shops, grocery stores, other retail outlets, restaurants, bars and pubs, government stores, etc.) and the rules governing their operations. They might try to influence those policies (e.g., supporting more relaxed rules for importing into the jurisdiction); and, to the extent possible, they might modify their choices to reduce the impact of such restrictions (e.g., favor shopping in jurisdictions with less government intervention, use domestic production—make wine at home rather than "importing" commercially made wine from a shop or producer).

## GOVERNMENTS' CHOICES

In discussing producers' and consumers' choices, we have already alluded to some of the choices governments make—trade policies that affect producers' access to markets, taxation, regulation of production decisions from the vineyard to the retail shop. Beyond decisions in the private market, governments—or its politicians and officials—must choose the extent to which they will intervene in private behavior. As the varieties of public policy over history indicate, the possibilities for public intervention in the private sector are seemingly endless. Since publicly controlled resources are also scarce, governments must decide where to put them. Their role consists of two broad activities: (1) developing the content of the public role and (2) enforcing any interventions that are chosen (taken to include imposing consequences upon those who do not cooperate with the public authority).

In contrast to the view that a clear and accepted view of the proper public role molds public policy and its enforcement—or that a few such views of the proper public role exist, and the majority decides which will prevail, at least in a democracy—the prevailing view of "the economics of politics" is that public policy is, in effect, a product of government that is bought and sold. The buyers are all those with an interest in influencing the rules governing any aspect of the particular commercial market— for example, various interest groups (e.g., vignerons, wineries, all those selling wine, consumers, temperance groups)—and the sellers are politicians and other officials who can produce and enforce the rules: this is a highly simplified version of the theory of public choice and rent-seeking (e.g., Buchanan, Tullock, and Tollison 1980).

Do we treat wine differently from other beverages? If so, do we regulate its price or its quantity—including the possibility of prohibition—or both? How much of the production process do we choose to regulate— permissible varieties, agricultural methods (e.g., irrigation allowed?), vinification (e.g., additives allowed?), packaging and labeling? Do we treat imported wine differently from domestic wine (e.g., tariffs, labels)? Do we treat it differently from other alcoholic beverages? From other narcotics? With public policy, the relevant scarcity is not that of limited raw materials or fixed technology or the scarcity of time. Instead, one form of intervention in the marketplace—whether promoting or deterring transactions— often precludes others, especially if one hopes to pursue some consistent public policy, so the scarcity is the nature of government intervention that can exist at any given time.

We could continue since decision making is choice making—in deciding, one selects one alternative over others—and all actors in this industry make an endless number of decisions. Scarcity is pervasive, the world of wine is necessarily full of choices, and such choices are all potentially the subject of economic scrutiny.

## HOW WE ALLOCATE: MARKETS AND ALTERNATIVES TO MARKETS

Because we never have enough of everything, choices must be made. Notice the introduction of the passive voice: choices must be made, but they might not be ours, and we need to consider some alternative choice-making or allocation or rationing mechanisms. Much of what we have just discussed suggests the existence of markets which are one of four mechanisms we discuss and the one where the individual's choices are likely the most important. We shall briefly consider three more, all of which also have some relevance to wine: Random, Queuing, and Authority. We shall say more, briefly for now, about market-based allocation—rationing through transactions of buying and selling based upon market-set prices—because it is relatively familiar to most of us, seems to be increasingly popular in the global economy, and is in fact an important mechanism not only in wine markets but also in various markets that influence wine markets (e.g., foreign exchange). Then we shall discuss the other, perhaps less familiar mechanisms to illustrate their importance to wine.

First, we can acknowledge that scarce resources will always be allocated somehow. At any given moment, the resources of a community—perhaps a family, perhaps a nation, perhaps the world—are allocated and being either used or, if possible, stored for future use or perhaps discarded. That allocation reflects the one or more mechanisms that currently operate, and their operation reflects some default mechanism such as a seemingly random allocation and/or one or more mechanisms that the community has adopted, perhaps through elected representatives, perhaps through deference to some authority such as a monarch, dictator, or body like a church or central committee.

With market-based allocation, we expect that resources gravitate toward their highest and best use through market transactions: in effect, they go to the highest bidder. The most familiar examples of this are markets we witness and perhaps experience regularly—retail transactions, hiring and firing in employment—although the "gravitating to highest and best use" might not be apparent. While they could have either sold their goods to others or not used resources to produce goods in the first place, farmers and perhaps food processors use scarce resources to bring food to market—the local grocer, for example—with the idea that their revenues will exceed their costs: the goods supplied have a higher value than the next best use of those resources so they are going to a higher and better use than that alternative. If there is truly no higher value, then the food supplied is the highest and best use. Market-based allocation provides valuable incentives both to produce what is most valued by buyers and employers and to produce that at the lowest cost, that is, most efficiently. On the other hand, one of the most persistent concerns about markets is the fairness of their allocation as suggested by characterizing it as "survival of the fittest". Markets reward some behaviors and punish others: if one disagrees with those treatments, then one might consider markets unfair.

Markets of different sizes and degrees of sophistication are pervasive around the world, though we should note at least four concerns about their efficiency. First, the market's capacity to perform well depends upon the quality and completeness of the information to the decision makers: "highest and best" assumes that both suppliers and buyers know all their alternatives as well as all the important information about the product itself. Ignorance and inaccuracies are always threats to the best market performance—other products available and their prices, missed or unknown or unreliable information about product characteristics, alternative technologies, availability of other supplies, and so forth. Information quality and completeness is particularly challenging in the wine market where significant production uncertainties like weather are so important, and product characteristics can change from year to year and are difficult to know and communicate.

Second, market valuations depend upon the size and distribution of purchasing power. We can imagine that some markets either do not exist or are "too small" because those to whom a product might be vitally important—perhaps literally life-saving—express no value in the marketplace because they have no purchasing power. We may have too little of a life-saving drug—or pharmaceutical companies may not even develop it in the first place—if those who value it cannot pay for it. Unlike healthcare or personal safety, wine is not a necessity so we are less concerned that some wine markets are missing or "too small" or "too large", but the role of the income distribution in the distribution of wine production is noteworthy. For example, the market for the wines of Central and Eastern European countries (CEEC) such as the Czech Republic and Slovakia is probably at a disadvantage because its consumers have relatively low incomes (cf. Chapter 8) while, at the other extreme, the markets for the wines of Bordeaux and Burgundy have been stimulated in recent years from their relative popularity with increasingly affluent Asian consumers, at least in part because of the status associated with being able to afford expensive wines.

The concern here is not market operation per se but the distribution of income or purchasing power influencing it, and it is not one that is easily addressed. "Perfect" markets respond to the preferences and purchasing power of interested consumers along with other influences. Assuming that we have no concerns about their preferences (e.g., they are well informed and rational), they will have access to products that "should" be readily available to all—healthcare, education, food, housing, legal representation, for example—*unless* they cannot afford them: they lack the purchasing power to express themselves "adequately" in the relevant markets. Clearly, these are value-laden judgments—normative questions for economists, not technical mistakes that can be corrected. Many economists have supported "correcting" the income distribution to address this problem, and a discussion of that and its alternatives (e.g., subsidizing purchases, providing benefits in kind) would take us to a large literature and far afield.

The more relevant application for us is not that consumers may not be able to buy enough wine or good enough wine. It is instead that, lacking "adequate" demand, the quality and size of wine production may be too small in cultures in which it is important. Like museums and orchestras, wine production may be a cultural good whose production should not be left entirely to market forces. Knowing what else should be done is not straightforward (see Chapter 8).

Third, the market's tendency to produce what consumers want at the lowest cost depends upon the degree of competition. In some markets, the issue is too few buyers: producers have limited selling opportunities and depend upon only a few or perhaps only one buyer. Amazon.com may have such monopsony power over book publishers. This can stunt the size and efficiency of the industry. A more familiar concern about the extent of competition is too few sellers in the presence of many buyers—the extreme case being monopoly or a single seller—which can also stunt the size and efficiency of the industry and reduce the benefits to consumers as the monopolist faces no competitive threat and might treat customers accordingly.

Several markets support wine—for example, the market for vineyards, the market for fruit, the wholesale market for wine, the retail market, and the market for policy. As we shall discuss in Chapter 5, one of the most important competitive issues is excess competition—so much that, aside from other market challenges, wine production has difficulty earning enough profit to survive.

Fourth, certain types of products and production present more challenges to the best market outcomes than others. Beyond information difficulties, markets tend to fail or under-perform under certain conditions. Left entirely to itself (no market-specific government regulation), the market's ability to move resources to their highest and best use can be complicated:

● By costs or benefits from either production or consumption that neither party to the transaction considers (e.g., benefits and/or costs from the transaction that are external to the buyers and sellers—like unrecognized pollution from production, e.g., fertilizer or pesticide runoff from a vineyard, or uncompensated spillover benefits from one resident's actions to her neighbors such as a popular winery attracting visitors who learn of and decide to patronize neighboring, less known wineries);

- By failing to trade adequately—or perhaps at all—goods that cannot easily depend upon the consumer paying something related to benefit received and which thus may be too limited or perhaps completely unavailable. For example, would market forces alone yield an efficient level of police and fire protection or national defense? Does an appellation's collective pride in its production and reputation provide enough incentive for it to develop its properties attractively, perhaps to attract tourists, or does it need an extra incentive to reflect that community benefit?; and
- By the existence of goods which may be overused because we cannot easily limit access or define property rights (e.g., roads, pastures, reputations).

Markets can work well, but they are not foolproof.

Even if we could banish the quirks and qualifications that complicate the operation of markets, we still could not expect markets to govern all allocation of goods and resources. Other allocation mechanisms dominate various parts of our lives. For example, while our knowledge and understanding of genetics has increased dramatically, the benefits and burdens allocated by our genetic inheritance often seem and sometimes are accidental: this allocation is *random*. These are not truly random since some regularities exist—for example, they run in families—but as of now we cannot do much to alter that inheritance. The benefits and burdens allocated by apparent accidents—from natural disasters to random discoveries—are difficult to manage. Some of the wine industry's performance reflects apparently random allocation—from weather events to the global distribution of *terroir* to the distribution of good winemaking genes. Statistical studies of wine production and pricing, for example, consistently relegate a considerable share of the variations they study to "random events". We try to learn about such occurrences and the processes producing them so that their allocation is not random, in part because truly random allocation forgoes potentially valuable incentives. More predictable events might provide opportunities for us to harness useful incentives.

For example, our ancestors might have believed that many conditions affecting the success of the hunt or agricultural production (e.g., weather, natural disasters like earthquakes, and the arrival of pests) were random. Perhaps the resulting sense of futility of controlling such conditions led them to believe that they were influenced by some higher being like "the gods" which gave them an incentive to please the gods—or for some to persuade the others of how the gods worked and manage behavior and incentives to their benefit through those stories (e.g., they understood the gods and could work with them in exchange for an offering). Among other things, the lack of success of, and abuses from, that system has provided incentives to develop the sciences that help us understand and, to some extent, manage these phenomena more scientifically by revealing nature's incentives for good management.

Against the idea of harnessing the process of allocation, some argue that the vicissitudes of nature are valuable to wine production—much like appreciating the variety of the human race instead of controlling production in a laboratory. While all major wine regions involve some level of government regulation in the process, the allowable degree of intervention with nature varies across regions—and, within that, allowable designations—because of different attitudes toward such manipulation. France has relatively restrictive rules about intervention (e.g., prohibition of irrigation); some have criticized the Australian wine industry as pursuing the "cultural depletion" of wine production in the pursuit of "clean wine" that involves excessive intervention (Aylward 2008: 376).

The allocation method that awards resources to those who "arrive first" is *queuing* which provides an incentive to get ahead of the crowd. We know that retailers sometimes offer goods "first come, first served" (FCFS)—"available to the first 100 customers" or "while supplies last". Other examples can be more significant such as the best land going to the first settlers or the first recipients of government permits to do business getting them for little or nothing (e.g., licenses to produce or sell alcoholic beverages) or of appellation designations when first created. FCFS allocation is not inherently efficient (for example, cost minimizing or net benefit maximizing) since the first arrivals might not place the highest value on a resource or put it to its most valuable use. Also the process of queuing can itself use valuable resources (e.g., the resources used to arrive first or to wait in line). However, when coupled with market-based allocation and related institutions such as the determination and protection of property rights, it can create valuable incentives (e.g., encourage discovery by granting property rights (e.g., land title, patents) to discoverers, explorers, and pioneers; allow reallocation to higher uses through secondary markets).

Finally, sometimes because of the concern about the fairness either of the market or of some other mechanism or because of a political interest in the allocation of resources, we relegate the allocation function to an *authority*—perhaps some level of government or various managers within an organization or perhaps the head of the family as a particularly familiar example. Those who own a resource or are responsible for its allocation turn to an authority to allocate when they want the allocation to go to the "right" people, to those who are "deserving" in contrast to market-based allocation where, conceptually, the voluntary, mutually beneficial transaction is the heart of the allocation mechanism. Some of the earliest examples of the delegation of allocation to an authority involve religion such as that noted earlier in the discussion of random allocation. While it is perhaps ironic as a second example, a more recent example of a similar idea is the adoption of communism which gives pervasive control of allocation to an authority.

Various authorities—especially governments and their branches and agencies—play central roles in the wine market. Some of them are created for the wine industry—grape marketing boards, appellation enforcement authorities, agricultural stations dedicated to vignerons—and some like legislatures and courts would exist anyway but take actions of central importance to the market, including determination of the rules of trade (e.g., rules governing imports and exports) and delegating authority to private organizations (e.g., determining who is allowed to produce, sell, or buy wine and the conditions governing those transactions).

While much of the discussion in this book focuses upon market-based allocation, discussion of the role of authority, especially through government, receives considerable attention, especially in Chapter 6.

## A SNAPSHOT OF THE RELEVANCE OF ECONOMICS

Professor Karl Storchmann has been one of the leaders of the community of wine economists. His research agenda has included wine research throughout his career, and he is the founding Managing Editor of the *Journal of Wine Economics*. In a recent paper entitled simply "Wine Economics" (2012), he has provided a useful discussion of many of the areas of research that demonstrate the relevance of economics to wine markets. He focuses upon three which he considers the "major research topics" of wine economics: finance, climate change, and expert opinion. He adds that an econometric relationship developed by another leading wine economist, Professor Orley Ashenfelter, "contains the main seeds of wine economics" (p. 9) and these research topics. The equation presents a quantitative relationship between the (natural logarithm of) London auction prices of red Bordeaux wine and two wine characteristics: its age and the weather conditions when its grapes were harvested. (While the relationship is for red Bordeaux, many would argue that these are two key determinants of value for the majority of fine wines.) The relationship reflects (a) a key relationship of finance to wine markets by suggesting the annual return to wine as an investment (estimated at 2.4 percent for each year of age); (b) the importance of the allocation of weather to wine markets by measuring the significant positive effect upon wine values of higher temperatures (within limits) during the growing season but not particularly during harvest, less rainfall in the month before harvest, and more rainfall in the months preceding the growing season (October–March); and perhaps the relatively minor importance of expert opinion since age and weather variations account for over 80 percent of the variation in value in Ashenfelter's sample with all other influences, including expert opinion, accounting for the rest.

We shall note that it is easier to agree with this characterization of the major research topics as being finance, climate, and expertise if we focus upon wine value—the focus of Ashenfelter's equation—than if we expand the discussion of wine economics to include topics such as regulation of the industry and the importance of wine as a cultural good that appear later in this volume.

What is the relevance of wine to finance? A small proportion of wine production is "investment grade" because, like all financial assets, it is durable and is designed to improve with age up to a point. Since wine is a durable good and ownership can be bought and sold, people can use it as an investment just like any other investment instrument. Some argue that wine's investment value is enhanced because, unlike many assets, it can be consumed and enjoyed. Storchmann's review of this literature focuses upon the evidence of the performance of the asset class rather than a conceptual analysis of asset characteristics, unique risks, etc. Also he does not consider the relative value of financial assets related to the wine industry (e.g., share prices of corporations such as Constellation Brands, Inc., involved heavily in the wine market).

The prospect of significant climate change generates a wide range of research questions in economics—from the economics of pollution which considers human contributions to climate change and their costs, possible benefits, and the distribution thereof to the development of policies to manage polluting behavior. Like other economic phenomena, polluting behavior represents a choice, and one of the most widely accepted roles of government is to manage the circumstances under which those choices are made—for example, identify and enforce the ownership of private and public property and the rights that flow from that. Since weather is such an integral part of the wine production process—and "climate is the description of the long-term pattern of weather in a particular area" (http://www.nasa.gov/mission_pages/noaa-n/climate/climate_weather.html), patterns of climate change are obviously important to the performance of wine markets. Storchmann's discussion of climate change and the wine market begins by observing that some of the earliest writing on wine discusses the sensitivity of grape quality to vintage weather. Also, some of the most significant early work in modern wine economics emerged from Ashenfelter's pioneering research which studied the role of weather in affecting the price of Bordeaux wines.

Storchmann's discussion does not pronounce on the existence of climate change but, instead, considers the impact upon the global wine market if climate change develops. Because primary effects include increases in temperatures and changes in precipitation around the world, a general effect is a redistribution of vineyard growing patterns (e.g., the warming of cooler climates changes the varietals to which they are best suited (for example, the increased production and quality of pinot noir (or spätburgunder) in Germany) and would decrease and potentially eliminate the suitability of existing regions to grow their traditional varietals).

Finally, economists study few markets other than wine where the role of imperfect knowledge is more significant. Its importance is comparable in related markets such as fine art and antiques. Since knowledge matters so much to good decision making, Storchmann discusses the role of a popular source of wine information in affecting wine prices—namely, tasting notes and ratings from wine experts. While it is often the best third-party information we have about wine quality, its value—including its value in predicting wine prices—is limited. Because of the significance of this topic, we devote Chapter 7 to discussing it further.

## CONCLUDING THOUGHTS

Presenting material of this scope requires selectivity and coverage at varying depths. This book is not encyclopedic in its coverage of the breadth and depth of wine economics: some topics are either missing or treated briefly just as Storchmann's survey excludes some topics. No treatment of a subject of this breadth is comprehensive and immutable, especially in a young field. While the discussion assumes very little prior technical knowledge of economics, it is probably easier to grasp if one has that. However, the ubiquity of the role of choice and related tradeoffs in the world of wine becomes obvious as one studies the chapters that follow.

# 3. Comparative advantage and why we transact

## INTRODUCTION

One focus of this book and one of the fundamental ideas in economics is the motivation to transact—our propensity to turn to others to supply our needs and wants rather than attempting to supply them ourselves. Many of the choices described in Chapter 2 involve transactions with others. Given that meaning, the concept of transaction transcends economics and has been applied in other fields such as Transactional Analysis in psychology (e.g., Lapworth and Sills 2011) and the variety of exchanges that occur within personal relationships. One could argue that the logic that steers us to transact with others in commercial relationships applies as well to the costs and benefits considered in our personal relationships.

The economic theory of *comparative advantage* predicts that trade, or transacting, occurs when the costs of producing goods internally (or domestically)—in effect, doing it ourselves—is different from the costs of external production. We want goods and perhaps can even produce everything we want ourselves, but it might be better—indeed, mutually beneficial—to trade with others if they can make it at lower cost. This logic applies in a variety of significant contexts. Ricardo's original application is the mix of products that different economies produce and in which they specialize and their corresponding patterns of imports and exports as they buy internationally to address domestic shortages and sell internationally from domestic surpluses. Other applications flow from the same logic when we realize that the "producers" in the original application need not be countries and potential international trading partners: for example, they might be firms, sub-units within a firm, and even households and individuals. Thus, the idea illuminates the firm's decision to produce in house or to outsource and a household's similar decision about producing "in house" literally—"doing it yourself"—or purchasing from an outsider. Put simply to help us understand the motivation to transact, if others can produce a good for less than it costs us to do it ourselves, then we might be better off buying the good from them rather than producing it ourselves. Similarly, they will want to sell to us if, when we consider our cost of doing it ourselves, we can pay less than that to an outsider but still cover, perhaps amply, their cost of production.

Given these contexts, one can imagine a host of applications to the wine market—patterns of wine imports and exports both international and intranational, a winery's choice to keep a variety of activities in house (e.g., vineyard acquisition and management to winemaking and bottling to sales and distribution) or to outsource, and even a consumer's decision to purchase wine or make wine herself. The idea of opportunity cost at the heart of the comparative advantage model also illuminates a related variety of applications such as a firm's decision about its most profitable product mix, a vigneron's allocation of vineyard to different varietals, and a retailer's allocation of shelf space to wine and non-wine products or among different wines. We shall explore some of these applications below.

## THE BASIC MODEL OF TRADE

A relatively simple example of this trading model involves two countries which produce initially only for domestic consumption and consume only domestic production but might find trade mutually beneficial. Imagine that, given its productive resources, France can produce either 2,000 gallons of wine or 400 trucks. The US can produce either 1,200 gallons of wine or 600 trucks. To keep the example simple, we want to make several assumptions: (a) production in either country can move between wine and truck production freely so that, in effect, France forgoes five gallons of wine for every truck it produces (or 0.2 trucks for every gallon of wine produced), and the US forgoes two gallons of wine for every truck it produces (or 0.5 trucks for every gallon of wine); (b) the goods produced are the same and perfectly substitutable (a strong assumption when discussing trucks and wine from the US and France)—only the location of production differs; (c) all trade is barter—goods for goods—and (d) transportation is free. These assumptions are obviously unrealistic in the context of international trade, but they allow us to focus upon the core logic of the analysis. Moreover, analogous assumptions are more realistic for some of our other applications of the analysis.

Assume further that each country wants to consume some of each good and that, initially, each is devoting half of its resources to each good. Thus, France is producing 1,000 gallons of wine and 200 trucks, and the US is producing 600 gallons of wine and 300 trucks.

Table 3.1 indicates each country's capacity to produce each good and its initial output mix which is also its initial consumption. Table 3.2 indicates the cost of each unit of each good in terms of forgone units of the other

*Table 3.1    Output capacity for France and the US*

|                                                              | France      | US      |
| ------------------------------------------------------------ | ----------- | ------- |
| Maximum output: Wine                                         | 2,000       | 1,200   |
| Maximum output: Trucks                                       | 400         | 600     |
| Nontrade output mix (Wine/Trucks) (equals domestic consumption) | 1,000/200   | 600/300 |

*Table 3.2    Output opportunity costs for France and the US*

| Opportunity Cost (in terms of the other) | France | US  |
| ---------------------------------------- | ------ | --- |
| Wine cost of one Truck                   | 5      | 2   |
| Truck cost of one Wine                   | 0.2    | 0.5 |

good—that is, the opportunity cost of producing one unit of a good in terms of forgone units of the other good. Notice that, in terms of capacity to produce either good, neither economy seems to be larger: France is a larger economy if only wine is produced, but the US is a larger economy if only trucks are produced. Typically, we compare the size of economies by looking at the total value of the goods they produce, but we are omitting prices from this discussion for now.

Neither economy is larger, but we see that France forgoes more wine per truck when it produces trucks, and the US forgoes more trucks per wine when it produces wine. Herein lies the basis for gains from trade.

One lesson from this analysis is the reciprocal nature of these trade advantages. Production conditions in France are such that its sacrifice of trucks to produce wine is smaller (0.2 trucks per unit of wine versus 0.5 for the US): it is relatively "easy"—less costly—for France to produce wine, or it does not forgo as many trucks when it makes wine. It must follow, then, that if France decides to produce trucks, it does not get as much truck when it forgoes a gallon of wine, and it must forgo relatively more gallons (than the US in our example) to produce a truck. It is relatively "difficult"—more costly—for France to produce trucks. By comparison, the US forgoes relatively more trucks to produce wine; if it forgoes a gallon of wine, it gets more truck production than France. As long as we find such differences in costs, the trade advantages will always be reciprocal: one trader will have a cost advantage in one good, and the other must have an advantage in the other.

Since France forgoes more wine per truck (five) when it produces its own trucks, it realizes from its information about US wine and truck production that it might gain from trade with the US by buying its trucks if it can "pay" the US fewer than five wines for a truck. This should get the attention of the US since it forgoes two wines per truck and should be willing to produce extra trucks for export to France if France's only alternative is domestic production, and it is interested at any cost per truck less than five wines.

The mutual interest of the two countries arises from the cost differential. When they consider the prospect of buying and selling trucks, France and the US see the potential for mutually beneficial trade. France is interested in any trucks that cost less than the five wines it must forgo to produce its own trucks, and the US is interested in producing extra trucks for any customer willing to pay more than its two-wine cost. Moreover, within this range, there is no magic number of wines per truck that the two potential trading partners must discover. Any price of trucks between two wines and five wines appeals to both parties: if France can import trucks for less than five wines, then it is forgoing less wine per truck than its domestic production would require so it has more wine; and if the US can produce extra trucks and export them for more than its two-wine cost, it also has more wine. An unlimited number of prices work here.

Careful consideration reveals that we already have the basic logic of any motivation to transact: the buyer is willing to buy if the cost is smaller than the cost of doing it oneself, and the seller is willing to sell as long as the buyer's offer more than covers her cost. Myriad additional considerations bear upon the logic of a particular transaction—for example, the buyer finding the lowest price among those available and the seller finding the highest price among those offered—but this logic is the heart of the decision to transact.

Consider the impact of the two countries settling upon a price of four wines per truck. First, this appeals to both. If France imports only one truck instead of producing it, it has one more gallon of wine: it can produce five more wines but needs only four to pay the US for the truck. If the US produces one extra truck to export to France, it must forgo two wines, but it receives four wines in payment so it is ahead by two gallons of wine. If, instead, France decides to import 100 of its desired 200 trucks at the four-wine price, then it is ahead by 100 gallons of wine; and, by the same logic, the US is ahead by 200 gallons of wine. Compared with their original production for domestic consumption only, a 100-truck trade means that France still has 200 trucks but 1,100 gallons of wine; and the US still has 300 trucks but 800 gallons of wine. It is as if we have created something from nothing, but actually we have only altered the locus of production so that the lower cost producer is doing more of the production.

We can also see why the logic of comparative advantage provides an incentive to specialize in what one does relatively well. Indeed, in this simple model, both countries have an incentive to move production entirely to the good in which they have a comparative advantage, export any surplus beyond domestic demand, and import the other goods desired by the domestic economy. In our example, that would mean that France would produce only wine, and the US would produce only trucks.

With complete specialization, how do they get back to the mix of domestic consumption that they had? If we assume the price of four wines per truck, then France with 2,000 gallons can import its original 200 trucks for 800 gallons and still have 1,200 gallons left over: it is 200 gallons better off. Alternatively, it could use some of those extra gallons and import some extra trucks and have more of both wine and trucks relative to its original no-trade production for domestic consumption.

The US could produce only trucks—600 of them—and export 150 of them in exchange for its original quantity of 600 gallons of wine, thus having 150 extra trucks for consumption in addition to the 300 it was consuming originally. Alternatively, it could export more trucks and have more of both wine and trucks relative to its original no-trade production.

One might wonder what would happen if the US decided that it wanted to trade all 600 of its trucks for wine. At the price of four gallons per truck, France could not satisfy that demand for 2,400 gallons since it can produce only 2,000 gallons. We then need to make a simple amendment to our model that also makes it more realistic: allow for many countries willing to trade at the price—perhaps similar to the US and France—so that importers and exporters can trade all they want at the world price. Indeed, international markets often involve many importing and many exporting countries for the goods being traded. In our example, we would simply need "one more France" if the US wanted all wine and no trucks.

What happens if the parties agree upon a different price and what influences the price they choose? Perhaps it is easier now to see why any price within the range of two to five wines per truck appeals to both parties, though neither is indifferent to which price is chosen within the range. Consider the impact of choosing the price of three wines per truck. Now France saves two wines per truck by importing. The US receives less wine per truck but still more than its cost.

At three wines per truck, France could buy its 200 trucks for 600 gallons and have 1,400 gallons left over or buy more trucks and still have more wine. Specializing and producing only trucks, the US would now need to export 200 trucks to get its 600 gallons so it would have only 100 extra trucks—or some mix of extra trucks and extra wine. Not surprisingly, the lower price of trucks, while still mutually beneficial relative to no trade, expands France's options and decreases those of the US: lower mutually beneficial prices are better for buyers/importers and worse for sellers/ exporters and vice versa for higher prices.

The barter price that we have been discussing is sometimes called the *terms of trade*. The particular terms obviously matter to the parties involved with sellers wanting them higher and buyers wanting them lower. Then what determines the terms of trade other than the boundaries that we have noted, namely, the seller's cost of production and the buyer's cost of doing it herself? Like any price, a variety of factors can have an impact, but one operative principle is bargaining power. The price will tend to be higher when the sellers have more bargaining power—for example, when many buyers want to buy from a single seller which is the industry structure we know as monopoly. In this case in principle, all the buyers would still be willing to buy if the price were just below their cost of domestic production. At the other extreme, the price will tend to be lower when many sellers want to sell to a single buyer—an industry structure called monopsony—to the point where the buyer could offer to pay just a bit more than the sellers' cost of production. Compared with either of these extremes, if the same market has many buyers and many sellers, then generally we would expect the price to be somewhere between the extremes.

Such characterizations of the number of buyers and sellers beg the question of the definition of the market. The more narrowly we define the product, the more likely we are to define a market in which there is a single seller (or buyer)—for example, the newest vintage of a small-production wine that is sold only to members of the winery's mailing list. Among the variety of markets related to wine, it is more difficult to find familiar examples of many sellers trying to sell to one buyer, although we hear of buyers with considerable bargaining power such as retail chains that buy all the production of some wineries or are the largest wholesale purchaser of wine in a major market (e.g., the Costco chain of "warehouse stores" in the US that might be its largest wine retailer, government monopolies as in Sweden or the Canadian provinces). By contrast, in the competitive global wine market, thousands of producers want to transact "wine" with millions of consumers. Of course, outside of retail, the transactions actually occur between many and varied sellers (e.g., producers and exporters) and many and varied buyers (e.g., distributors and importers).

In a simple story involving trucks and wine, there is no substitutability in consumption between the products. If we think about actual international trade in wine and vehicles, however, we realize that the breadth of the market depends upon how narrowly or broadly we define the product so that the bargaining power of buyers and sellers will depend upon their willingness to substitute.

Of course, dropping our simplifying assumptions to allow for complications such as costs of transportation, search, and trade-driven adjustments of industry complicates the analysis, but the logic of the motivation to trade is compelling.

By the way, we can consider the mirror image of this trading arrangement. We have just seen the logic of France importing and the US exporting trucks at a price of, say, four gallons per truck. However, this is not different from the US importing and France exporting wine at a price of 0.25 trucks per wine. We could perform the analysis the same way but treat wine as the traded good and, in that context, reverse the exporter and importer labels of France and the US.

Aside from the general appeal of this analysis as an explanation of international trade, we can see applications to wine markets. A variety of factors affect the domestic tradeoff between two products—the opportunity cost of producing one good instead of another. When we compare countries like France and Sweden, we can understand why France is a relatively low-cost producer of certain wines, and Sweden is a relatively low-cost producer of certain precision equipment (https://www.cia.gov/library/publications/the-world-factbook/geos/sw.html). It is more efficient for France to export wine and import equipment (and vice versa for Sweden) than for either to depend entirely upon domestic production.[1]

## THE ANALYSIS WITH MONEY PRICES

Illustrating trade as barter simplifies our story but overlooks the important roles of money, money prices, and currency exchange rates in the global economy and wine markets in particular. While all are topics too vast to explore thoroughly here, one can begin to appreciate their importance with a brief discussion of their relevance.

Adding money to the story means that we can talk about buying and selling trucks and wine with money prices. Given the variety of goods available globally, transacting with money facilitates the process considerably because it avoids the problem of "the double coincidence of wants": barter is mutually beneficial only when the buyer and seller want each other's goods at the same time. In our story, this required the assumption that the two countries' goods were interchangeable and, implicitly, that consumption was current: each was as satisfied with an import as with its domestic alternative. When money is accepted as a *medium of exchange*, buyers and sellers who lack the double coincidence—for example, the buyer lacks something the seller wants—can still transact goods (to the buyer) for money (to the seller) which can then be used for some subsequent transaction when the seller wants to buy something from another seller who accepts money. One can see how the availability of money facilitates transactions as long as the money is widely trusted and accepted.[2]

We can add money prices to the story by assuming a global currency (call them "douros" (DS)) and a price for one of the goods: say, the price of wine in France is 100 DS. An equilibrium price for trucks in France in the absence of trade would then be 500 DS (since the production tradeoff of wines per truck in France is five, the equilibrium prices of each would need to reflect that tradeoff). With a global currency, the wine price in the US would also need to be 100 DS, and the US price of trucks would be 200 DS, reflecting the US domestic tradeoff. France would see the value of buying trucks from the US, offering something between 200 and 500 DS per truck—something between its domestic price and the US domestic price which would perhaps increase. For example, offering 400 DS would be like offering four wines as in our barter story.

Once we introduce money into the trading environment, the next step is to allow different monies—or different currencies—such as US dollars (USD) and French euros (EUR). While the sources of different currencies have changed throughout history (e.g., tribes, banks, companies, online (Bitcoin)), their importance in modern wine markets arises largely from international trade. It is likely self-evident that a significant share of global wine production is traded across national boundaries. More specifically, most of the major wine-producing regions in the world export a large proportion of their production: in 2009, Italy and Spain exported about 40 percent of their production, and New World producers such as Chile and Australia exported closer to two-thirds of their production (Anderson and Nelgen 2014, Table 51). Unless they are trading with countries using the same currency (e.g., within the Eurozone), then part of the import–export transaction involves an exchange of currencies, and changes in exchange rates can have as much or more influence upon wine prices to the consumer as any other market influence.

The importance of exchange rates in international transactions is that the currency available to the buyer might not be the same as the currency required by the seller. A US consumer whose purchasing power is in USD cannot use dollars to buy wine from a French chateau which needs its local currency to pay both its expenses and the income of its owners: the French producer requires payment in the currency it can use in France. Assume, for example, that the French producer sells its wine for €200 per case, and the USD-per-EUR exchange rate is 2—that is, €1 costs $2. Then the USD price of the case is $400. If the exchange rate of USD-per-EUR changed from 2 to 1, then the chateau would sell its case for the same €200, but it would be half-price to the US consumer—$200 instead of $400. One can see how fluctuations in exchange rates can have a significant effect upon prices and costs.

If this were simply two names for the same currency, then exchange rates would not fluctuate, and the existence of different currencies would be difficult to understand on grounds other than, perhaps, national pride. However, currencies are different and are traded just like other goods. For example, for a given supply of a currency (e.g., EUR), an increase in demand for it by those holding some other currency (e.g., USD) will increase how much they must pay for it. If the great wine regions of Western Europe had a widespread "vintage of the century", then US consumers wanting that wine would need to buy EUR with their USD in order to buy the European wines. While the vicissitudes of wine markets are typically not important enough in international trade to influence exchange rates, if the increased demand were great enough, then US consumers would find themselves having to pay more USD per case—perhaps because the EUR price was rising because of increased demand but also because, for a given EUR price, the USD-per-EUR rate was rising.

Say the initial price of the case is €200, and the initial USD-per-EUR exchange rate is 2 (so the initial USD price of the case is $400). If increased demand for the wine pushes the price in Europe to €300 and the increased demand for EUR pushes the exchange rate to 2.5, then the final price to the US consumer rises from $400 to $750 (= €300 × $2.50/€).

Of course, this discussion begs the question of the need for different currencies. Clearly, the existence of different currencies increases the riskiness of inter-currency—largely international—transactions: aside from all the other sources of uncertainty in transactions, why do we add this one? The discussion of "optimal currency areas" (e.g., Mundell 1961 and subsequent literature)—identifying the boundaries of an economy (perhaps international such as the Eurozone) that work best with a single currency—is more than we can cover here, but we can identify some of the costs and benefits of a common currency. We see already that a common currency reduces transaction risk since, aside from the influence of other market forces, one avoids exchange rate risk. A common currency also avoids foreign exchange transaction costs and political pressures to manipulate a currency against potential trade partners who otherwise would have a different currency. On the other hand, It requires a common monetary policy (e.g., management of interest rates) which might have significantly different impacts if the economic sectors included are sufficiently heterogeneous (e.g., capital intensive versus labor intensive). In general, we can speculate that the more closely economies are linked through trade and legal structure, the more likely are net benefits from a common currency (e.g., the state economies of the US or Australia or India, the provincial economies of Canada or South Africa).

The decision of some members of the European Union not to adopt the euro (e.g., the UK, Sweden) reflects the idea that some economies are, or think they are, sufficiently different that they want to maintain their relative monetary independence. The monetary difficulties within the Eurozone involving Greece and other heavily indebted countries highlighted some of the difficulties of maintaining a common currency (e.g., O'Rourke and Taylor 2013).

Expanding our analysis to allow for monetized transactions instead of barter has complicated the application of our trading story to international markets, but it has not challenged the basic logic of mutually beneficial trade driven by comparative advantage. However, other considerations might, and we consider this later in the chapter.

## OUTSOURCING

We have just examined a relationship in which two potential traders wanted goods and could produce them but found it mutually beneficial to specialize in one and import the other. If we change the labels, our example would illustrate a firm's decision to outsource or subcontract some production that could be done internally—a decision that has multiple applications within the wine industry.

Jacques and Maria both own vineyards and want to produce wine from both merlot and chardonnay grapes. We assume for simplicity that they can sell all they produce at a constant price per ton. Each has 100 acres. Table 3.3 indicates the capacity (in tons) of each vineyard to produce the grapes; they might differ because of the different soil, drainage, slope, and aspect of their particular sites.

We assume for now that weather conditions for the two vineyards are similar; but if they are not or if microclimates are fine enough that small distances matter, then weather would represent another reason for differences in production. Table 3.4 indicates the opportunity cost of producing either of the grapes in terms of forgone units of the other: Jacques has a

*Table 3.3   Vineyard output capacity for Jacques and Maria*

|  | Jacques | Maria |
|---|---|---|
| Maximum output: Chardonnay | 400 | 800 |
| Maximum output: Merlot | 200 | 200 |

*Table 3.4   Output opportunity costs for Jacques and Maria*

| Opportunity cost (in terms of the other) | Jacques | Maria |
|---|---|---|
| Chardonnay cost of merlot | 2.0 | 4.0 |
| Merlot cost of chardonnay | 0.5 | 0.25 |

comparative advantage in producing merlot—half the loss of chardonnay production of Maria—and Maria has a comparative advantage in producing chardonnay. Once again, we see the reciprocal cost (or trade) advantages: Jacques is relatively good at producing merlot, and Maria is relatively good at producing chardonnay. If they both want to produce wines from both grapes, then—once again assuming equal quality from each of them—Maria should produce all chardonnay and subcontract merlot production to Jacques. She could offer Jacques, say, three gallons of chardonnay per gallon of merlot and thereby offer it at a lower cost than if she produced her own merlot at a loss of four gallons of chardonnay. Assuming that he wants to sell merlot, Jacques would find this offer attractive: he forgoes two gallons of chardonnay to produce extra merlot, but Maria is offering him three.

This relationship is equivalent to Jacques playing to his strength by producing all merlot and, in the interest of keeping chardonnay wine in his product line, offering Maria 0.33 gallons of merlot for a gallon of her chardonnay, thus subcontracting his chardonnay production to her. Since this more than covers her lost merlot production from producing chardonnay surplus to her needs, she would find this attractive.

Before one objects that such trading does not sound like subcontracting, we should think more broadly about the logic of these relationships. The logic says that countries, or firms, will tend to specialize in producing the products in which they have a comparative advantage—for which they are relatively low-cost producers. They might have a comparative advantage in producing a number of products relative to other sources. Complications like transportation costs, quality comparability, and transaction costs (e.g., information collection and contract negotiation) confound outsiders' cost advantages, but—left to the opportunity to trade freely—they will gravitate toward allowing lower-cost outsiders to produce some of what they want. Once we realize that all that goes into a firm taking one or more products to market requires production of a number of "products"—some intermediate (that is, used only as inputs into a later stage of production) and some final (that is, the final product sold to the buyer)—we can understand better why a firm that has relatively low cost for one step in the process might subcontract all of its other needs.

If, for example, we can simplify the stages of getting a wine to market to include growing grapes, processing grapes, winemaking, bottling, storage, marketing, distribution, and retailing; then we can imagine any or all of these steps being subcontracted (see below).

This assumes that such transacting is legal. More specifically, because place is so important in identifying wine, appellation requirements and labeling laws have a significant impact upon management decisions affecting wine production. We shall have more to say about this later.

It is common for winemakers to contract for grapes, including long-term contracts (e.g., Thornton 2013: 74–77). Even within the process of providing grapes, it is common for vignerons to subcontract harvesting and even vineyard maintenance. In addition, one can buy grapes or bulk wine from brokers (e.g., the Turrentine Brokerage based in California, http://www.turrentinebrokerage.com/). Companies like The Wine Foundry based in Sonoma, California (http://www.thewinefoundry.com/, the successor to Crushpad which went bankrupt in 2012) offer services from grape acquisition and crush to production of the final labeled bottle. Winemakers such as Michel Rolland, Bernard Magrez, and Stephane Derenoncourt are "subcontractors" who advise wineries and are among the most prominent of numerous consulting enologists. Small wineries regularly use mobile bottling plants rather than build their own which would sit idle most of the year. Ultimately every function of wine production and sales can be outsourced: perhaps the only in-house requirement is a vision for producing wine.

## THE CHOICE OF PRODUCT MIX: FROM VINEYARD TO SHELF SPACE

Our discussion has focused upon the desire to transact with others where the theory depends upon the concept of opportunity cost: we turn to others if they can produce for us at a cost lower than our cost of doing it ourselves. One way to describe the outcome is that a producer will replace one source of production (her own) with another's if it costs less: if the producer is selling the product, this is equivalent to saying that she makes more profit (revenue minus costs) by making such a substitution.

Connected to our earlier discussion is the related question of the producer's most desirable product mix. In the same spirit in which we were asking what the producer should produce in house and what should she import or outsource, we can ask whether a firm's current product mix—which might be only one product—is better than any alternative. Instead of asking if she can do better replacing her own production with an import, we now ask whether she can do better replacing one product with another (with the source of production now being a subordinate question).

We can take another look at our vignerons Jacques and Maria. Given the information in Tables 3.3 and 3.4, we realized that, if both wanted to sell both chardonnay and merlot wines, then they could do better by specializing and trading with each other than each growing both varietals. What happens if we add some price information to this example? If, for example, each grape sells for $2,000/ton, then both Jacques and Maria will produce all chardonnay: they can produce more of it than merlot, but more precisely producing any merlot involves losing 2–4 times that revenue from forgoing the corresponding amount of chardonnay. On the other hand, if chardonnay sells for $1,000/ton and merlot sells for $5,000/ton, both will produce all merlot: even Maria who gives up twice as much chardonnay per ton of merlot as Jacques, will earn more this way because otherwise she would forgo $5,000 for every ton of merlot not produced in order to earn $4,000 (4 × $1,000) to produce chardonnay. Obviously, prices matter. More precisely, relative prices matter: if one's opportunity costs—say, chardonnay lost per ton of merlot produced ($\Delta C/\Delta M$)—exceeds the ratio of the (negative of the) grapes' prices (in this case, merlot price to chardonnay price), then they grow merlot.[3] The extent to which merlot displaces chardonnay in this example reflects the proportion of vignerons who face that kind of relative price relationship in their choices of vineyard.

Given these examples, what prices would yield some production of each grape? Since Jacques is the lower cost merlot producer (he forgoes two units of chardonnay for every unit of merlot compared with four for Maria), he will grow merlot as long as its price is more than twice that of chardonnay: as long as merlot earns more than twice as much as chardonnay, Jacques will produce merlot—and only merlot, since his opportunity cost of growing merlot (in terms of lost chardonnay production) remains constant. Only when merlot's price is more than four times that of chardonnay do we lose all chardonnay since, at that price, Maria also grows merlot. Thus, if we have a price of merlot grapes that is two to four times that of chardonnay, we expect to find both grapes produced, though our two vignerons would still specialize. For example, if the price of chardonnay is $1,500/ton, then a price of merlot between $3,000 and $6,000/ton should convince only Maria to produce chardonnay.

We see the role of opportunity cost in guiding the vignerons' choices of crop, and we see support for this kind of crop selection (e.g., a shift in taste from merlot to pinot noir: http://www.winesandvines.com/template.cfm?htitle=Red%20Flag%20for%20Merlot%3F&content=96673&section=news) and, relatedly, the supply response to changes in grape prices (Volpe et al. 2010). Of course, the same kind of analysis helps explain decisions to change one's crop from grapes to something else (e.g., reducing grape production in Australia, http://www.adelaidenow. com.au/news/south-australia/grape-prices-to-force-growers-off-the-land/ story-e6frea83-1225980629909).

As we saw with international trade, practical considerations complicate the actual crop selection decision. For example, such adjustments of production must account for the time required to plant vineyards and allow them to mature. Vines require time to mature enough to produce usable fruit; and, within limits, older vines produce better fruit (e.g., Heymann and Noble 1987). Also, given that and other costs associated with crop adjustment, one wants to see evidence of a long-term trend in changes in relative prices, not some aberration from a continuing pattern. Furthermore, it is unlikely that one's opportunity cost of one grape in terms of another is the same throughout a property. For example, one might have a large farm with varying growing conditions throughout. Rather than convincing the vigneron to switch from all of one grape to all of another, a secular price change might be more likely to lead to a change in the proportion of vineyards used for a particular grape. While our example suggests that Jacques and Maria will grow only one grape or another, it is often more likely that the vigneron grows a variety of grapes (e.g., regarding vineyard site evaluation: http://arcserver2.iagt.org/vll/learnmore.aspx).

To see the effects of prices in another example of product mix, imagine that Jacques and Maria merge their vineyards into one—JM Enterprises— which is probably not a bad analogy to large vineyard holdings by producers like E. and J. Gallo in California or Australian Vintage Ltd. in Australia. For simplicity, we assume that the reason for the merger is something other than increased vineyard productivity of their respective vineyards (e.g., they decide to do joint management) so that JM's capacity is simply the combined capacity of the two vineyards.

We continue to assume that JM can sell all it produces at the current market price. Table 3.5 provides useful information about JM's productivity

*Table 3.5   JM Enterprises production data*

| | | |
|---|---|---|
| Merlot capacity=400 | 0–200 tons of Merlot | 201–400 tons of Merlot |
| Chardonnay cost of merlot | 2.0 | 4.0 |
| Chardonnay capacity=1200 | 0–800 tons of Chardonnay | 801–1,200 tons of Chardonnay |
| Merlot cost of chardonnay | 0.25 | 0.5 |

and tradeoffs. JM's capacity is the sum of Jacques's and Maria's individual capacities and their tradeoffs between the crops are taken from Table 3.4. The opportunity costs reflect the differences we saw with Jacques and Maria. Recall that Jacques's vineyard has lower cost merlot so, if market conditions support it, JM would produce the first 200 tons of merlot in Jacques's vineyard—his maximum production. JM would use Maria's vineyard for additional merlot production up to an additional 200 tons if market prices justified that more costly production. If chardonnay prices rose enough relative to merlot prices, then JM would move out of merlot production into chardonnay. If it were producing all merlot, then the less costly chardonnay is Maria's whose production per ton (up to 800 tons) displaces 0.25 tons of merlot. Only if the chardonnay price rises enough would JM also turn Jacques's vineyard to chardonnay production.

How might such prices work? Assume, for example, that chardonnay currently sells for $1,500/ton and, as a starting point, JM is currently producing only chardonnay. What is the lowest long-term price for merlot, to the nearest dollar, that would convince JM to convert some vineyard capacity to merlot if we assume that the changeover costs are negligible? Since JM must forgo at least two tons of chardonnay to produce a ton of merlot and each ton of chardonnay sells for $1,500, it must earn more than $3,000/ton to more than cover that lost revenue—so $3,001/ton, to suggest an easy target price. If merlot prices maintained that level or more, how much merlot would JM supply? Certainly it would supply 200 tons since that is the "two tons of chardonnay" merlot production. Why not produce more merlot? The next ton—ton number 201—must come from Maria's vineyard and displaces four tons of chardonnay worth $6,000. JM would add her vineyard to merlot production only when the merlot price rises above $6,000.

We can extract from this analysis a simple but accurate "supply curve" of merlot from JM Enterprises—that is, a graphic representation of JM's revenue-maximizing quantity of merlot at all possible merlot prices, given JM's cost of providing it (i.e., the lost revenue from forgone chardonnay sales). Given a chardonnay price ($P_C$) of $1,500/ton, JM will not supply merlot until its price exceeds $3,000/ton, and then it is willing to supply up to 200 tons. It will gladly accept a higher price for merlot, but it will not supply more until its price exceeds $6,000/ton at which price it will increase production another 200 tons (from Maria's vineyard) to its capacity. Of course, it will accept an even higher price for merlot, but it cannot produce more with its current vineyards. This supply curve ($S_M(P_C=\$1,500/\text{ton})$) is depicted in Figure 3.1.

What does this relationship indicate? It reflects the idea that supply is forthcoming as long as the available price covers the producer's opportunity cost—her marginal or incremental cost of producing the

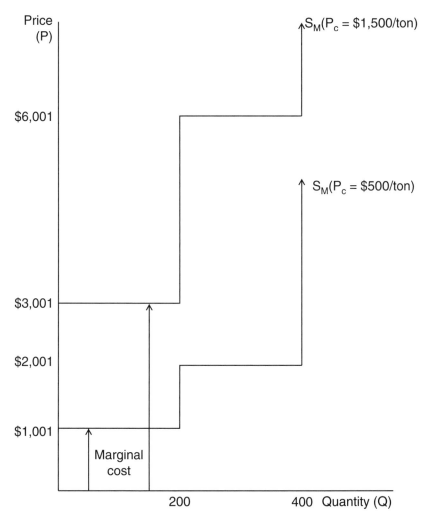

*Figure 3.1    The JM Enterprises merlot supply curve ($S_M$) (Price of chardonnay/ton: $1,500; $500)*

product—and more supply is forthcoming despite rising production costs if a product's price rises to cover them. This is the same logic that informed our finding the terms of trade as the basis for transacting between two countries in our earlier international trade example.

JM's supply response reflects rising costs in the JM vineyards: since, in our simple model, JM's cost of supplying a grape is constant over a range of output, its supply curve looks like stair steps with a range of output at each price threshold followed by no additional supply (a vertical section) until price hits the next price-to-cost threshold. It also captures the idea of the vertical distance at any quantity reflecting the marginal cost of that unit of production—like the terms of trade covering the exporter's cost. In this example, the marginal cost is the forgone revenue from chardonnay sales; it should not be surprising that this is a cost. Forgoing the revenue from some alternative production is just as much a cost as forgoing funds that are used to purchase labor, fertilizer, and other inputs.

Figure 3.1 also illustrates the effect of a chardonnay price decrease from $1,500 to $500/ton. Using our "dollar more" requirement, the threshold price for offering merlot drops to $1,001, and JM is willing to produce only merlot if the chardonnay price gets above $2,000.

If we imagine that JM has extensive vineyards with a wide range of tradeoffs—a wide range of lost chardonnay production per ton of merlot—then we can imagine many "stair steps" or, more generally, rising marginal costs of production as depicted in Figure 3.2 which, once again, shows the willingness to supply for the two prices of chardonnay.

Can we extract a general pricing strategy from this analysis? It helps to recall the relationship between opportunity cost and relative prices noted earlier, namely, that relative prices matter: if one's opportunity costs—say, chardonnay lost per ton of merlot ($\Delta C/\Delta M$)—exceeds the negative of the ratio of the grapes' prices (in this case, merlot price to chardonnay price), then they grow merlot. In our example, JM loses at least two tons of chardonnay per ton of merlot; and, sure enough, JM does not begin producing merlot until its price is more than twice that of chardonnay.

The decision becomes more complicated, and more realistic, when we allow for significant changeover costs, uncertainty about key data such as the duration of price changes and weather, and other practical considerations.

If this approach helps us understand the allocation of vineyard to different grapes, then it should be helpful in analyzing other capacity allocation questions—for example, the allocation of shelf space to different products in a wine shop. If one has a given shelf space capacity, then one first wants to stock it with items that are profitable. However, one also wants to replace less profitable bottles with the more profitable ones just as JM altered its mix of chardonnay and merlot depending upon their relative profitability. It might seem obvious that, among a variety of products one could stock, one chooses those that yield the greatest return (revenue minus cost) per linear foot of shelving. However, such decisions can be more complicated (e.g., stocking items such as "loss leaders" or low-margin locally produced products as part of a public relations or larger marketing strategy to attract customers).

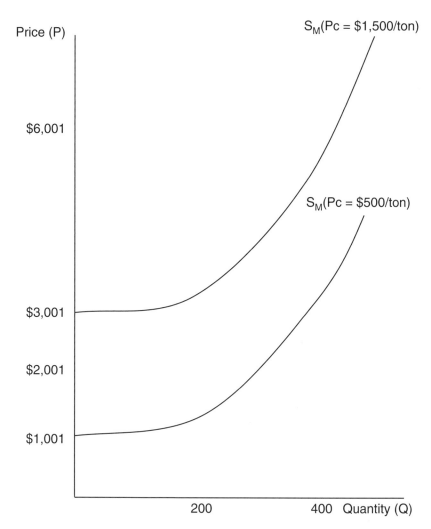

*Figure 3.2   The JM Enterprises merlot supply curve ($S_M$) (Continuously rising marginal cost)*

## OBJECTIONS TO TRADE

Our discussion describes a variety of contexts in which the logic of comparative advantage supports transacting—from international trade to outsourcing to household management. We have extended the benefit–cost logic of comparative advantage to an analysis of the allocation of scarce capacity to the most profitable product mix—another version of greater value displacing lesser.

Relative costs of production are not all that governs decisions and public policy about transacting. A number of further considerations complicate the decision to transact, especially when it becomes important to consider who is transacting and their relationships. Arguments for the freedom to transact (including "free trade") and against it ("protectionism" in the case of international trade) have persisted for centuries. The most popular arguments against free trade, often international, include:

- Strategic goods: Free trade assumes a willingness to depend upon outside production. Such dependence upon imports might be problematic if (a) they are strategically important (e.g., at the economy-wide level: technology, weapons, energy) and (b) they come from only a few or one source(s), especially if the trade relationship is fragile (e.g., due to political differences).
- The reliability of relative cost information: Differences in cost drive the logic of transacting. If the local cost disadvantage reflects the immaturity of the local industry (e.g., learning by doing, achievement of economies of scale), then threatening it prematurely with outside competition might diminish or eliminate it prematurely. Also, if the outside cost advantage is not real but instead reflects some commercial strategy (e.g., tax advantages or other subsidies from another government or an outside producer's ability to cross-subsidize sales in one market with profits made in another (like predatory pricing)), then free trade might diminish or eliminate a local sector which is, in fact, competitive (e.g., the concern about "dumping" and predatory pricing).
- Employment effects: Starting from a position of commercial isolation, introducing free trade will displace investment and employment in sectors that cannot compete with goods from outside. Local resources shift away from those sectors toward those in which the economy has comparative advantage. This might be economically efficient but politically unacceptable. Such trade shifts and displacements are typically more acceptable within an economy—the normal process of more efficient producers driving out less efficient ones—but more problematic between economies where foreign production displaces domestic production.

Unlike sectors such as manufacturing, technology, or agriculture generally, the wine industry in most countries is either not large enough or not threatened enough to drive its trade policy, though protection of the local wine industry is surprisingly visible in some countries (e.g., Mexico). However, applications to the wine industry of related concerns about transacting freely are appropriate. We consider three types of extenuating circumstances: alternative suppliers as substitutes, the reliability of external supply, and discomfort with a reallocation of production.

## ALTERNATIVE SUPPLIERS AS SUBSTITUTES

At the heart of transacting is the willingness to substitute someone else's production for one's own. Our willingness to shop demonstrates that we are often willing to do this.

An application of comparative advantage that illustrates the potential difficulty of that prospect is production within the household. Typically, households can produce many of the goods and services they desire—for example, meal preparation, storage, gardening, housecleaning, and personal grooming. However, they also import a number of these products for the same reasons of cost advantage that we have discussed—for example, lawn maintenance, auto maintenance and repair, and grooming. Like prepared meals, they can also produce many of the items they use—fresh vegetables from the garden, canned foods, homemade furniture and toys, sewn clothing—but they often import from lower-cost producers. In particular, households can make their own wine; but most find the cost of producing in house relative to "importing" for a given quality to be prohibitive.

It is likely, however, that households are unwilling to import some services which would seem, on the face of it, to be more efficiently provided by outsiders—for example, child care or elder care. In effect, these are strategic goods to the household, and it decides that it is unwilling to become dependent upon outside suppliers for these goods. Correspondingly, they might decide that there is no acceptable substitute for the kind of personal attention and dedication that family members can provide in such cases. Even wealthy and highly paid individuals still want to play a significant role in raising their own children. Even with winemaking, some households feel that no imported product can replace what can be done "domestically".

It is likely so with many, often smaller wineries. They can subcontract many of the production steps that they need, but they might resist dependence upon others or doubt the quality of the market alternative for some of these steps—perhaps maintenance of the vineyard, perhaps grape selection, perhaps winemaking. Some might even feel that no distributor can establish the kind of relationship and communication that they desire with

their customers so they insist upon doing it themselves (e.g., small producers who travel through a region meeting potential buyers and also invite
buyers to visit them to sample the wines).

Producers might resist outsourcing some or all of the winemaking
process, but their willingness to do it will depend upon their ability to
afford not to. Assuming that the producer's objective is to maximize
profit is standard in economics, but Thornton (2013) reminds us that
wine producers might think otherwise (pp. 14–17). The nature of wine
production—especially small production—is that some or all of the
process might produce enjoyment per se. Producers might be willing to
forgo profits in order to produce and enjoy "nonmarket goods [which]
may include nepotism, living the wine proprietor's lifestyle and the aesthetic value of making a high-quality wine" (p. 16). Some can afford this
because wine production attracts those with considerable wealth made
outside of and/or prior to entering the industry (e.g., Sullivan 2012). In
effect, the producer chooses not to transact because the external supply
cannot substitute for doing it oneself (like raising one's own children).

While data on the profitability and survival of smaller winery ownership is difficult to find (e.g., Stang 2012), two scholars of the industry have
noted that the first wine miracle was Jesus' miraculous transformation of
water into wine at the wedding at Cana, and the second "will be making
a consistent profit from wine" (Heien and Martin 2002: 33). For some
unknown proportion of wineries, profitability is likely not required for
their survival.

Another concern about transacting involves the role of place. Recall
that our discussion of trade assumed that the goods being produced were
the same: all that differed was the site of production. For many products,
the location of production is largely irrelevant: a certain grade of lumber is
effectively the same whether it comes from British Columbia or Alabama.
If wine were like lumber and consumers could not tell whether their cabernet wine was produced in Bordeaux or the Maipo Valley or Napa Valley
or the Brda Valley, then we would expect them to choose the least expensive among the four (assumed) perfect substitutes: French cabernet lovers
would simply choose the least expensive alternative—perhaps Chilean—
and French cabernet production would be displaced by some other French
sector, not necessarily wine.

The claim is that such perfect substitution is impossible: place matters
to many participants in wine markets. Educated palates can tell the difference among cabernets, and only French production can taste like French
cabernet: wine from elsewhere being a perfect substitute is a contradiction.
This is an element of the concept of *terroir* which supports the provisions
of French wine law that impose strict rules on what grapes can be grown

where and the content requirements that must be met before one can use an appellation name on one's wine label. Moreover, the principles behind such laws have been adopted to some extent by all the major wine producing regions of the world. In general, place names play a crucial role in determining the price (perhaps value) of a wine because wine quality and reputation are invariably associated with places, and regulations are strict about what must be in the bottle before a place name can be used. Also, more specific place names correlate directly with price: as one moves to smaller and smaller divisions within an appellation (e.g., from appellation to village to vineyard to parcel), price usually increases, although more "nested" places do not necessarily produce better wine.

One wonders whether the *terroir* argument is simply a protectionist illusion. Given the potential gains from producing a perfect substitute for French cabernet at a lower cost and the failure to do that over the centuries, one expects that the *terroir* argument has some merit. On the other hand, we lack evidence that consumers can easily distinguish wines of a given type that are produced in very different wine regions. While the incentive to find a lower cost perfect substitute apparently has not succeeded, the search has resulted in the extraordinary growth of New World wine regions which produce different, and still delicious, cabernet.

An example of the importance of place is Aylward's (2008) argument about the growth of "cola" wines in Australia's production—the expansion of the industry and homogenization of content that has disregarded many of the distinctive qualities of the various wine areas of the country. We shall have more to say about this when we discuss the cultural content of wine in Chapter 8.

## RELIABILITY OF SUPPLY

If legal, the decision to outsource to lower cost alternatives depends upon the reliability of the supply. Of course, the aforementioned concerns about political differences which deter trade for strategic goods are unlikely to threaten one's alternative grape supplies, but a variety of other conditions can (e.g., weather, changes of ownership, and contracts with competing producers). Our discussion of comparative advantage implicitly assumed ideal spot markets: the perfectly informed potential traders weigh relative costs, reach agreement upon some mutually beneficial terms of trade, consummate the trade instantaneously, and walk away. However, markets connected to the wine trade are not so ideal. Also, while they exist, spot markets for grapes represent only a part of the grape market—recently less than half, according to Thornton (2013: 74–77; Goodhue et al. 2002).

Depending upon what one wants to put onto one's label legally (e.g., "Estate Grown"), spot markets are convenient, but long-term contracts can be desirable and can involve considerable levels of cooperation between grape growers and the wine producers they supply. However, a vigneron might decide not to transact with an external supplier if the cost of finding mutually beneficial terms of a contract, including duration of the commitment, are high enough.

The literature on contracts in both economics and law addresses a vast number of incentive and enforcement issues that arise once one hopes to negotiate a contract (e.g., Salanié 2005). One approach to grasping the complexity of contracting is to realize that, in a contract, one hopes to find an external decision maker who is, in effect, oneself—or better. The assumption in our simple model of comparative advantage that the goods traded are identical—what the external supplier provides is exactly what would be provided internally—avoids this complication. However, questioning that assumption goes to the heart of the challenge of actual contracting—for example, the specifications of the deliverable and the timing of the delivery. A winery that contracts for grapes, for example, wants "perfect grapes" for its purposes (e.g., ripeness, sugar content, color), but the winemaker's idea of perfection might not match the external vigneron's idea, and neither party can control an outcome affected by unknown events like weather and pests. The contract can specify the extent of collaboration between the parties—and often does (e.g., yield, extent of green harvest, irrigation, use of pesticides and fungicides)—but it is difficult to guarantee an outcome ideal for both parties.

Such contracts generally represent Principal–Agent relationships where the principal is contracting with the agent to act as if she is the principal, but the agent has incentives of her own (e.g., minimizing the cost of performance). A variety of structural challenges threaten such contracts. For example, moral hazard risks exist—that is, incentives for the agent to fall short of the principal's goal for a variety of reasons such as (a) the principal cannot tell the difference timely and (b) the suboptimal performance serves the agent (e.g., costs less to achieve). Adverse selection risks are a challenge: among the possible sources of supply, the low bidder might be a supplier who is most adept at getting away with suboptimal performance. Correspondingly, among the possible buyers, the highest bidders might be those who represent the greatest risk of actually paying. Reputations are important, but, like the quality of fine wine, they are difficult to know and to establish and sustain. Another risk is that it is difficult or impossible to produce a contract that is complete—that deals with all possible contingencies.

Given the costs of making good contracts, long-term contracts might exist in part because parties want to preserve a contract that works. On the other hand, parties will be reluctant to enter into a long-term relationship in the first place until they feel that they can trust the contract.

## REALLOCATIVE EFFECTS

We can characterize the decision to transact as, on the demand side, a decision to opt for an external supplier over internal production or, on the supply side, to produce surplus to one's own requirements. The former case is likely the source of most of the complications in the wine industry.

At the national level, free trade might be politically sensitive or effectively not possible. A familiar example is the well-established objection to liberalized international trade or, conversely, a familiar basis for protectionist trade policy. The availability of imports at lower cost than domestic production means that domestic productive capacity is allocated away from that sector and toward one's own comparative advantage, but the transition of the resources from one sector to another is not costless. Since firms might have political influence per se (e.g., through financial support of politicians) and their workers are voters and might be members of trade unions wielding political influence, allowing domestic production to be displaced by imports by supporting free trade might encounter political opposition resulting in various forms of trade interference such as taxes on imports (tariffs), import quantity limits (quotas) or outright prohibitions on imports, and various "non-tariff barriers" that effectively raise the cost of imports relative to domestic production (e.g., Krugman et al. 2015): the list of potential interferences is limited only by the imaginations of politicians and bureaucrats and perhaps a nation's constitution. We return to this in Chapter 6.

We usually hear about such displacements in the context of international trade. However, displacement by domestic competition concerned Bordeaux wine producers in the sixteenth to eighteenth centuries so that they erected various non-tariff barriers to access to the port at Bordeaux (Pitte 2008: 36). During that same period and earlier, local governments levied domestic tariffs (*octroi*) on certain products, including wine, coming into the jurisdiction (e.g., Gilbey 1869: 25). Jancis Robinson (1997) has written that the producers of Gaillac, an appellation about 250 km southeast of the city of Bordeaux are "still smarting centuries later from having its wines taxed so punitively by the protectionist merchants of Bordeaux (a long way) downriver" (p. 253). These taxes raised revenue—perhaps their primary purpose—but, either intentionally or not, they disadvantaged wine produced outside the jurisdiction relative to that produced within and thus might have protected local winemakers.

Producers might also forgo transactions to preserve employment of family members or friends either aside from, or even in spite of, concerns about wine quality. Preserving this version of "domestic production" over external production could be another dimension of the producer's selection of personal satisfaction over profit.

## CONCLUSION

This chapter has provided a logical basis for the desire to transact along with some of the special considerations that affect that behavior in wine markets. We have considered a variety of contexts in which transactions are mutually beneficial as well as some circumstances where the cost of transacting as well as benefits and costs external to the actual transaction complicate the choice. We turn next to a more thorough discussion of the behavior on either side of the transaction, in particular, a consumer's decision whether to buy wine and how much as well as the producer's decision to supply it.

## NOTES

1.  The logic of comparative advantage is compelling, and the scholarly trade literature that flows from it—from theoretical complications to policy analysis—is vast. A useful single resource is Krugman, Obstfeld, and Melitz (2015). Krugman (1993) provides an informed and supportive perspective on the enduring appeal of the basic theory.
2.  A thorough discussion of the role of money would take us far afield. In addition to its importance as a medium of exchange, its two other generally recognized and invaluable roles in society are as a store of value (so that we can bank future purchasing power rather than vest it in goods currently) and as a unit of account (so that we have some standard for measuring commercial value). For example, see Mankiw (2015: 609–615).
3.  This relationship between chardonnay lost per ton of additional merlot ($\Delta C/\Delta M$) and the ratio of the negative of the grapes' prices ($-P(\text{merlot})/P(\text{chardonnay})$) is unlikely to be intuitive to the non-economist. For example, the production tradeoff has chardonnay on top ($\Delta C$) while the price ratio has merlot on top ($-P(\text{merlot})$). How can this make sense? The first expression is a negative value (since any increase in merlot production requires a corresponding decrease in chardonnay production) capturing the tradeoff in production that the vigneron faces. For example, if $\Delta M = +1$ pound and $\Delta C = -2$ pounds, then nature says that the vigneron loses two pounds of chardonnay for every additional pound of merlot grown.

    The second expression involving prices is the tradeoff that the market offers. For example, if the merlot price is \$2 and the chardonnay price is \$1, then the market is saying that it will swap two units of chardonnay for one unit of merlot: one can buy one pound of merlot and is implicitly not buying two pounds of chardonnay instead, or one could forgo the merlot and buy the chardonnay for the same money instead. Since the relationship is necessarily inverse—that is, buying more of one implicitly means forgoing the other for a given expenditure—it is negative. Since prices are positive, their ratio is positive so we need to include the negative sign with the price ratio.

We can cast this market relationship using the $\Delta$-notation. Buying one pound of merlot ($\Delta M = +1$) at the stated prices means forgoing two pounds of chardonnay ($\Delta C = -2$) unless one wants to spend more money. That is, the vigneron knows her production tradeoff of chardonnay lost per extra merlot, and the market presents its tradeoff as chardonnay (forgone) per merlot (purchased).

If these two tradeoffs do not match, then the vigneron can adjust production to make more money. Consider the example in the text ($\Delta C/\Delta M$ exceeds ($-P(\text{merlot})/P(\text{chardonnay})$)). One must be careful here: since both expressions are negative, "exceeds" means "is less negative than". Say the former is $-2$ and the latter is $-4$ (for example, chardonnay is \$1 and merlot is \$4) so that the production tradeoff—gain one M by giving up two Cs—is less negative than the market tradeoff—gain one M (at \$4 each) by giving up four Cs (at \$1 each). If the vigneron can gain one merlot at the cost of two chardonnays in production, she should: she could earn \$4 in revenue from merlot by losing only \$2 ($2 \times \$1$) from the corresponding reduced sales of chardonnay. As long as this mismatch exists, the vigneron will increase revenue by replacing chardonnay production with merlot production.

Thus, the ratio of merlot price to chardonnay price actually captures the market's rate of replacing lost chardonnay revenue with additional merlot revenue.

# 4. Some basic tools of economics: consumer behavior and demand

## INTRODUCTION

Economics is about decision making, and every type of decision maker involved with wine is the focus of a field in economics; all the choices described in Chapter 2 involve economics. One way to learn about the economist's analytic tools is to review the field in the order in which most of us have learned about wine: we start with the economics of the consumer and consumer demand and study the demand side of transactions. We move next to wine production—the nature of the organization, or firm, that produces wine and the industry of which it is a part. In the sense that a transaction requires simply a buyer and a seller, this is the seller, or supply, side of the market. Chapter 3 discussed the logic of transacting, and this chapter and the next look more closely at the logic of behavior on either side of the transaction.

## CONSUMERS: THE IDEA OF A MODEL

Wine is produced primarily to be sold to consumers for consumption and, as such, is a final good. That is, it is not primarily an intermediate good produced as an input into some further productive process, although it sometimes has that role—for example, when restaurants offer wine as a complement to their meals. Unlike most consumer goods, however, some wines also qualify as financial assets or investments whose value may vary over time. In this case, the consumer as investor hopes that the value increases and, moreover, that it increases more than other available assets— that is, that its appreciation rate is relatively high—more on this later.

One complication in studying consumers and wine is that our models of consumer behavior depend upon the motive for buying: immediate consumption, consumption over time, or investment. Does s/he use the good immediately, does s/he extract a stream of services from the good over time (as with consumer durables such as appliances or automobiles), or is the purchase a form of savings—that is, a source of future purchasing power either for oneself or as an endowment for someone else such as one's children. Sometimes we can infer the motive from the nature of the purchase. The large majority by volume of wines purchased are for immediate consumption since the wine involved is both widely available and at its peak quality at the time of purchase or soon thereafter. Some investment funds consist of wine purchased only as an investment (e.g., the Bottled Asset Fund (Gelles 2014)): investors buy units of a fund based upon the purchase price of a collection of fine wines and are then paid their return when the wine is sold at the end of a fixed term (e.g., five years). The investors never see, touch, taste, or technically own the wine itself. For these two extreme cases, one can infer the very different motives for the purchase. However, for cases in between, the motivation may be murkier, even in the consumer's own mind, and the motive for keeping a wine may change from the initial motive for buying it—for example, when one learns that a favorite wine has appreciated unexpectedly well and has become "too expensive to drink".

In addition to managing carefully the time required to enjoy the goods they purchase, we assume that consumers pursue some goal in their purchasing decisions: they want to "make the most" of both the money they have available and their other assets (e.g., labor skills) that can be converted into money. This is the consumer's purchasing power. Economists model that pursuit as the effort to maximize *utility*, where utility represents the overall sense of benefit or pleasure or satisfaction that comes from one's expenditures.

What will affect the move from the goal to the purchase—from trying to make the most of one's purchasing power to actually spending money? The process that takes a consumer from an ability to purchase to actually purchasing varies as much as the number of consumers: indeed, anyone would be hard pressed to describe that process exactly even for oneself, and we cannot hope to describe in detail a process that would be widely accepted as both an explanation of that behavior and a reliable predictor of it. Instead, we try to capture the essence of the process by describing a *model* of consumer behavior.

Pursued as a science, economics embraces the scientific method as an approach to identifying, articulating, and attempting to answer questions deemed interesting to the profession and perhaps the wider community. Much of the effort of scholars in the natural sciences such as physics or biology is to identify an interesting question about the way the world works, perhaps pose it in an "If . . . then . . ." framework (e.g., "If one reduces one's daily caloric intake, then one's weight will decrease, *ceteris paribus*"), and then collect the data that seem relevant to the question (e.g., daily caloric intake, body weight, other determinants of weight for which one must control such as amount and type of exercise). The *ceteris paribus* (abbreviated to *cet. par.*) condition ("with other things equal") highlights the central role of isolating the relationship between only two variables—in this example, calories and weight—in testing the hypothesis or answering the question (Is caloric intake directly correlated with weight?): without recognizing the importance of that isolation, one or more other influences may be overlooked while still affecting the outcome (weight) and confounding any conclusions about the role of calories (e.g., exercise and other activity levels of various sorts, metabolism).

In this same spirit, a model in economics is generally a logical explanation of behavior that leads to some testable—and thus refutable—predictions about behavior, typically with the following primary components:

1. A statement of the decision maker's objective or desired outcome (e.g., "make the most of what I can spend") or of a question one wants to answer (e.g., "How will consumers respond if product price decreases?" where the outcome of interest is quantity sold) or a testable hypothesis ("If the consumer is maximizing utility, then s/he will buy more of a product when its price decreases, *cet. par.*");
2. A selection of the key influences or variables related to that objective or outcome—one or more variables that represent both it (e.g., the quantity purchased) and the influences upon it (e.g., the good's price, the consumer's income, advertising);
3. A statement of assumptions that allow us to avoid both unimportant and insurmountable real-world complications (e.g., the consumer thinks logically and has complete information about the product: if we do not assume that, how much of the complexity of decision making do we try to capture?);
4. A logical explanation that incorporates the assumptions and shows how the chosen key variables are related to the objective(s), perhaps presented mathematically (e.g., $Q = a + bP + cM$ where $Q$ is consumers' quantity desired, $P$ is the good's price, and $M$ is a measure of consumer income: thus, the equation says that desired quantity is driven only by price and income and relates to them linearly);
5. One or more hypotheses, or predictions, generated by that explanation (e.g., when its price falls, the consumer buys more of the good: this amounts to a prediction that the coefficient $b$ in the equation above has a negative sign); and
6. Collection and analysis of data on the outcome and key variables (Step 2) that allow us to see if variations in the outcome actually vary systematically and as predicted with variations in the other key variables that we think affect it.

Since a model is a simplification of reality, one must exercise judgment in walking the fine line between simplicity and reality, most clearly in steps such as the number and choice of assumptions and the identification of key variables: a more realistic model becomes more complex and probably less tractable, but a simpler model may be too far removed from reality to have much relevance (the metaphor of Ockham's Razor comes to mind).

The best model of some behavior is simply our best story, carefully presented, of the logical connection between all the key influences and the outcome. Often when we try to understand behavior, we talk as if we do: in particular, we talk as if we know or expect that one or more events *cause* or at least influence another. Rain causes us to wear raincoats. Traffic congestion causes us to feel frustrated. Products used by glamorous people cause us to want them. A lower price causes the modal consumer to buy more. But the question of causality is a significant and elusive one. On the one hand, if we can prove causality, then we should be able to manipulate behavior: if certain influences actually cause some outcome, then controlling those influences should allow us to control that outcome. However, in the behavioral sciences, we tend to be—or ought to be—humble about imputing causality: it is difficult to know enough about behavior to arrange outcomes reliably, to know fully what causes decision makers to behave in various ways. This is one reason why designing economic policy and predicting its effects are so difficult.

Even the natural sciences proceed cautiously when imputing causality. Like economic theories, scientific theories are "best stories" that are subject to revision as research tests and refines—and sometimes overturns—the current best story of the logical connection between influences and outcomes (e.g., medical theories of treatments as "cures"). Their advantage is that they can often test predictions in laboratories whereas it is considerably more difficult, if not impossible, for economists and social scientists generally to find laboratories for testing their theories fully.

If we are careful, economists do not assert that that they know what causes various economic behaviors such as consumer demand or firm or industry supply or government policy. One of the key steps in the development of economic models is testing our predictions by collecting data on the key variables, including the outcomes, and seeing how well the data fit the behavior "explained" by the model. Once we have a model, the first challenge is knowing exactly what we mean by its key components. What do we mean by price? Income? Advertising? What do we mean by "wine"—or some other product whose market we are trying to understand? A careful reading of any good-quality empirical economic analysis will provide a detailed discussion of all the gaps between the concepts captured in the model and the data available to represent those concepts—although the existence of such gaps is so widely assumed in the profession that such discussions often focus only upon the longest stretches between concept and data. One of the easiest ways to appreciate why economists are often characterized as ambidextrous because they must handle so many hands ("on the one hand, on the other hand") is to ask a competent practitioner exactly what we mean by some everyday concept like cost.

Beyond the challenge of finding good data to test models, the statistical methods needed to test correctly are often complex, requiring the skills of a specialist in econometrics. The seemingly simple idea of isolating a relationship in movements between some influence upon an outcome and the outcome itself in the midst of other influences raises challenges such as (a) isolating the role of one influence when it, in turn, may be affected by the other influences (e.g., expert rating and producer may both influence wine price, but they may also influence each other) and (b) isolating the effect of an influence upon an outcome when the relationship may also run the other way (e.g., price is likely to influence quantity supplied, but supply is also likely to influence price). A look at a modern econometrics text (e.g., Green 2011) will convince one quickly of the potential—even likely—complexity of careful statistical analysis.

An issue that is both conceptual and statistical is a determination of a comprehensive list of the relevant influences. Conceptually, the requirement of Step 2 in building a complete model is identifying *all* of the influences upon an outcome: failure to be complete means that changes in an outcome will be left unexplained which we want to avoid. A potential explanation for the poor explanatory power of any model is that some important influence has been omitted from consideration (e.g., attempting to explain changes in sales based upon changes in one's price that fails to consider the potential impact of competitors' prices); indeed, one of the best arguments for developing and testing a model is to force one to decide if it includes everything important. That said, we will never identify all of the influences upon some outcome so Step 2 requires finding the *key* influences where drawing that line reflects both good judgment and experience with the market being considered.

Attempting to be comprehensive in describing the market and its influences can also present a uniquely statistical challenge: the data for some key variable may simply not exist—or its closest proxy may be so remotely related that its use is questionable (e.g., missing weather information for some appellation or availability only from some distant station with a different microclimate). One may have no alternative but to work around this "omitted variable" and attempt to correct the resulting imprecision to the extent possible.

Even with a good model, good data, and skillful analysis, our empirical analysis can, at best, test only for apparent shared movements between influences and outcomes. It may seem limiting, but we can find only correlations, not causation. We return to the recognition that we usually do not truly understand why things happen.

Given the care with which we must study and use models and the imperfect tools and "raw materials" (data) at our disposal, we believe that they are still helpful relative to the alternative of ignoring patterns of behavior. Here is a simple example of this process. The consumer's goal is to make the most of her weekly spending on food and wine. We would like to measure an outcome—something like "pleasure per dollar spent". We assume that only food and wine prices and the consumer's budget determine how much total pleasure she experiences: all other complications in the world are assumed irrelevant to achieving that pleasure. Since it would allow the consumer to buy more with a given budget, we predict that lower wine prices will increase the consumer's overall pleasure since she can buy more wine or more food or more of both. Since the budget is constant, this must mean more pleasure per dollar. In this example, testing the model with data is practically difficult because we cannot measure "pleasure", but we would expect an opinion survey to show that consumers feel they "get more for their money" when a price falls (especially if it is sizeable).

This discussion of models might sound academic, but we all model our behavior this way every day. We have goals, or desired outcomes, and we go about finding ways to reach them which amounts to numerous predictions like: I predict that I can achieve A if I do B and C as long as various "real world" complications of various importance and probability do not interfere. We regularly test our models by informally collecting data on influences and outcomes and checking regularly that our predictions work: "Assuming the car starts and that all road, weather, and traffic conditions are normal, it should take me 20 minutes to get to the office." A particularly vivid reminder of our instinctive use of models is our reaction when our predictions are incorrect, and we are late or unsuccessful or surprised or disappointed by an outcome: our models might prove unreliable, and we need to revise them.

## DETERMINANTS OF CONSUMER DEMAND

### Tastes and Preferences

Since we cannot observe—and certainly cannot measure objectively—the consumer's satisfaction with a good, we focus upon the good itself: the consumer's selection of goods and the quantity of each. Consistent with our paradigm of model building, we start by identifying several key influences upon the choice of goods and the quantity desired. In our discussion of these influences, we shall treat each in isolation from all other influences: that is, we consider its impact or the impact if it changes as if all other influences stay the same (*cet. par.*).

First, the consumer's particular *tastes and preferences* narrow the universe of goods into those that are appealing: our focus is upon those whose interests include wine. This raises one of the most profound issues on the demand side of the wine market: what determines the consumer's preferences and how do they influence the choice of product—for example, the particular wine? Especially for products with which one is unfamiliar—such as fine wine—where one might have never experienced the particular wine and where quality can vary at least from vintage to vintage and from winemaker to winemaker, one may search widely for knowledge to guide one's choice or may settle for "rules of thumb" to guide purchases. Among many goods that are difficult to know, consumers hope that price varies directly with quality: a more expensive version is a better quality version. This phenomenon is particularly relevant for items that are popular gift items. The consumer is buying something for someone else; even though s/he may not know the product or how much the recipient would appreciate it, giving an apparently expensive gift signals at least that the giver is generous even if s/he does not know what s/he is giving.

Since we expect that a variety of influences from advertising to peer pressure to "expert" evaluations and recommendations exert such influence, we shall have more to say about this later (Chapter 7): for now, we assume that choosing wine is as simple as choosing canned peas. One can choose among several brands, but the range of choice is limited; the brands are similar; and one perceives that the product changes little over time—perhaps even over one's lifetime—so that one comes to know a product's characteristics. Among wines, beverage wines purchased as a frequently used casual beverage or refreshment are likely the best example of this.

### Own Price, Willingness to Pay, and Consumer Surplus

Once we are interested in a product, its *price* ("own price") matters. The first test is whether one can find the item at a price at or below one's willingness to pay (WTP)—the amount that one is ready, willing, and able to pay where the good is available. We usually assume that the consumer knows her WTP, but this seems unlikely. We are most likely to have a sense of WTP for familiar, frequently transacted goods; but we may not know our maximum WTP except for familiar goods whose prices sometimes rise so much as to make them unaffordable. We are also more likely to know WTP for relatively costly, infrequently traded items (e.g., owned homes, vehicles) whose purchases reward careful market research. Otherwise, we know instinctively that price is less than some vague sense of WTP whenever a purchase seems "worth it". Of course, our WTP for a particular item depends upon the prices of all the related items that we might purchase along with or instead of it (e.g., competing, substitute goods and complementary goods used jointly).

We shall note also the potential uncertainty of WTP when, for example, we have not experienced the product and/or we have little information of what others might pay. Even if prices are negotiable, we ultimately know the actual price that we must pay. We are less likely to know our WTP.

While people vary in the extent to which they change how much they want of something as its price varies—the own price elasticity of their demand (more on this later)—we expect that generally people's demands are sensitive to the price variations of at least some goods. In a way, this is obvious: taken with one's purchasing power, price determines the ceiling on one's access to a good.

But the impact of price goes beyond that. For example, we expect that a consumer's WTP for something will reflect its relative value to her—for example, consumers will be willing to pay twice as much for one good over another if they value it twice as much as the other good. In fact, this is the basis for a concept of consumer equilibrium—an outcome of decision making that is stable and from which the consumer feels no impulse to move. In particular, we would expect consumers to arrange their purchases at any point in time so that the benefit per dollar is about the same, given all the choices made. If this were not true—if one product were yielding noticeably more benefit per dollar than another—then we would expect a reallocation of purchases toward the product yielding more benefit per dollar and away from the one yielding less.

Moreover, when prices change, we expect two kinds of reactions. Consider a price increase. We expect that the good becomes relatively less appealing so that the consumer finds other goods—potential substitutes—relatively more appealing. We also expect that we are more likely to respond as the size of the increase grows. If the price of one's usual choice for an everyday white wine doubles, then one is more likely to re-consider that choice and look for an alternative. Conversely, if an alternative is half-price, then one may buy more of it and less of other wines. This kind of price sensitivity is the *substitution effect*: price changes in one direction lead to changes in the quantity demanded of a good in the opposite direction.

Beyond the substitution effect, a price change also affects the extent of one's purchasing power. A price increase decreases one's purchasing power and conversely for a price decrease. This may seem odd: prices change all the time—and in both directions—but our reactions to such changes typically do not include a sense that we have lost or gained purchasing power. Or do they? If we consider a price change that is (a) sizeable and (b) applies to some good that represents a significant proportion of our typical spending (e.g., housing), then we begin to understand the impact price changes can have upon our sense of our money's purchasing power. If one third of one's income goes for rent and that rent doubles, then one will feel poorer and likely decrease the amount of housing purchased[1] perhaps along with decreases in purchases of other goods. A wine aficionado who devotes a significant share of monthly expenditures to ageworthy Bordeaux will certainly feel an "income effect" of decreased purchasing power if those prices double—or, preferably, if they plummet (unless s/he collects only for investment value rather than personal consumption). Similar price changes for a bottle of table wine bought occasionally to drink with a pizza would have no such impact upon the consumer. (Changes in the aggregate price level in the economy—inflation or deflation—lead to similar feelings: for example, the general concern about price inflation, especially if it grows, is that it diminishes our purchasing power, and we all feel poorer.) In this sense, price changes can make us feel richer or poorer; this may be unfamiliar if we have not experienced price changes of such significance (e.g., hyperinflations such as postwar China or Germany during the 1920s).

Notwithstanding its possible unfamiliarity, we acknowledge that price changes can influence our sense of the extent of our purchasing power. This *income effect* of a price change operates in a predictable manner: conceptually, a price increase reduces the amount of our purchasing power (our money does not go as far—we feel poorer), and a price decrease increases the amount of our purchasing power (our money goes farther—we feel richer). We predict that this effect operates like actual changes in income. If we have more income, then we can imagine wanting more of many goods; if a price decreases so that we *feel* like we have more income—or our money goes farther—then we also buy more (and vice versa for income decreases or price increases). Do we expect the same reaction for all goods?

Another consideration that we only mention here is that our impulse to buy more as our income increases (or less with decreases) does not apply to all goods. For example, with sufficiently large increases in their usual income, wine aficionados tend to increase their purchases of premium or fine wines and decrease their purchases of ordinary or beverage wines; their minimum acceptable quality may change so that they may stop buying some wines altogether. This pattern of buying illustrates the economist's distinction between two types of goods: *normal goods* whose consumption varies directly with income and *inferior goods* whose consumption varies inversely with income (to be comprehensive, we can allow a third category—independent goods—whose consumption is independent of income changes). It is easy to understand the idea of normal goods; and, with sufficient experience as a consumer, we can recognize inferior goods beyond beverage wines—used cars, generic brands of groceries and clothing, less tender cuts of meat, rental housing, fast food. Note that the designation as "inferior" is not intentionally pejorative, and the designation "normal" is not intentionally complimentary: inferior goods may be good quality, excellent value, and reliable; and normal goods may be frivolous, wasteful, and offensive. The normal/inferior distinction is empirical, indicating only the direct or inverse relationship between demand changes and income changes.

It is fair to say that, because magnitudes matter, we may feel more familiar with the substitution effect than the income effect of the price changes that we usually encounter: our tendency to change how much we buy in the direction opposite the price change (e.g., buy less when the price rises) may more typically reflect our substituting (buying another product instead) than any feeling that we cannot "afford" as much or that we can afford much more.

Thus, we predict that a price change will have both a substitution effect and an income effect. Allowing for both effects yields an important and fundamental prediction about consumer behavior, very much in the spirit of model-building discussed earlier: for a normal good, changes in the quantity demanded move inversely with price changes. For example, if the price decreases, then the substitution effect suggests that the consumer will want more (substituting additional units of this good for units of other goods whose prices are unchanged), and the (normal good) income effect also suggests that the consumer will want more (feeling "richer" from the lower price, the consumer wants more of all normal goods). The two effects reinforce each other and lead to the prediction of the inverse price/quantity demanded relationship.

This is the logic behind the *demand curve* D depicted in Figure 4.1 where we identify the good's price (P) along the vertical axis of the graph and the number of units of the good—the quantity (Q)—along the horizontal axis.

If we assume that the product is standard bottles (750 ml) of red wine—perhaps some particular brand and vintage—then a point on the demand curve like A identifies the following predicted behavior: If the price of a bottle of red wine is $12, then the consumers in the market are ready, willing, and able to purchase 60 bottles. Substitution and income effects provide the logic behind the curve's downward sloping shape: assuming it

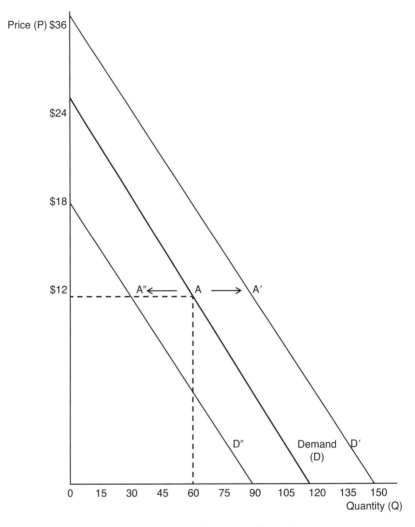

*Figure 4.1   The demand curve and changes in demand*

is a normal good, price decreases increase the quantity demanded, price increases decrease the quantity demanded.

Getting comfortable with graphic presentations of predicted behavior can be convenient: instead of presenting lists of prices and desired quantities, a graph can capture all that information in one picture.

The picture tells us—and helps us visualize—more. Recall that we have identified these pairs of prices and quantities as the outcome of some consumer decision-making process. In many market settings, consumers are told the price, and they respond with the quantity desired (we consider markets with price flexibility later). It is important to bear in mind that the quantity is the most desired quantity—the utility- or satisfaction-maximizing quantity: we started this discussion by assuming that the consumer wanted to make the most of her purchasing power (and similarly, by aggregating, for a group of consumers), and the quantity associated with a price is the outcome of that decision-making process—the best quantity at that price. We can infer that any quantity different from 60 is not as satisfying to the consumers. If only 50 bottles are available at $12, then the consumers get less than they want (a shortage, or excess demand): they can purchase some bottles but not all they want so, while some are better than none, they are disappointed. More difficult to imagine would be buying 80 bottles at $12 (a surplus, or excess supply relative to their desired quantity)—which would require coercion. The consumers might be willing to do it—within limits, having too many is better than having none—but they would rather have only the 60 bottles. Buying more or less than the most desired quantity is a less desirable outcome for the consumers. Understanding the optimality to consumers of being "on the demand curve"—and not off—at a given price will help us understand the concept of market equilibrium that we discuss later (Chapter 5).

Not only does point A tell us that consumers are happiest buying 60 bottles for $12 each, it also embeds the initial idea that consumers are willing to purchase because they have a taste for this wine. However, a price of $24 would extinguish demand: quantity demanded decreases to zero (maximum quantity demanded is 120 bottles at zero price—likely unrealistic but a reflection of our simplified assumption of a linear demand curve).

If consumers had a stronger desire or taste/preference—perhaps as a result of advertising or some expert's recommendation—then they would want more bottles at the same price, and point A would move to the right to reflect that. While the size of that positive influence on demand might depend upon the particular price, we expect that it would apply at almost any price so that the entire demand curve would shift right as reflected by the demand curve D'. We see also that the most anyone would pay likely increases. Conversely, some other change in the market setting such as unfavorable reviews or health reports about the risks of wine consumption might decrease consumers' desire at this price and shift point A—and, once again, the entire demand curve—to the left to D''. At every price consumers want less; also, demand is extinguished at a lower price.

From this, one can also see a fundamental reason why markets disappear, have not yet appeared, or may come and go. If the highest price anyone is willing to pay—perhaps decreasing because of decreased popularity, adverse publicity (e.g., health warnings), or some other reason—is less than the lowest price a producer is willing to charge, then no transactions occur so there is no market. An increased willingness to pay and/or falling production costs can create or revive a "missing market".

What about markets where the price is not set? We shall consider two cases briefly at this point. First, if the price is negotiable—say it can only fall during negotiation—then one might decide to buy more if the final price is lower so the price is no longer $12: if the wine merchant agrees to give a 20 percent discount, then consumers receiving the discount may buy more bottles (likely the merchant's reason for offering the discount). Second, if the price is negotiable and the quantity is fixed, then we can still infer that consumers want 60 bottles if the price is $12/bottle. However, they would willingly pay less if possible. This suggests an important concept that we shall find useful: if a consumer can purchase an item for less than her willingness to pay (WTP) for it, then she receives *consumer surplus*—defined as the difference between WTP and actual price, another important concept covered in standard introductory economics texts (e.g., Mankiw 2015: 136–140).

Introducing this concept requires special care: consumer surplus conveys the idea that the consumer is receiving value beyond what she pays—she is willing to pay more than she must pay and receives a surplus or a benefit net of expense. Any time we are prepared to purchase something at one price but actually pay less, we receive consumer surplus. This is distinctly different from, and essentially unrelated to, the concept of surplus as "excess supply" that we used earlier—an amount of a good available at a given price that exceeds the quantity demanded.

The importance of this concept is difficult to overstate. In effect, consumer surplus represents the consumer's benefit from transacting: it is what s/he takes from the transaction net of what s/he dispenses. If our focus is "transacting the elixir of life", then this is critical to the consumer's decision to transact. As we shall see, consumer surplus is conceptually the consumer analogue to producers' profit (which, we shall see, is not necessarily purely pecuniary). If we can acknowledge and appreciate the importance of some version of profit to motivating producers, then we are on the way to understanding the importance of consumer surplus to motivating consumers.

We can use curve D in Figure 4.1 and point A to calculate an approximate but convenient measure of consumer surplus to illustrate its meaning. Consumers want 60 bottles of wine when the price is $12; by the same reasoning and considering the shape of the demand curve, say that they want 59 bottles when the price is $12.20/bottle. Generally, we predict that, as the price per bottle increases, their desired quantity decreases (we shall assume, as a simplified but convenient example, that each $0.20 increase in price reduces the quantity demanded by one bottle and similarly for price decreases). That suggests that, at a given price, the "last" bottle purchased is, approximately, the "breakeven" bottle—that is, the price is approximately the consumer's WTP for that bottle. That price is too high to convince consumers to demand even one more bottle but low enough to add the last bottle to the desired quantity relative to the quantity desired at a slightly higher price. At $12, that price exceeds the WTP for the next bottle—bottle 61—which is why the consumers stop at bottle 60; and $12 is below the WTP for bottle 59 and, in fact, all inframarginal bottles (bottles 1–59).

Following this, we can interpret the price at every quantity on the demand curve as consumers' WTP *for that bottle* and the difference between that vertical distance and the actual price as consumers' surplus for that bottle (which is negative—like "consumer's deficit"—if we consider bottles beyond what consumers want at a given price). In this example, if the price is $12, then a consumer gets $0.20 consumer surplus for bottle 59. If consumers want 58 bottles if the price is $12.40—but the price is actually $12—then consumers get $0.40 consumer surplus on bottle 58, $0.20 consumer surplus on bottle 59, and break even on bottle 60.

If we extrapolate from this analysis, then we can approximate the aggregate consumer surplus (ACS) generated when consumers buy 60 bottles when the price is $12/bottle as the area below the demand curve and above the stated price; in Figure 4.2 with its linear demand curve, the shaded triangle represents this.

It is useful that we can measure this: given the assumed shape, the demand curve will intersect the P axis when the price is $24—the lowest integer price that extinguishes demand for the wine and just above the highest price anyone is willing to pay for the wine—and the ACS at a $12 price is, by our approximate measure, $360 (the area of a triangle with base of 60 and height of $12). If we could charge WTP for each of the 60 bottles (i.e., perfect price discrimination), then consumers would pay about $360 more for the 60 bottles than they do when the price is simply $12/bottle.[2,3]

Understanding the concept of consumer surplus provides a variety of insights into consumer behavior and firm pricing strategies. For example, acknowledging the existence of consumer surplus challenges the idea that "you get what you pay for". If that were true, then one could not receive consumer surplus since it requires that one pay for all the benefit one receives. To the extent that one finds a bargain or can negotiate a price lower than one's WTP, then one gets more than one pays for. Indeed, it would seem unreasonable to believe sincerely that one can get only what

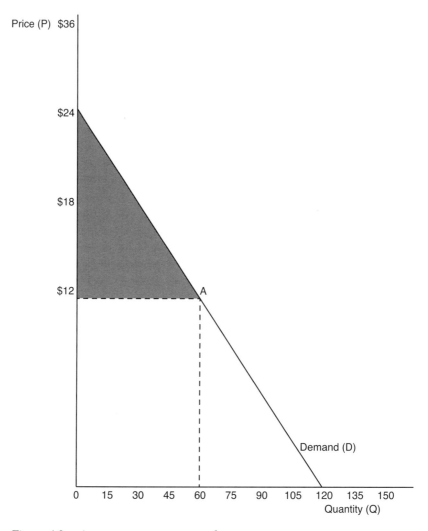

*Figure 4.2    Aggregate consumer surplus*

one pays for and should therefore avoid bargains, surprisingly lower prices, and negotiating for lower prices—or the deals on wines discussed in Chapter 2 that are offloaded by producers and rebranded to avoid diluting a brand.[4]

Realizing that consumers are likely to enjoy consumer surplus when they find a bargain, producers can try to capture some of that as profit by charging an "entrance fee" to markets that offer bargains—a membership fee for a discount retailer, an entry fee for access to discounted or "free" goods (e.g., free rides at an amusement park, "free food" at an all-you-can-eat restaurant). This is so-called two-part pricing (e.g., Baye 2010: 408–410) where Part I allows the buyer access to the relevant market (e.g., an entrance or admission fee, a cover charge) and Part II is the price per unit of the good being sold. With sufficiently careful analysis of the consumers' demand curve, one can make more profit with two-part pricing than by allowing free access to the good and selling it at a fixed price.

Figure 4.2 can illustrate a straightforward application of this pricing strategy. If we assume that the demand curve applies to an individual consumer rather than a market, then it tells us that the consumer would be willing to pay about $360 more than the market requires when s/he buys 60 bottles of this wine at $12 apiece (the Part II price). That suggests that the supplier of this wine—the producer, a retailer, a wine club organized by a broker—could charge this consumer up to $360 for the opportunity to buy this wine for $12, perhaps calling the charge a membership fee or a purchasing license (the Part I price).

Given this example, one might wonder where we see such pricing in the wine market: it may not sound familiar. One reason it is unfamiliar requires us to recall the idea of WTP. Recall that the height of the demand curve at any quantity indicates WTP for that unit of the good. In a well-developed retail wine market, consumers have extensive choice of wines: typically, between the number of producers and vintages available, one might not be willing to pay much above the asking price for many bottles of a given wine because one has so many alternatives. That is, the demand curve for any given wine might be almost horizontal so the ACS from purchases of that wine is too small to make two-part pricing practical.

Another reason is that capturing ACS from the (ultimate) buyer can appear in other ways. For example, access to some highly prized ("cult") wines is limited to those on the seller's mailing list. Assuming demand for the wine supports it, selling places on the mailing list amounts to charging a Part I price. Such a policy is unknown or certainly not widespread—sellers tend to use non-price allocation such as first-come-first-served or authority (to those who deserve a place)—but those on the mailing list have been known to sell their places (e.g., McCoy 2009). The seller is not charging the Part I price, but someone is. Different but related ways of capturing ACS include "flipping" such allocated wines—buying them at the mailing list price and then selling them immediately for a capital gain (e.g., Taylor 2013). Other related techniques for turning consumer surplus into profit would include requiring a buyer to purchase either excess wine or unwanted wine in order to get the desired wine—in effect, offsetting some or all of the ACS from one purchase with a "consumer deficit" (paying more than one's WTP) on another purchase, presumably for a wine that the seller is having difficulty selling at its current price.[5]

## Other Key Variables Affecting Consumer Demand

Third after tastes and price, the consumer must live within her means which is available *purchasing power* (we can include credit—which is current purchasing power for which one usually pays a premium (interest) since it is borrowed). Here we consider some typical source of purchasing power such as annual *income* (distinct from the income effect that we discussed in the context of the impact of price changes).

We would expect demand for many goods to depend upon purchasing power and to respond to changes in income. Higher incomes—found from comparing different markets or from monitoring markets during the business cycle and watching them rise during recovery—tend to increase demand, but demand sensitivity may vary widely. Wine demand may be more income sensitive than demand for electricity among the middle class. Also, identifying wine as a normal or inferior good is an empirical question. While we expect wine demand to vary directly with income—it is a normal good—we expect an inverse relationship between income changes and demand for sub-groups of wines. If consumers buy more fine wine (e.g., classified Bordeaux) with higher income and less non-vintage and jug wine, then the former is a normal good and the latter is an inferior good. As in that example, the normal/inferior designation may seem to conform to general perceptions of quality; but, as noted earlier, it does not reflect any inherent information about quality. It is simply an indication of the correlation between income changes and demand changes.

We can represent the influence of purchasing power on demand using Figure 4.1. Now that we have acknowledged the importance of income on demand, we realize that point A indicates the influence of tastes, price, and income on demand. If wine is a normal good and income increases, then point A would move to the right—and similarly in principle at every price—so that now a shift such as D to D′ could reflect this impact of higher income. For normal goods, higher incomes increase demand. However, if this is a demand curve for a wine with diminishing appeal as consumer income increases and they prefer something different—if we observe from market behavior that this wine is an inferior good—then point A would shift to the left with higher income and similarly at every price (and D shifts to D″).

Fourth, the *prices of other goods* matter. When we consider a purchase, we consider the price of the good itself—"own" price—but we also may consider the prices of other goods "related" to it. If other goods are similar and we might be able to use them instead—if they are potential *substitutes*—then we might choose one of them if they are less expensive and provide the same benefit: in a large urban market where wine is widely available, consumers looking for a bottle of everyday wine can choose among an abundance of substitutes—wines that they consider essentially interchangeable. If we have a favorite everyday wine and all such substitutes are more expensive and interchangeable, then we skip them. Why would we pay more without getting any more benefit from the purchase? Similarly, if the price of a substitute decreases—for example, it is on sale or closeout—then we are more likely to choose it: we buy more of the substitute and less of our usual choice.

From this it follows that we expect the demand for a good to vary directly with the price of a substitute: for example, if one decreases, then the other decreases. If a substitute wine is on sale, we tend to buy more of it and less of our usual choice, *cet. par.* We can represent this in Figure 4.1: if point A represents current market conditions and the corresponding consumer behavior toward Wine R, then a significant decrease in the price of a substitute would convince consumers to buy less Wine R at a price of $12. In effect, point A would shift to the left. Since we can extend this logic to any point on the demand curve, we expect that a decrease in the price of a substitute shifts the entire demand curve to the left. Knowing details such as the size of the shift and its sensitivity to the price level is more complicated. The existence and size of the shift require that consumers respond—the price change must get their attention—and the size of the shift reflects, in part, the extent to which they consider the two wines substitutable.

On the other hand, the purchase of one good often involves or even requires the purchase of another good: if we plan to purchase an automobile, then we will need fuel for it, and it will require maintenance and repairs from time to time. When we select certain cuisines, we may be likely to want wine to accompany the food. These goods whose purchase accompanies some other purchase are *complements*. The use of the term for this type of good reflects the role they play relative to some other good: complements are goods that "complete" the use of some other good. After enough experience with complementary goods, consumers become more sensitive to the financial implications of purchases. For example, purchasing a relatively expensive, fuel-inefficient automobile often entails purchasing an associated series of relatively expensive maintenance and repairs—and more fuel per mile. Expensive cars tend to have more expensive tires and oil changes and overhauls. However, sometimes the relationship is inverse so that relatively expensive goods have relatively inexpensive complements and vice versa: inexpensive computer printers may have expensive ink cartridges.

The idea of complementarity is particularly important with wine. For example, once one's interest extends beyond beverage wines, one is likely to seek wine information and knowledge to improve the reliability of one's wine purchases. Also, much of wine appreciation involves wine and food pairings. This traditional role for wine arose, at least in part, because the most successful wines in a region were those that complemented the local cuisine in regions where both wine and food production were viable. Certain wines were good complements for seafood (e.g., Loire Valley sauvignon blanc or Muscadet with shellfish); others went well with local meat or cheese. The importance of this pairing depends not only upon individual tastes but also upon the type of wine. The former is typically more important: our palate tells us the foods whose flavor is enhanced with a given wine and those whose flavor clashes. Some such beneficial pairings are well established, and some are to be avoided such as sweet desserts and dry wines or raw apples and virtually any wine. More challenging perhaps are "food wines"—wines whose impact are traditionally enhanced significantly with food and whose full impact is lost without it.

If these pairings were strict—like printers and ink cartridges—then we could imagine that the demand for the appropriate wine could be heavily influenced by the price of its complementary food: if the price of oysters jumped and consumers bought fewer oysters, then we might expect that the demand for Muscadet might decrease. Of course, such pairings are not so strict so it would be difficult to isolate such a relationship. Most wines and foods are complementary with a number of alternatives—or substitutes. Moreover, for a variety of reasons such as the lower cost of shipping and producing more durable wines, the idea of pairing has receded so that wine is increasingly perceived as a beverage to enjoy on its own. The weakening of the wine–food connection has weakened the role of complementarity as an influence on demand.

Price changes for complements have an inverse relationship to the demand for a good. We can represent this in Figure 4.1: if point A represents current market conditions and the corresponding consumer behavior, then a significant decrease in the price of a complement would convince consumers to buy more at a price of $12. In effect, point A would shift to the right. Since we can extend this logic to any point on the demand curve, we expect that a decrease in the price of a complement shifts the entire demand curve to the right. Once again, the existence and size of the shift require that consumers respond and the size of the shift reflects, in part, the extent to which they consider the two products complementary. For example, finding oysters on sale could lead consumers to buy more oysters (move down their demand curve for oysters) and also to buy more Muscadet at its usual price (the Muscadet demand curve shifts right when oyster prices decrease).

An important lesson to take from this is that other goods' prices may affect the demand for a given wine more significantly than the wine's own price.

While the logic of substitutes and complements is instinctive, the identification of substitutes and complements is actually empirical: two goods have that relationship only if market behavior demonstrates it. If we see merlot sales increase when cabernet sauvignon prices increase, *cet. par.*, then we have evidence that the two varietals are substitutes (and conversely if cabernet prices decrease). While probably less intuitive, we would say the same if chardonnay sales and cabernet prices behaved similarly. We would support a claim that Muscadet and oysters are complements by looking for corresponding price change/demand change relationships.

These four influences—consumer preferences, own price, purchasing power, and prices of related goods—affect demand without regard to the role of time. Consumers respond to these influences and changes in them, but often—perhaps typically—they also look ahead and have expectations: the fifth influence is consumer *expectations* about the future. While some of our consumption decisions seem spontaneous or impulsive with no sense of planning or thoughts for the future and some are virtually independent of such concerns, our expectations often influence our current consumption decisions. When someone receives a significant raise or wins a large lottery prize, we expect them to have much more purchasing power in the future and to change at least some of their current consumption patterns and generally to consume more (normal) goods. If we consider this carefully, then we can say that such changes in consumption will appear in the "current" market. Certainly we expect to consume more tomorrow, next week, and next year; but, once we have the changed information, we likely will buy more now.

While we can imagine a number of applications of the role of expectations to wine demand, some are more subtle than others. For example, news of a large or small harvest or a particularly high or low quality vintage in some prominent wine area such as Bordeaux—or perhaps the release of expert opinion about that vintage—is likely to affect expectations about the future price of the wines upon release and, in turn, the current price of the corresponding wine futures (e.g., Ali, Lecocq, and Visser 2010) (see below). Such news may suggest, in effect, a windfall increase (for a good vintage) in the future supply of good wine with implications for the markets for, and market prices of, substitutes and complements. For example, current prices for competing, substitute wines may either decrease or slow their rate of increase with news of increased future supplies. On the other hand, news of a poor or unusually small vintage might increase current prices of competing wines.

Perhaps more obviously, an expectation of considerably higher income leads consumers to demand more of certain wines. More precisely, the net effect upon the demand curve for a given wine reflects the aggregation of all consumers' demand responses: with generally rising incomes, lower income consumers might increase their demand for a wine at the same time that higher income consumers move on to higher quality and reduce their demand for the same wine—certainly one consumer's normal good may be another's inferior good, and what may be a normal good for me now may become an inferior good if my income rises enough.

Once again, we can turn to Figure 4.1 to illustrate this effect. Point A on curve D represents consumers' *current* most desired quantity at $12 per bottle and, we can add, reflects given values or "settings" for preferences, income, and the prices of any goods somehow connected to this wine. Any change in one of these values could move point A to the right or left: more or less wine desired at the given price of $12 per bottle. We can also add that it reflects given expectations about the future—not necessarily that everything stays the same, just that expectations are fixed (e.g., wine prices remain the same indefinitely or, alternatively, will rise by 5 percent annually from now on).

How do we capture the effect of a change in expectations? Conceptually, any change in our expectations about the future could increase or decrease the amount of wine we want now. If a local retailer announces a significant sale starting next week—in effect, if they can reliably expect that prices will be lower next week than they are this week—then consumers may postpone some or all of their purchases until the sale. If Figure 4.1 represents this week's wine market, then point A would move to the left and similarly for the entire demand curve. A new expectation of decreased future wine prices decreases current demand. Wine collectors who have just learned that they have a terminal disease so that their expected "years remaining" decrease are likely to reduce their current demand for wines whose maturity is years in the future. Those who just received unexpected salary increases or won the lottery and now expect to have more purchasing power from now on are likely to increase their current demand—a rightward shift of point A and the entire demand curve, assuming wine is a normal good.

In principle, changes in a variety of expectations can shift the demand curve. Consumers' current demand is conditioned by all sorts of plans for the future—their health, their personal and social situation (e.g., marriage, parenting), their economic situation (e.g., employment stability), their level of knowledge. One of the most familiar expectations involves prices. Most consumers are sensitive to the expected movements in at least some prices, especially for goods that are storable, that is, that can be purchased at one time and used later. If consumers learn of an upcoming sale, then they may postpone their purchase—decrease current demand—until the sale. If they begin to feel that prices are increasing, then they may accelerate their purchases before the increase: for example, rising housing prices influence consumers as they hope to buy something before they are "priced out of the market". As many have learned, reactions to such expectations can be self-fulfilling as increased demand does indeed lead to higher prices—until, perhaps, the bubble bursts.

A more subtle example of the role of expectations involves wine futures—contracts to purchase wine well in advance of its release by the producer similar to futures contracts for commodities. Wine futures are typically promoted as a way of securing access to a wine at a price below the price expected when the wine is actually released—the release price. The market for Bordeaux futures is one of the most established such markets where brokers of Bordeaux wines—at least those with the best reputations—offer futures contracts in the spring following a vintage for delivery, or release, approximately two years ahead.

Futures markets exist because of expectations: for the Bordeaux market, consumers are willing to pay now for delivery in two years because they expect the price in two years to be sufficiently higher that current payment is more appealing than waiting, despite the "costs" of current payment such as losing the income those funds might earn (e.g., in an investment) and the risk that they might never receive the wine (e.g., if their futures vendor goes bankrupt before the wine is delivered). With futures markets, the price expectations are the reason for the market: they explain the futures demand curve, but they do not shift it. However, if consumers come to expect that the release price will be different from their initial expectation, then we expect the demand for futures to shift in the same direction as their changed expectations: for example, they will increase their demand for futures if the expected release price increases.

Another reason sometimes given for futures purchases is to secure an allocation of the wine for fear that it will "sell out" upon release (e.g., Parker 1993: 171). But this is usually not a different reason for purchasing futures. For widely traded wines such as good Bordeaux, consumers will be able to buy it upon release—as long as they are willing to pay the market price at that time. The wine is unlikely to become completely unavailable—sell out—unless we mean by implication that it will sell out at "the old price" or the original price or some such. Thus, a concern about the wine being sold out is another way of saying that the wine's expected price at release will be so high that buying futures now is preferred.

In markets involving international trade among countries using different currencies—certainly a characteristic of wine markets—a sixth influence upon demand is the *foreign exchange rate*. About one-third of global wine production is exported to other countries (Anderson and Nelgen 2014: 32, Table I-3). Not all of this trade occurs between countries using different currencies—intra-Eurozone trade is likely to be the largest exception—but most of it does, and thus it is important to understand the role of exchange rates as an influence upon international wine markets.

In this context, it becomes important to designate the currency in which the price in Figure 4.1 is denominated. We shall assume for now that it is US dollars (USD). Thus, point A in Figure 4.1 says that consumers worldwide want 60 bottles when the price is 12 USD per bottle. What if some of the consumers responding to that price have purchasing power in a currency other than USD? For example, German consumers may enjoy California cabernet wines. However, most German consumers have purchasing power denominated only in euros. If we assume for simplicity that the euro and the USD are trading at par—one euro per USD—then the $12 price is also 12 euros. However, if the rate of exchange between euros and USD changes—say, the euro appreciates against the USD so that one euro buys two USD—then the wine is, in effect, "half price" to German consumers. Initially, the $12 price meant that it was 12 euros per bottle, but with the revised exchange rate their price is only 6 euros. For those consumers using euros, the price has decreased, and we expect them to buy more wine: point A would move to the right as would the entire demand curve with the size of the shift depending upon the size of the German market for the cabernet.

If the change in the exchange rate went the other way—for example, the euro could buy only half a USD instead of one—then the $12 price taken with the now-weaker euro would now represent a 24-euro price, and consumers with euros would buy less: the demand curve would shift left. Given the importance of international trade in the global wine market, the importance of changes in exchange rates is clear. For example, the UK imports almost all its wine from countries which use a different currency. Traditionally, a significant share of US wine purchases are imports; for example, it imported 35 percent of its wine in 2012 (Veseth 2013).

Finally, all of the influences on demand discussed thus far apply to the individual decision maker and, by extension, to all the consumers in the market. Since the market consists of all participating consumers, if they change their demand, then the market demand curve will change according to the net effect of the sum of the individual changes. Even if individual demand is unchanged, however, if the *number of consumers* changes, then the quantity sold marketwide at any price will change in the same direction: more consumers joining the market shifts market demand right, consumers leaving the market shifts market demand left. This is another source of shifts in the market's demand curve.

In addition, like many consumer goods, each consumer's demand may be affected by knowledge of who else is or is not in the market—a form of external influence of one consumer's purchases upon another (a form of economic *externality*). If the influence is the participation, or lack thereof, of some celebrity or expert, would we want to add that to the list of key variables in our model like other prices or expectations? That could depend upon the market we are studying. For goods for which this is a prominent influence upon consumer decisions—for example, goods for which celebrity endorsements are traditionally important such as sporting goods or processed foods—then adding that to the model may be advisable. The question of whether endorsements are sufficiently distinct from general advertising to warrant special recognition will again depend upon the product.

The importance of the participation of others may be more idiosyncratic. The extent of our interest may depend upon the endorsement, or lack thereof, of someone we know and whose judgment we trust. A different form of the influence of others is the general popularity of a product: the likelihood and magnitude of our market participation may depend upon what "everyone else" thinks. As the number of market participants grows, then our interest may increase. The advent and popularity of social media is a reflection of our interest in what others think as we make our market decisions. It is more difficult to model these influences upon our behavior, but it is worth acknowledging their importance.

## CONCLUSION

We have begun our study of wine economics by considering the methodology of economics—essentially, the scientific method which is closely related to the way we address our personal challenges and questions and search for reliable predictions, both every day and lifelong. The concept of modeling involves a number of important principles: (1) Stating the objective or the question to be answered exactly; (2) Judging carefully between the influences to include and the ones to exclude; (3) Moving logically from assumptions and influences to predictions about the outcome, paying attention to their relationship to each other; (4) Both collecting data representing the influences and outcome and applying it carefully;

and (5) Keeping an open mind, willing to modify the model in every way to improve its reliability.

Our first application of that method has been a model of consumer behavior with a focus upon consumer demand and predictions related to it. We have discussed consumer demand with an emphasis on a handful of influences that tend to be important—in most markets, in one form or another. The actual influences on demand will depend upon the product and the market: for example, expert opinion may influence demand significantly in fine wine markets but be largely irrelevant in the "beverage wine" market.

Next, we consider the other side of the market—the behavior of those who supply the goods consumers want.

# APPENDIX: A NOTE ON ELASTICITY

It should be apparent that a central focus in economics is reactions. How do consumers respond to changes in prices or changes in their incomes? How do producers respond to changes in their production costs or a competitor's price? Up to now, we have been discussing reactions either in simple qualitative terms—consumers bought less when the price increased, firms produced more after a decrease in raw materials prices—or in comparable quantitative terms (perhaps with the help of a mathematical model of the market) such as a $100 increase in income increased demand by 800 units (always bearing in mind that these statements assume *cet. par.*).

Economists regularly use another measure of responsiveness that can provide a fuller understanding of the size of some reaction. To appreciate its value, consider the following simple "Annual Report" from a hypothetical one-wine winery:

- "CEO Philippine Matour presented First Quarter results for Chateau Lafite Brion today. After a price increase of $1 per bottle for Ch. Lafite Brion Rouge this quarter, sales fell by 500 bottles. Merci!"

If our interest is the business performance of Ch. Lafite Brion, would we consider this news good or bad? Does Ms. Matour deserve a bonus or a termination notice? Lost sales are bad news, but a higher price per bottle is good news (once again, we assume all else is constant so that the extra dollar per bottle goes into profit). Depending upon which result occurs to us first, we might conclude either bad or good news respectively—but, since both those observations are valid, that suggests that the correct answer is "it depends" and that what we want is "net news" since what we want to know is the net effect of both impacts of a higher price per bottle.

Ms. Matour has provided information that is consistent with something we know about markets so it makes sense: higher prices decrease the quantity demanded. But what further information would bring us closer to resolving the question of the meaning of this news? For example, if Ch. Lafite Brion has been selling 1,000,000 bottles per quarter at the original price of $10/bottle (total revenue = $10,000,000), then earning an extra dollar per bottle and reducing sales by only 500 bottles would increase revenue by $994,500 to $10,994,500—and the increase is all profit which is certainly a good outcome: the net news is good. On the other hand, if it has been selling only 10,000 bottles per quarter for $1,000/bottle (once again, total revenue = $10,000,000), then this is not a good outcome: total revenue has fallen by $490,500 to $9,509,500.

Apparently, we have net good news for a "high volume, low price" product but net bad news for a relatively "low volume, high price" product: if the added revenue from the remaining sales more than offsets the lost revenue from the lost sales, then we are ahead—and conversely. Put another way, the price increase increases revenue if the percentage increase in price is larger than the percentage decrease in units sold. However, the mathematics behind that last conclusion may not be obvious.

We must also add that the price changes we consider must be small enough so that they are "reasonable": for example, a large enough price increase could extinguish sales entirely.

This example illustrates the more general principle that we are often interested in not only the directions of changes—changes in price and quantity demanded in our example—but also their relative sizes. One concept that helps capture relative movements is elasticity. Measuring changes—for example, price and quantity changes—can be useful, but measuring the relative size of such movements can, too; and it can often add additional valuable information.

The generic definition of elasticity is the percentage change in some outcome divided by the percentage change in some key variable, usually one that is expected to affect the outcome: it is the ratio of the percentage change in the outcome per unit percentage change in the influence which is clearly consistent with the goal of measuring responsiveness. References to elasticity later in the text will always refer to a ratio of this kind where the outcome and influence will be clear from the context. In our example, the outcome is the quantity of bottles demanded and the key variable is the bottle price. Our results suggest that a price increase will increase total revenue if the percentage decrease in the quantity demanded is smaller than the percentage increase in the price—for example, relatively speaking, if we raise price a lot and sales fall just a little (both in percentage terms), then revenue is likely to increase. An extreme example would be if sales did not fall at all—the case of a vertical demand curve—where it is obvious that a price increase yields good results for the firm.

If we change Ms. Matour's price change from a $1 increase to a $1 decrease (with a corresponding change in the direction but not the size of the change in sales) and do the same comparison, we find that this is the strategy that raises revenue for the high price/low volume wine. A reasonable price decrease will increase total revenue if the percentage increase in the quantity demanded is larger than the percentage decrease in price: the increased revenue from more bottles sold more than covers the lost revenue from charging the lower price.

# THE OWN-PRICE ELASTICITY OF DEMAND

We have just introduced the own-price elasticity of demand (Ed) with our story of Madame Matour. As our analysis of the impact of her decision suggests, the net effect of her decision to increase the price of Ch. Lafite Brion can be either increased or decreased revenue. We shall see below how we can tell which to expect.

By definition, Ed is the ratio of the percentage change in quantity demanded (Q) divided by the percentage change in own price (P):

$$Ed = (change\ in\ Q/Q)/(change\ in\ P/P) \qquad (4A.1)$$

which we can also write as (using $\Delta$ for "change in")

$$= (\Delta Q/\Delta P) \times (P/Q) \qquad (4A.2)$$

where we measure the change in the variable between two points on the demand curve and treat P and Q as the average of the two values. We know that this number is negative or zero since the value of a change in Q that corresponds to any change in P must have the opposite sign: when P rises, Q falls, and conversely. We know that the slope of the demand curve over some portion—with P on the vertical axis and Q on the horizontal—either equals $(\Delta P/\Delta Q)$ if the demand curve is linear or averages that if the demand curve is curved. Since we can show that $(b/a) = (1/(a/b))$, we can write $(\Delta Q/\Delta P)$ as $(1/(\Delta P/\Delta Q))$ and equation (A4.2) as

$$Ed = (1/slope) \times (P/Q) \qquad (4A.3)$$

where "slope" represents the slope of the consumer demand curve. This indicates that, for a given value of average P and Q, the own-price elasticity of demand varies inversely with the slope of the demand curve. If the demand curve is steep—the slope is a large negative number (e.g., $-50$)—then elasticity will be closer to zero than if the demand curve is flat (a relatively small negative number (e.g., $-3$)). The steepest demand curve is vertical—no change in Q with changes in P—so Ed = 0; and the flattest demand curve is horizontal so Ed = $-\infty$ since the percentage change in Q is infinitely larger than the percentage change in P (which approaches 0).

It helps to know the terms used to describe values of Ed that fall within a certain range:

$$Ed = 0: \qquad \text{Completely inelastic}$$
$$0 \geq \; Ed \geq\rangle -1 \qquad \text{Inelastic}$$
$$Ed = -1 \qquad \text{Unit elastic}$$
$$-1 \geq Ed \geq -\infty \qquad \text{Elastic}$$
$$Ed = -\infty \qquad \text{Completely or infinitely elastic}$$

Thus, we can say that, for given values of P and Q, demand is more elastic as the slope of the demand curve for those values becomes less negative, or flatter: for given P and Q, a flatter demand curve depicts more relative quantity responsiveness to changes in own price than a steeper one.

We can also draw a useful conclusion about price changes and changes in total revenue using this terminology and the results we illustrated above. For reasonable (small enough) price changes, revenue changes and price changes move in the same direction when demand is inelastic and in the opposite direction when demand is elastic. Ms. Matour's success with the price increase in the high volume/low price regime amounts to raising price with inelastic demand; the success with the price decrease occurred with low volume/high price regime where demand was elastic.

Interest in estimating elasticities related to alcohol consumption is well established for a variety of reasons. For example, aside from commercial interest in consumer responsiveness to price changes, governments study the extent to which alcohol taxation—which obviously affects beverage prices—affects both alcohol consumption and tax revenue. As long as demand is inelastic, price increases reflecting tax increases will yield tax revenue. In a particularly useful paper related to an interest in that policy question, Nelson (2013) reviewed 104 studies that generated estimates of Ed and the income elasticity of demand (Em)—percentage change in demand divided by percentage change in income. He found significant differences among countries and country groups (e.g., US, Europe), but his overall estimate for Ed was −0.45—clearly inelastic—and +1.00 for Em, indicating that demand for wine changes in step with income changes, though this is not inconsistent with different normal and inferior good buying patterns among sub-groups of wines. Also, it is again important to bear in mind national and regional differences (e.g., European demand is more price elastic than US demand).

To some extent, the robust estimate of price inelastic demand reflects the impact of addiction on overall demand for alcohol. Addicted consumers are, of course, notoriously insensitive to price changes. Price-inelastic demand also bodes well for raising revenue through taxation. Thus, we have the suggestion of a public policy dilemma with alcohol: governments might simultaneously encourage and discourage alcohol consumption. This is a topic for Chapter 6.

## NOTES

1. The idea of decreasing the quantity of one's housing consumption is subtle. This could mean renting a smaller unit, but it could also mean renting a lower quality unit or a unit in a less desirable neighborhood or "less housing" along any of a number of dimensions that one might use to define the quantity of housing one consumes.

2. Using our vertical distance measure of WTP—the P value at each quantity equals WTP, and CS is the difference between that and the assumed $12 price—the total of all the CS measures is $0 + $0.20 + $0.40 + $0.60 + $0.80 + . . . + $11.80 = $354. Why the difference with the triangle's area? If one thinks of each WTP distance as a unit-wide rectangle (for the one bottle it represents) with height equal to WTP, then one constructs an area with base of 60, height on one end of $12 and the other end of $23.80, and a "stair step" top edge. The difference between the area of the triangle ($360) and the sum of the 60 one-unit-wide rectangles is a set of little triangles at the top of each rectangle, each with an area of $1 \times 0.20 \times 0.5$, or $.10. Sixty of these sum to $6, the difference in the two areas. As we increase the quantity we measure for a given distance of horizontal axis and a given price range—say, 600 bottles instead of 60 (so each $.02 change changes quantity demanded by one bottle)—the triangles get smaller and so does the discrepancy. In the limit, they disappear, and the two measures are the same.

3. The measure of consumer surplus is actually slightly different from the quantity indicated. The demand curve says that consumers maximize their utility if they can buy 60 bottles when the price is $12. To simplify, assume that this is a single consumer. In our example, saying that he would buy 60 bottles at $12 is not the same as saying that, if we were charging WTP for each bottle (starting with, say, $23.80 for the first and so forth), he would still be willing to pay $12 for the sixtieth: he wants 60 at $12 when he gets each bottle for $12. Instinctively, one can see that, if we started charging WTP for each bottle, his WTP for the sixtieth would likely be lower than $12—and slightly lower for all inframarginal bottles. Buying all 60 for $12 apiece has a "feeling richer" income effect (which stimulates demand for normal goods) which is lost if we charge WTP for each bottle. A steeper, income-compensated demand curve—that, starting with the first bottle, would tilt below the ordinary demand curve in Figure 4.2—is the one we should use to calculate ACS. However, the difference between the two measures is typically small since income effects of price changes in this context are small so economists tend to allow the measurement using the ordinary demand curve. See Willig 1976.

4. "You get what you pay for" is often heard from someone trying to sell something, attempting to nudge the buyer to accept the current price and/or stop negotiating. We also say it to ourselves to rationalize paying what we might suspect is more than we should have. That said, we must often pay full price if we want something badly enough. Paying more than necessary for an item that is widely available in identical form from equally convenient and reliable suppliers seems questionable. However, the modifiers in the previous sentence often do not apply. Given the value of time, paying more for convenience, reliability, and service is commonplace and rational. Also, the content of products like services where the provider's attitude may determine product content (especially when monitoring performance and quality is costly and warranties are weak and/or costly to enforce) may be more likely to reflect what one pays (e.g., auto or home repairs).

5. Something analogous happens when distributors require retailers to purchase low- or negative-margin wines in order to receive an "allocation" of high-margin wines.

# 5. Some basic tools of economics: firm behavior, supply, and equilibrium in a market

## INTRODUCTION

An underlying theme of this book is transactions. Our closer look at the decision to transact has begun with the one most familiar to most of us, namely, buying and selling consumer goods such as bottles of wine. We have already discussed the consumer side of that transaction, and we turn now to the supplier of those goods. Who supplies the goods that consumers want? One way or another, they are producers—organizations ("businesses") that acquire and manage productive resources from raw materials and employees to machines, land, structures, and advertising to produce and sell goods usually to make a profit which, for now, we consider to be sales revenues exceeding production costs.

In this chapter, we analyze supply behavior and then put buyers and sellers together to see how the market works. While the demand side of markets tends to be relatively unorganized, industry structure on the supply side can make a difference, and we discuss that. We close the chapter with a discussion of the challenge of asymmetric information.

## FIRMS

To an economist, a firm is any organization that assembles resources to achieve one or more identifiable objectives—for example, producing a product to be offered in a market. If we think broadly about the meanings of "product", "offer", and "market", then we can consider a wide range of organizations to be firms—from the familiar organizations with which we transact regularly such as grocery stores and gas stations to universities, churches, and charities such as the Red Cross. They all acquire resources and transform them so that their "customers" have access to what they are producing. In a pioneering paper, Ronald Coase (1937) defined a firm as "the system of relationships which comes into existence when the direction of resources is dependent upon an entrepreneur" (p. 393). Since an entrepreneur is simply someone who organizes and manages resources in the presence of risk for the sake of achieving one or more objectives, we can see how broadly the idea of a firm can be applied.

At the outset, we shall assume that the objective of firms is to maximize profit. While this goal likely dominates the various sectors of the wine industry—from vignerons (grape farmers) to distributors and retailers—we shall also allow for alternative objectives later (e.g., owner satisfaction) while noting that minimizing the cost of achieving any objective is always desirable. These other objectives that "wine suppliers" may pursue enrich our model of wine supply and help us understand why wine economics deserves special treatment.

As we developed our discussion of consumers in the context of understanding transactions, it was useful to describe how much consumers are ready, willing, and able to buy at a given price. In the same spirit, it is useful to describe how much firms are willing to sell at a given price. Beyond the logic of transacting, we can draw further upon our analysis from Chapter 3 where we explained the logic of a supply curve by appealing to the idea of a vigneron willing to grow and sell merlot grapes depending upon its price and the price it could receive from selling chardonnay, its alterative product.

Consider Figure 5.1 which resembles Figure 3.2 in that it represents the quantities that a firm—say, a winery—is ready, willing, and able to supply at various prices.

Once again, we identify prices (P—again in USD) measured on the vertical axis and quantities (Q) of the product, or good, measured on the horizontal axis; and we shall continue the example of bottles of wine that we used in talking about consumers. The firm is unwilling to supply any bottles until the price exceeds $3, the lowest cost at which it can produce a bottle of wine. As we saw in Figure 3.1, that could be the firm's cost that the price must cover over some range of production—the supply curve would be horizontal over that range of output—but we have assumed that the marginal cost of production rises continuously with production; with its linear shape, the supply curve assumes, only for simplicity, a constant rate of cost increase with increased output.

Point B describes a particular combination of P and Q describing supply behavior: at a price of $12, the firm is ready, willing, and able to supply 900 bottles. However, this point represents more: it reflects the firm's *best* quantity response—its profit-maximizing response—to a given price; and, in that sense, it is the supply side analogue to a point as "best point" on the consumer's demand curve. Thus, settling for any quantity other than 900

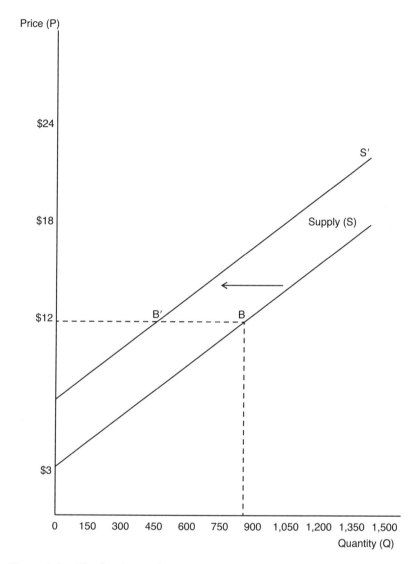

*Figure 5.1    The firm's supply*

when the price is $12 leaves the producer worse off. If she is unable to sell all 900 at that price, then she will be disappointed and will not make as much profit. Similarly, if somehow she must sell more than 900 at that price, then her profits fall on this product because, since her marginal cost exceeds $12, she is losing money on the units beyond 900 that she sells. Thus, the quantity represented by point B is optimal for the firm at that price.

If the firm is willing to sell wine for as little as $3 a bottle, or perhaps just more than that, but is actually selling it for $12 a bottle, then it is more than covering its costs: actual price less marginal cost is the definition of its *producer surplus*. This concept resembles one we introduced when discussing consumers and the demand curve and the idea of the "breakeven" bottle. For a given price, any quantity other than the one on the supply curve is less desirable—for suppliers, less profitable—either because the firm falls short of its most profitable sales or it is forced into sales at a loss. This means that the price at any point on the supply curve—in addition to representing the price that is most desirable for the firm's objectives (e.g., maximizes profits) at the corresponding level of sales—also just covers the production cost of the last unit sold at that price. The firm can offer any quantity at that price, but the quantity chosen must be one whose last unit sold costs just enough to be covered by that price: otherwise, with rising marginal cost, that unit costs more than the price and reduces profits, or it costs less than the price, and selling more units increases profits. That is, for the firm's breakeven bottle—that is, the last one it wants to sell at a given price (analogous to the last one consumers want to buy at a given price)— that price is approximately equal to the cost of producing that last unit (the marginal cost) of output at that price. This reminds us of the interpretation of vertical distance as marginal cost in the discussion of Figure 3.1.

With an upward sloping supply curve reflecting rising marginal cost with increasing output, the price required to elicit more output is increasing and, correspondingly, lower prices reduce desired output because they cover only lower marginal costs. Following our analysis and example, it follows that the marginal cost of producing bottle number 900 in the market depicted in Figure 5.1 is $12: it is the breakeven bottle that the firm wants to sell when the price is $12. If the price turns out to be $14, then we expect the firm to increase its desired sales if possible. However, we also know that the firm would have been willing to sell bottle number 900 for $12: if it sells for $14, then the difference of $2 is its producer surplus for bottle number 900. It should not be surprising that this "revenue minus cost" concept resembles profit.

We can extend this measurement to all the units sold at a given price to make a useful calculation. As drawn, Figure 5.1 indicates that, at a price of $12/bottle, the firm wants to sell 900 bottles. All infra-marginal bottles have a marginal cost below $12 and so earn producer surplus. Thus, the aggregate producer surplus resulting from the firm's desired sales is represented approximately by the triangular area between the horizontal $12 price "line" and the supply curve; Figure 5.2 depicts this.

Since the supply curve intersects the price axis at a price of $3—just below the lowest price at which the firm is willing to supply any bottles—then this

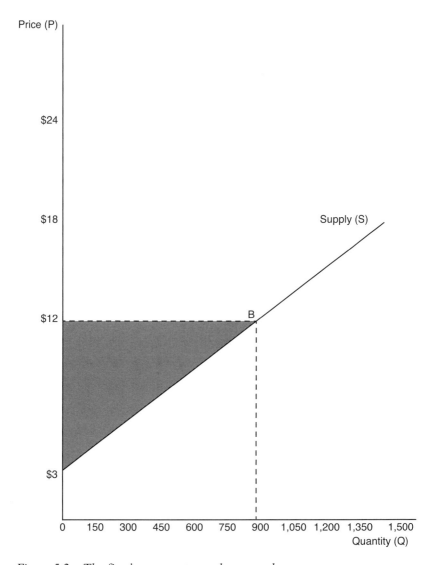

*Figure 5.2    The firm's aggregate producer surplus*

aggregate producer surplus is approximately \$4050 (= \$9 × 900 × 0.5). This is an estimate of the profit earned net of its opportunity costs when the firm produces and sells at point B on its supply curve.

Just as the market demand curve aggregates the demands of all individual consumers into one market-wide quantity at each price, we can

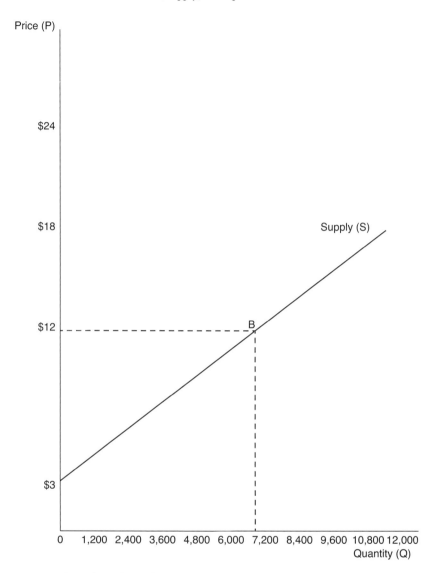

*Figure 5.3    The industry's supply (8 identical firms)*

aggregate the supply from all firms in a market into a market supply curve by "adding horizontally"—that is, each firm's quantity supplied at a given price—to find the aggregate quantity available at each price.

Figure 5.3 represents a market supply curve that assumes that the industry consists of eight identical firms, each with a supply curve like that in

Figure 5.1: the quantity available at any price is eight times as large as that for a single firm. Thus, for example, optimal supply for the industry is 7,200 bottles (8 x 900) when the price is $12.

## DETERMINANTS OF FIRM SUPPLY

With our model of demand, our story about consumer behavior started with consumer motivation and led to predictions about behavior based upon a handful of influences on behavior. Like demand, the pursuit of profit by supplying goods faces constraints and depends upon the impact of certain key influences. Like a recipe, actual production of most products involves a long list of "ingredients" that the firm must combine to produce its output. Since we want to model this process, we can abstract from long lists and identify a short list of widely acknowledged influences. A unifying theme in considering these influences is cost. If the goal is profit and the selling price is market-driven, then the firm focuses upon what it is best able to control which is cost. This is what we saw when we analyzed JM Enterprises' supply of merlot grapes in Chapter 3: the willingness to supply at various prices depended upon its cost in terms of lost revenue from chardonnay sales.

First, demand constrains the supplier. The supplier might be able to influence demand, but at any time, the supplier can sell only so much at any price. Initially, we shall assume that the demand curve is fixed: at any price, the supplier or the industry representing all suppliers, can sell only so much at a given (own) price, and once again *(own) price* is a key determinant. In Figure 5.1, point B indicates that the firm's optimal supply is 900 units when that price is $12.

How do we expect it to respond when price changes? The firm's ability to respond to price changes increases over time so we divide its choice of planning horizons into only two—the short run and the long run, the distinction being that its greater ability to adapt in the long run results from its ability to adjust all of its inputs (except its technology: changing that requires a period called the Very Long Run). In the short run, the firm finds adjustment more difficult because only some of its inputs are variable: at least one is fixed (the economist's definition of the firm's short run).

In the short run, the firm can expand production, but being bound by a fixed supply of one or more inputs means that ultimately its capacity is more constrained than if all inputs were adaptable. Production can increase as it uses more of the variable inputs, but the fixed input is a constraint on capacity. For example, a manufacturer may use more unskilled labor or buy more raw materials, but its equipment and, even more so, its plant are probably more difficult to expand. What are a winery's most and least variable inputs? That may depend upon its location and its products. If regulations allow it, a winery producing "homogenized" beverage wine, perhaps non-vintage (NV) so that vintages can be blended, might readily change almost anything in short order—from purchased bulk wine to bottles and labels to bottling capacity (if mobile bottlers are available) to storage and shipping.

These examples suggest constraints that, by contrast, fine wine producers might face. For example, an estate bottler has only limited interest in purchased juice, depending upon blending or content regulations. Since vine age affects grape characteristics, one cannot alter the number of one's "old vines" quickly. Also, some wines have vineyard designation (e.g., Burgundies, classified Bordeaux, and vineyard-specific bottlings from Napa Valley such as Heitz Cellars' "Martha's Vineyard" and "Bella Oaks" cabernet sauvignon bottlings): if the vineyard's location is legally defined, then one cannot expand its boundaries. More generally, appellations are geographically demarcated; regulators can alter those boundaries (e.g., Carvajal 2008), but that is unusual and a long-term proposition at best for the best appellations. Appellation size varies directly with aggregate production capacity, *cet. par.*, and production capacity affects price so current and potential producers are always sensitive to changes in boundaries.

Various types of labor are likely highly variable (e.g., unskilled labor), but changing one's access to highly skilled labor may be a bottleneck (e.g., winemakers with extensive experience and success with the wines of a particular appellation, experienced harvesters or sorters, especially for hand harvesting). If irrigation is allowed, then one may face constraints on water access that are difficult or virtually impossible to alter. If irrigation is illegal, then water access is perhaps even more challenging: it is left largely to nature.

The input that defines the firm's short run depends upon a number of considerations and may even vary over time.

The implication of such an ultimate limitation on the firm's short-run output is that the average production per unit of input—or average productivity—and the ability to increase output with greater use of any single input—or marginal productivity—must eventually decrease as the firm expands production. Using the relatively familiar example of labor productivity, if one continues to add more work hours to a fixed amount of another input, then labor's capacity to increase output will diminish. As the vigneron adds more pickers to the vineyard, the harvest per picker will eventually diminish. If pickers are paid a standard wage, then eventually falling productivity with a constant wage rate amounts to eventually rising marginal cost per unit of output. If the vigneron uses a piece-rate wage system, then that marginal labor cost of production may be constant—but eventually becomes infinite once there is nothing more to harvest.

This is another way of understanding the upward sloping shape of the supply curve. The idea that the firm's marginal cost eventually rises in the short run suggests that, at some level of production, the firm must receive a higher price to justify further production. As long as its unit costs are constant, it is willing to sell for the same price. It is willing to produce more in the presence of rising unit costs only if, at least eventually, it can successfully charge enough to cover those costs. Moreover, for at least some of its labels, a firm is unable to produce more regardless of cost beyond some point: in effect, it will gladly accept higher prices, but it is unable to provide any more product. The relationship between price and quantity supplied is eventually that price can continue to increase, but quantity supplied cannot.

The implication is that the firm's short-run supply curve is upward sloping beyond some level of production where it could offer more at the same price. If we realize that the industry consists simply of a number of firms facing similar conditions, then we can expect that the supply curve in Figure 5.3 provides an acceptable representation of the industry's short-run supply curve.

Changes in own price change the quantity supplied because of their direct relationship to the firm's ability to cover its costs of production: higher prices cover higher costs and vice versa. For a given price, however, changes in cost vary inversely with the firm's willingness to produce and sell: for a given price, the producer can respond to higher costs only by decreasing production (and vice versa for lower costs). If cost is a fundamental determinant of the firm's willingness to supply product, then we must consider the *prices of the industry's inputs* as a second key variable. Such inputs are everything the industry needs to supply the product from the obvious such as raw materials and labor to the subtle such as the unique sense of smell and taste of a master winemaker. The combination of their productivities and their prices (or wages in the case of labor) determine their contribution to the cost of producing a unit of product, and on average that must be below the product's price for the firm to be profitable.

How does a change in input prices affect supply? Assume for example that the price of labor—the wage rate and associated perquisites—doubles throughout the industry. If nothing else changes, then the unit cost of production increases. While the extent of that increase depends upon the share of cost that labor represents, higher cost means that the price required to support any given quantity increases—the price that now makes any quantity the most desirable to sell rises, the supply curve shifts up—or, equivalently, the optimal supply consistent with any given price decreases, and point B moves to the left like B' on S' and similarly for the entire supply curve as in Figure 5.1. Continuing to supply the same quantity at the same price while facing higher costs would reduce profits—perhaps below zero.

Note also that, using our concept of producer surplus, higher costs mean that, at a given price, the producer surplus decreases. If it decreases enough, then units with negative producer surplus are no longer supplied; units with positive producer surplus are still supplied, though the aggregate producer surplus is smaller; and the breakeven unit where price just covers marginal cost now occurs at a lower quantity supplied. This reminds us that producer surplus, as a measure of profitability, is a helpful measure of the benefits accruing to the firm and industry from market transactions. It is helpful to bear in mind this kind of producer surplus analysis as we proceed with discussions such as the determinants of the firms' costs and how markets operate.

The third influence is the *technology* or technologies that define the production process. Distinct from other inputs, the technology determines the productivity of the inputs perhaps by the selection of inputs it dictates or by the way in which it organizes the inputs. For example, producers may be able to use either labor- or capital-intensive methods of production as illustrated by the different blends of inputs that we observe in an economy over time or in countries like China compared with countries like Germany at a given time. Agricultural production often exhibits dramatic differences in input blends with wine grape production being no exception. For example, as labor costs have risen relative to the costs of most nonlabor inputs, vignerons have shifted to less labor-intensive vineyard maintenance and harvesting, although the feasibility and extent of such substitution depends upon numerous factors such as the nature of the accompanying inputs (e.g., harvesting the relatively flat vineyards of southern Washington compared with the steep vineyards along the banks of the Mosel or the Rhine).

One distinct characteristic of technology is that, if it is voluntarily adopted to produce a given product, it is cost-reducing in the very long run (that is, once the firm has had an opportunity to adapt fully to it). Changes in the other key variables can raise or lower costs, but a change in technology is always expected to reduce cost eventually: otherwise, it would not be adopted. Thus, a change in technology lowers the price needed to make any given quantity supplied optimal; or, alternatively, it shifts the supply curve to the right.

The fourth influence on the quantity supplied to a given market is the *prices of other products* the suppliers could supply. This is the element of cost that was our focus in Chapter 3. How does the wine retailer decide which bottles to stock and how many? For a given amount of shelf space, supplying any or more of Wine A requires stocking less or none of Wine B. Similarly, with a given amount of land, the vintner can grow a desired amount of cabernet sauvignon only by forgoing cultivation of some amount of another grape such as merlot or malbec. By measures such as yield and quality, a given vineyard may be best suited for a particular grape such as cabernet sauvignon, but as the price of merlot grapes increases, the opportunity cost of continuing to grow cabernet increases: the prices of alternative products that one forgoes represent a cost of producing one's current product.

If we think of Figure 5.3 as representing the supply of a particular wine—say, a sauvignon blanc varietal—then increased demand for some alternative such as semillon with a corresponding increase in its price raises the price at which a given supply of sauvignon blanc is still optimal (as if the cost of producing it had risen): the supply curve shifts left (and conversely if the demand for semillon, and therefore its price, decreased).

As with consumers, our understanding of the producers' side of the market becomes more complex and more realistic once we introduce concern about the future. For storable products such as wine, whether bottled or bulk, that can be stored or sold, *producer expectations* capture another dimension of cost: a product sold today cannot be sold tomorrow so a cost of selling at one time is the revenue forgone from not selling at another time.

If we treat Figure 5.1 as, say, the August market supply for champagne reflecting some initial set of expectations, then the realization among producers that some future event is likely to increase the demand for champagne in December along with its price (e.g., the turn of the millennium to the year 2000), then the cost of selling champagne in August increases—by selling in August, one is forgoing more future revenue than originally anticipated: a producer reduces the supply available in the August market (e.g., the shift from S to S') and increases the amount available in the December market.

Analyzing reallocation between markets—such as this one between the August and the December—requires care. A decrease in the August supply to reflect the reallocation away from the August market in light of changed expectations—reduced target sales at every price—to the December market does not shift the supply curve for the December market to the right: that reallocation is what moves the quantity available along that December supply curve (note that changes in quantity in Figure 5.1 may be either shifts in the supply curve like those we have described—a different quantity for a given price—or they may be movements along a stationary supply curve—a different quantity at a different price). The increased demand in December with the corresponding expectation of increased prices elicits more quantity supplied—but that is what a movement along the December supply curve means. A higher price covers higher costs; and, with a supply curve like that in Figure 5.1, the best quantity at that higher price is an increased quantity. We shall examine this process in more detail later in the chapter.

As another supply side influence, *exchange rates* are important again. Their influence on the demand side reflected the inclusion of customers whose purchasing power is in a currency different from the good's price which represents a significant share of the global wine market. What is the relationship between exchange rates and the supply side's concern about cost? They influence costs for firms that either produce offshore or, short of complete offshore production which is unlikely with wine, purchase inputs in another currency. The examples are numerous—from the relatively obvious such as the US retailer who stocks primarily European wines to the more obscure such as the French producer who uses Wyoming bentonite to fine her wines.

Assume a highly simplified example that makes the point: our wine selling for $12 in the US is produced in Italy, the producer operates a shop in the US that sells all production to customers there, and the Italian producer pays all costs associated with production in euros. Assume further, for simplicity, that the dollar trades at par with the euro: one dollar buys one euro and vice versa. Retail revenue in the US is in dollars, and costs are ultimately paid in euros. If the exchange rate changes—for example, it now takes two dollars to buy a euro or half a euro to buy a dollar (the euro appreciates against the dollar—it buys more dollars)—then sale of a bottle of wine contributes only half as much as it did toward covering production costs: $12 translates into only 6 euros. Alternatively, we can say that it now takes twice as many dollars to cover euro costs as it did. In effect, cost measured in dollars has risen, and the producer either needs a higher dollar price to cover its costs; or only decreased production (at lower cost) is consistent with the current dollar price. As with our other examples of increased cost, supply decreases (S to S'). Of course, the world is more complicated than this story (e.g., the change in exchange rates could result in retail sales shifting away from the US toward retailers in the Eurozone), but one gets the point.

If the exchange rate moved the other way—it takes fewer dollars to buy a euro—then costs decrease, and supply increases. The extent of such shifts depends upon the degree to which costs are exposed to exchange rate fluctuations. Most of wine production occurs within a country or a currency zone; most of the exchange rate risk arises from trade between producing countries and consuming countries in different currency zones.

Finally, the supply available to the market depends upon the *number of firms in the industry* serving it. This is probably most easily understood if we assume that the firms have the same or similar costs so that, at a given price, each wants to supply a given quantity; but, with more firms, that means a greater quantity at that price: industry supply increases (and conversely if there are fewer firms). One can imagine industry supply increasing or decreasing as the number of producers increases or decreases. Figure 5.3 represents an industry supply curve where we assume that we have eight identical firms supplying a given wine: the quantity offered by the industry at any given price is eight times that offered by one of the firms.[1] One can imagine the industry supply curve shifting left if we had fewer firms or right if we had more.

We have discussed the relationship of own price to supply as well as the influence of a half dozen other influences which, in the context of a supply curve, are supply "shifters": we predict that a change in any one will increase or decrease supply for any given value of own price, *cet. par.*, in a manner logically identical to that of our demand shifters discussed earlier. The importance of understanding the role of these influences becomes clearer when we consider demand and supply together to understand the process of market price determination.

## THE RELATIONSHIP BETWEEN DEMAND AND SUPPLY

In discussing consumer behavior in Chapter 4 and producer supply behavior here, our representations of demand and supply graphically are behavioral models. In effect, the decision makers on either side of a potential transaction indicate to the world—or the relevant community—that they are ready, willing, and able to transact on those terms. Figure 5.3 represents an eight-firm industry's willingness to supply bottles of wine at various prices. Figure 5.4 indicates how that supply compares with an example of the quantities that consumers want at various prices.

While the industry is willing to supply 7,200 bottles when the price is $12, consumers want 12,000 bottles at that price. If the decision makers in this market had perfect information—if they could see that a shortage exists at $12—then somehow they might agree to increase the price to a level that would clear the market, that is, find a price at which quantity demanded matched quantity supplied. Figure 5.5 indicates what that would involve: the price would rise to $14.67, and sales would be 9,333

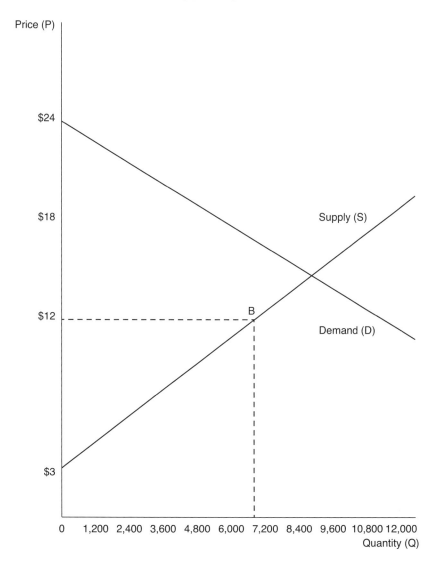

*Figure 5.4 Excess demand: price = $12*

bottles shown as point B″ in Figure 5.5 (for simplicity and clarity, we shall designate each bottle sold as a transaction).[2]

This would represent market equilibrium: we could find no alternative arrangement under the market conditions given where we could make any participant better off—in effect, more consumer or more producer surplus

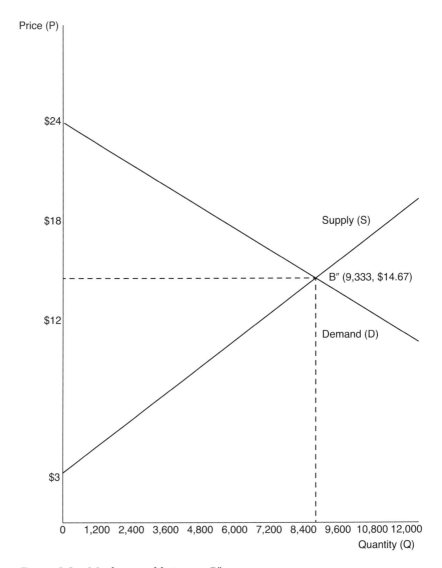

*Figure 5.5    Market equilibrium at B"*

(see below)—without making someone else worse off. Participants would
be willing to rearrange the outcome (e.g., producers charge a lower price)
only if they would be compensated for any losses from the change, and
that compensation would at least offset any gain to anyone else. This condition of exhausting all mutually beneficial transactions (e.g., voluntary

sales from producer to consumer) is Pareto optimal after the concept developed by the Italian scholar Vilfredo Pareto.

Postponing briefly the question of how a market might arrive at that outcome, one wonders why it might be appealing: several reasons come to mind. First, recall our interpretation of the demand curve as a "willingness to pay" curve and its height at any quantity indicating willingness to pay for that particular unit—that bottle of wine. Correspondingly, the height of the supply curve represents marginal (opportunity) cost. Notice that settling at the equilibrium price and quantity stops transactions at exactly the right point: the willingness to pay for the last bottle sold (this is marginal benefit to the buyer in this context) just covers the cost of its production. Any further transactions involve costs that exceed willingness to pay—a negative net value to the economy—and any fewer involves missing opportunities to meet someone's willingness to pay at a cost lower than that, thus forgoing a net positive value.

Second, standardizing so that each bottle sold is a transaction, we see that the equilibrium outcome maximizes the number of mutually beneficial transactions: we cannot get more. Mutual benefit necessitates each party entering into the transaction voluntarily, and we cannot find more mutually beneficial transactions than at the market-clearing price: at any other price, one party or the other becomes more reluctant to transact.

Third, the transactions accompanying the market equilibrium maximize the aggregate benefits going to participants. We can indicate the consumer and producer surplus generated in this market (sometimes called the Total Surplus) if we modify Figure 5.5 to highlight those measures as in Figure 5.6.

As a reminder of that calculation, the equilibrium transactions in the market generate \$43,556 value to consumers net of their expenditures (\$9.33 × 9,333 × 0.5 with some rounding error) and \$54,444 value to producers net of their costs (\$11.67 × 9,333 × 0.5). The aggregate producer surplus represents profit beyond what the industry could earn otherwise, and the aggregate consumer surplus is the consumer analogue to that— how much more consumers took from the transactions net of what they put into them. The Total Surplus is \$98,000.

As we shall see, it might be possible to help one side of the market or the other by overriding the equilibrium price, perhaps through government-regulated pricing, but any gains to one side are typically more than offset by losses to the other side and from lost transactions so that Total Surplus decreases. Unless it is in the public interest to favor one side or the other, decreasing Total Surplus is undesirable.

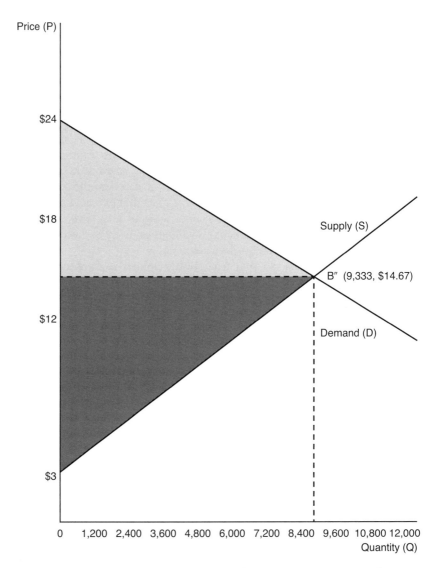

*Figure 5.6    Market equilibrium at B″ with aggregate consumer and*
*             producer surpluses*

# MARKETS AND AUCTIONS

Given the initial position presented in Figure 5.4, how does the market move toward that desirable equilibrium outcome of Figures 5.5 or 5.6? Frankly, we do not know. Our models of demand and supply are more models of market adjustment—the size and significance of the influences upon price and quantity—with the movement toward equilibrium assumed rather than confirming the actual achievement of equilibrium. We are better at understanding market changes than at finding equilibrium. Also, we expect that the movement toward equilibrium depends considerably upon the market setting.

For example, we can take a narrow view of a market and watch it move. Examples of this are formal auctions of various sorts: we shall consider three. First, ascending-bid (English) auctions are the familiar "bottom up" market where the auctioneer/broker presents some quantity of goods and perhaps suggests a starting price; and bidders usually respond, perhaps starting with lower prices, and bid against each other (assuming there is more than one) until only one bidder is left who wins the offered quantity with her winning bid. Within this narrow context, this market may be in equilibrium: the supply has been offered, and all of it has been sold at a price that is mutually agreeable to the available buyers and sellers. If buyers do not want more at the winning price, then there is no shortage— at the instant of the winning bid, only one buyer is willing to pay—and there is no surplus since everything offered has been sold. English auctions are a popular method of selling fine wines around the world through auction houses such as Christie's and Sotheby's (e.g., Hermacinski 2007).

Descending-bid (Dutch) auctions, named after the popular form of fresh flower auctions in the Netherlands, work in a similar manner except that the winning bid is the first, not the last, bid because the suggested price is supposed to start well above what anyone is expected to pay. Once again, the market, narrowly defined, clears as soon as the first bidder bids on the item on offer. Arguably, as an example, many retailers use a "Dutch auction" approach to moving wine inventory: offer a wine initially at the highest price one expects will sell and lower the price, as needed over time to attract customers, until the wine is sold (see below).

English and Dutch auctions are special cases of markets: at best, they illustrate market equilibrium for an instant for the narrow range of goods for which they are typically held. Because of that, they provide useful readings of market conditions, and auction results are among the most appealing data for studying the determinants of prices (e.g., Marks 2009 for fine wine prices). However, for a variety of reasons, they do not mimic the global market among all buyers and sellers for a particular good such as a bottle or case of a given fine wine: while it provides a useful benchmark, learning that a case of '82 Ch. Margaux sold for \$10,000 at a Sotheby's fine wine auction today does not say that the global market-clearing price of that wine is \$10,000 that day. Like all markets, auction market performance suffers from a variety of difficulties. For example, experience with them indicates that winning bids on otherwise identical items later in the auction may be at different prices. Moreover, there is no reason to expect that the quantity buyers want at any given price or the quantity sellers would be willing to sell at that price is the quantity transacted at that auction.

More generally, participants have imperfect information (e.g., is the world perfectly informed about the opportunity to buy and sell at the auction and the number of buyers and sellers involved and their demand and supply functions?) and face other difficulties such as negotiating terms of the transactions (e.g., payment, delivery) and the limited duration of the auction.

A third kind of auction reflects the work of the French economist Léon Walras. One version of the Walrasian auction asks buyers to submit their "demand curves" which allows the "Walrasian auctioneer" to compute the price at which buyers would purchase some available (fixed) supply, thus setting the equilibrium price. A market that bears some resemblance to this is the twice-daily London Gold Fix operated by the five London banks with the largest gold trading operations (Galmarley Ltd. 2014). In effect, the "Gold Fix Chairman"—a position that rotates among the five member banks—starts the process at each session by announcing a gold price (e.g., at or near the last Fix) and looking at the resulting buy and sell orders, including those of the banks themselves; no transactions occur until the quantity of gold demanded equals the quantity supplied. If the quantity demanded exceeds the quantity available at an announced price (a shortage), then the Chairman increases the price and allows revision of orders (and conversely if the quantity supplied exceeds the quantity demanded (a surplus)). The process iterates until the Chairman finds a market-clearing price at which price the orders are executed at that Gold Fix.

This sounds like a process that illustrates the movement toward competitive market equilibrium. It is a useful example, but it does not mimic a competitive market exactly for several reasons. For example, the five large banks are large enough to influence prices by their buying and selling behavior. The iterative process encourages strategic behavior (ibid.). The process excludes small traders since the units traded are 400 ounces of gold each, perhaps because of the transaction cost of including many smaller traders.

We cannot know whether some version of the market for wine—say, between consumers and wineries—could approach the competitive outcome depicted in Figure 5.5. When we discuss the role of government in wine markets in Chapter 6, we shall have even less reason to expect that result.

## MARKET OUTCOMES

While it is no more likely to be the outcome than the equilibrium we have described, we shall consider an outcome that is different from market equilibrium. When wine buyers and sellers transact, they do not know whether the current price, if left alone, is consistent with a shortage or a surplus or an equilibrium. Moreover, market conditions change sufficiently quickly that the equilibrium which might have emerged from today's market conditions is no longer the predicted outcome once the market processes tomorrow's new conditions (of course, market conditions and the associated prospective equilibrium can change more quickly than daily). The pattern of doing two Gold Fixes every weekday is only one indication of how rapidly market conditions can change in a relatively simple and formal market.

We shall assume that the market conditions of shortage at a price of $12 in Figure 5.4 persist: it is not apparent for now that suppliers will fall far short of potential demand at the $12 price; and, perhaps by the time that is knowledge, the market is sold out. This is a widespread result in a variety of markets: anyone who has arrived too late for a "limited to supplies on hand" sale understands this. For the sake of this example, we shall assume that we have the eight identical producers noted earlier with Figure 5.3 and some large number of consumers. The producers publish a bottle price of $12, and the consumers respond.

It will be useful to consider two alternative results in this scenario, recognizing first that invariably some customers will be disappointed when, whether recognized or not until it is too late, there is actually a shortage at the current price. Regardless of who buys the wine, the producers sell 7,200 bottles for $12, and their aggregate producer surplus is $32,400—considerably less than they could have earned ($54,444) if they had known how much more consumers would have been willing to buy and how much higher the price could have gone. One extreme assumption is that all the wine goes to those willing to pay the most for it which is depicted in Figure 5.7. The relevant willingness to pay in this case starts just short of $24 and decreases to $16.80 for bottle number 7,200.

The shaded trapezoid represents the total consumer surplus of

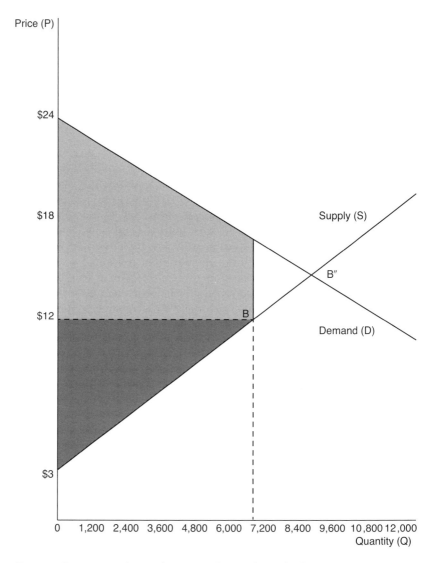

*Figure 5.7    Excess demand: price = $12, sales to highest WTP*

$60,480—considerably more than the $43,556 yielded at the market-clearing price. In this scenario which makes the most of the shortage for consumers (the available wine goes to those willing to pay the most for it), they have 2,133 fewer bottles of wine (which costs them some lost consumer surplus—about $2,275), but they pay $2.67 less per bottle for the

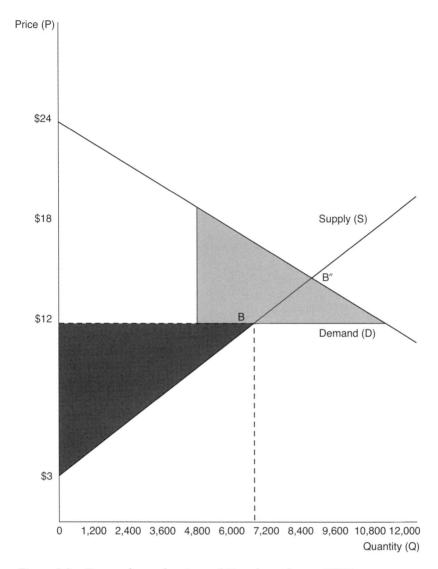

*Figure 5.8    Excess demand: price = $12, sales to lowest WTP*

bottles available, and that adds about $19,200 to their consumer surplus—for a net gain of about $16,925 ("about" because of rounding errors here).

On the other hand, if all the wine goes to those with the lowest willingness to pay—the scenario depicted in Figure 5.8—then the 7,200 bottles go to those willing to pay from $12 to $19.20 (the WTP values starting at the

12,000th bottle and working backwards for 7,200 bottles to bottle number 4,800). The consumer surplus drops to $25,920 which is over 40 percent less than the consumer benefit at the market-clearing price.

Transacting at a price that does not clear the market—likely a common occurrence in many markets—clearly affects the distribution of benefits. In this example of a price below the market-clearing level, producers lose unambiguously, and the distribution of benefits to consumers depends upon who gets the wine.

As noted earlier, this below-equilibrium price might benefit consumers and might reflect some conscious policy to do just that—say, for example, as a government-imposed price ceiling on this wine to make it more affordable or more "fairly priced". However, it hurts producers, and—even in the best case for consumers—Total Surplus is smaller ($60,480 + $32,400 = $92,880—less than the $98,000 achieved at the equilibrium price); as benefit to consumers decreases, the loss increases. This loss of Total Surplus will occur with any non-equilibrium price in a market exhibiting normal demand and supply behavior.

Despite its imperfections, one might wish for an arrangement similar to the London Gold Fix in selling wines—some process of iterating toward a market-clearing price if that is the price that generates the maximum Total Surplus. For beverage wines that are produced in large volume, sold at many outlets (often internationally), and are similar from vintage to vintage, that is likely unnecessary. Producers are more likely to have enough experience with transactions to avoid pricing that is far short or long of the mark. Shortages and surpluses are likely small relative to the total volume of the wine transacted.

For these wines, a new bottling (e.g., a new vintage) generally substitutes easily for a previous bottling, and buyers are often indifferent between the two. One often finds mixed vintages of large-volume wines on store shelves, and many vendors (e.g., the producer, retailers) will automatically substitute a newer vintage for an older unless instructed otherwise. Surpluses seem unusual as well—for example, one rarely sees an older vintage systematically rejected for a newer vintage on store shelves. However, one might observe various forms of downward price adjustment during the course of selling a particular bottling: the model resembles the Dutch auction. The vendor's initial offering is typically at a wine's highest expected price. If the market does not clear at that price, then the vendor can lower the price in various ways to increase the quantity demanded from those with lower willingness to pay—posting a sale price, offering a rebate, providing a quantity discount, presenting the wine as a "closeout", and so forth.

The example of fine, often collectable, wines is more challenging: they are produced at higher unit cost in smaller quantities, typically with more vintage-to-vintage variation, so a story about large volume, wide distribution, and easy substitutability is inappropriate. Following the example of gold, what about a "Fine Wine Fix" for collectable or fine wines? Nothing prevents that, but the cost of organizing and maintaining such a market is likely prohibitive because such wines, unlike gold, appear in much greater variety in much smaller quantities. A particular challenge for fine wine is that it is much more difficult for buyers and even sellers to know exactly what they are transacting so that, for example, arriving at an informed willingness to pay is problematic (see Chapter 7).

More fundamentally, at the time of release, the parties interested in such wines are not a variety of buyers and sellers submitting buy and sell orders and iterating toward a market-clearing price: the source of such wines is only the producer so the Fix analogy fails. The pure Walrasian alternative might be more attractive where the producer collects buyers' demand curves and calculates a market-clearing price from that. The difficulty there is that, unlike the Walrasian auctioneer, the producer may have an incentive to maximize her profit (aggregate producer surplus), not Total Surplus, and may make adjustments such as managing supply (e.g., selling "surplus" wine to avoid diluting the brand as discussed in Chapter 2). We lack a true Walrasian auctioneer.[3]

The difficulty of finding a market-clearing price in the fine wine market results in several adaptations. Because of its durability, wine can be re-traded in secondary markets after the original transaction. For beverage wine, this is not worthwhile. Transactions at non-clearing prices for fine wine might proceed as described earlier but might include additional strategies that lead to subsequent transactions. For example, commercial wine auctions, both live and online, exist internationally to serve as secondary markets to move wine to those with the greatest willingness to pay. Access to these auctions as a relatively efficient method for markets to work has spread dramatically since the mid-1990s with their growth in the US, their proliferation online, and their popularity in emerging fine wine markets in Asia.

Additionally, because the wine traded subsequently is not quite the same product that was traded originally—the wine has aged and, more importantly, the market's knowledge of its quality has probably increased—one could argue that the subsequent transactions operate more efficiently because there is better information.

Other adaptations have developed over time. Fine wine producers sometimes release a product slowly—for example, a new vintage of a wine—in order to get a reading of the market's valuation. It is not a Fix or even a Walrasian process, but it might improve market efficiency: we lack evidence to support that, but it is an established practice among many fine wine producers so one wonders why it would persist if it were not profitable. Likely the best known version of this occurs among Bordeaux producers (e.g., Parker 1993: 168–172). The chateau offers a première tranche ("first slice") of the new wine in the spring following the fall harvest as a test of market response. The chateau can adjust its pricing and rate of release depending upon market response to both the initial release and subsequent releases. Given the potential durability of a Bordeaux bottling, the producer's management of a given vintage can extend for years.

The practice certainly extends beyond Bordeaux. While data on inventory management by fine wine producers are not public, offers from vendors confirm that producers regularly provide "library releases" to distributors or negotiate releases from their aged inventories (e.g., numerous examples of wine offers from vintages 10 or more years old "directly from the winery" from the Seattle vendor Jonathan Rimmerman's Garagiste store website www.garagiste.com). Given its use as an investment by wine consumers, it is not surprising that producers approach fine wine inventory management as an investment as well.

We also observe producers selling all of their production directly to consumers without involving negociants, distributors, shops, or any other third party (other than shippers); for example, a number of California fine wine producers sell only through their mailing lists. One might consider that a market equilibrium if the producer sells all she wants, although that is unlikely to occur at a single price. If it does, then we are more likely to see a shortage because such a "sellout" often involves quantity restrictions to case or even bottle limits per buyer. In addition, it might also represent a shortage, given the number of producers who have waiting lists of those hoping to get onto their mailing lists. In such situations, we would also expect to find a market for places on these waiting lists—a clear sign of shortage at the producer's announced price. We are unlikely to observe this market because producers likely would remove buyers caught in such a transaction. The more attractive alternative is for those on the mailing list to sell the wine in a secondary transaction rather than the mailing list membership.

It is noteworthy that the idea of market equilibrium—or avoiding it—has an established if indirect role in wine marketing. A particularly vivid example of this is the use of "scarcity marketing" by the Laughing Stock Winery in British Columbia—"to produce less than you can sell . . . it was a good strategy" (Smith 2014). This is part of a more established marketing strategy of advertising limited supplies to create the impression of a risk of missing out ("only 50 cases made", "only 30 cases imported into the country"). Another example is the Wines Til Sold Out (WTSO) flash sale website in the US which, as its name suggests, purports to offer deeply discounted wines until "the wine is sold out", usually within a few hours of the offer ("About Us" tab at https://www.wtso.com/content.php?cms_id=2). The website also explains:

> I MISSED A WINE, CAN I STILL PURCHASE IT? No. The last product is discontinued at 11:59pm EST. We may get more at a later date, if we're lucky, but we cannot promise that we will get additional inventory of a specific wine . . .. In general, since every wine is only presented for a limited amount of time, if you see a wine that interests you, you should make your purchase. *"Snag it when you see it. It won't be there tomorrow."* Since every wine is guaranteed there is no risk. (ibid., emphasis added)

Wines appearing on the website often appear again, sometimes repeatedly, so the consumer has no way to determine if the wine is truly "sold out" when the current offer expires (or whether the vendor simply wants to stop sales now and make a new offer from existing inventory in the future).

Instead of highlighting the idea of sufficiency at the current price, the focus is encouraging an expectation of scarcity or shortage which, following our discussion of consumer behavior, might increase the demand for the wine and actually become a self-fulfilling prediction at the announced price. The strategy plays upon buyer risk aversion and tends to be more effective when the transaction price is consistent with relative quality (often difficult or impossible for the consumer to know), where finding close substitutes is more difficult, where the rationale for the declared scarcity is credible (e.g., small but unique vineyard, unusually good weather, accidental loss of part of production), where the scarcities seem to appear randomly, and where the strategy is not used widely. The producer's choice of target price and quantity is crucial to its profitability which we shall discuss later.

## THE MEANING OF PRICE

The focus of much of the preceding discussion is the central role of price in wine transactions and finding "the price" at which transactions occur; but, for anyone involved in any type of wine market—from retail transactions and beyond—the meaning of price in that sense is not straightforward. In any aspect of wine markets, one does not take transacting seriously until one learns something about price.

Perhaps the closest thing to a simple price is the price charged by the producer "at the cellar door" where only a small proportion of sales occur. More generally, we have no data on the proportion of any producer's sales that occur at any announced regular price, and therefore, except perhaps for commercial auctions, it is hypothetical to talk about choosing a market clearing price. More generally, transactions for a particular wine invariably involve transactions at a variety of prices.

We shall learn in the chapter on government (Chapter 6) that, of course, government policy affects the transaction price—whether directly through taxation or indirectly through the myriad forms of regulation that alter demand and supply conditions and thereby alter the price that will clear the market. Even the cellar door price usually reflects government policy (e.g., charging tax).

At the retail level, selling below "regular price" is widespread. We lack data on the frequency with which wine sales occur at prices below regular or suggested retail price, but it is unusual in the US for wines not to sell at a discount in that sense. That approach to announcing pricing is more of a marketing technique than an honest attempt to signal to the market the producer's estimate of a market-clearing price, especially for wines above beverage quality. This serves two marketing purposes: (1) Given consumer ignorance of what is in the bottle, especially for fine wine, the tendency is to judge that "regular price" correlates directly with quality; and (2) The prospect of getting a discount increases quantity demanded. These are seemingly contradictory signals to the consumer, but it is a widespread marketing technique: "This wine is high quality because it has a high regular price—but you can buy it at a discount: you are getting a deal (in more technical terms, you are getting significant consumer surplus)." The consumer surplus may reflect a WTP based upon psychological factors (e.g., risk aversion, status seeking) rather than actual experience with the wine; but, until one becomes informed to the contrary through actual tasting perhaps, it is consumer surplus nonetheless.

One particularly vivid example of this occurs in retailing. Especially for closeouts of fine wines, the owner judges what price s/he thinks will clear the market represented by the shop, and then increases that, perhaps by some multiple, for the price tag and then marks the wine with a deep discount back to the expected market-clearing price. When many or most consumers do not actually know the wine, this is clever marketing.

Of course, accurate pricing data are crucial to a careful analysis of buying and selling behavior such as consumer responsiveness to prices, complementarity and substitutability between wine and other products (including other wines), the impact of alcohol taxation (which affects prices), and the actual relationship between price and perceived quality such as studies of the effects of expert ratings on wine prices. Given the consumer's problem in knowing fine wine, this last relationship is a pivotal one in analyzing those wine transactions. If we do not have accurate readings of the prices at which wines are actually being transacted, then the conclusions drawn from analysis of behavioral responses to prices are shaken.

This is a major reason why, notwithstanding the limited market they represent, auction prices are relatively desirable for wine research involving price, and analysis of prices in studies of transactions of grapes, bulk wine, and vineyards are more reliable: they are relatively clear of distortions from marketing and the level of expertise is more symmetric in the transaction so that manipulation of price as a symbol carries less importance. However, if we are looking for price data to help us test our hypotheses about widespread wine market outcomes, auction results represent only a tiny part of the wine market and suffer from their own challenges of interpretation (e.g., Marks 2009; Marks and Welsch forthcoming).

We also do not know, but would like to learn, about cultural differences in the manipulation of price. In North America, "discounting" and the illusion of discounting of wine are widespread—and would be more widespread but for Canadian provincial monopolies with pricing structures driven largely by the significant federal and provincial taxes on alcohol.[4] Some cultures seem more comfortable than others with thinking of price as flexible, of prices as being negotiable. Perhaps it depends upon the relative importance (e.g., market share) and number of casual or small shop markets versus large stores or government vendors where there is a longer distance between the owner or perhaps a manager who makes pricing decisions and the shop floor with or without sales staff available. Public policy, which might reflect the culture, could also limit pricing flexibility. Pricing in the traditional wine producing countries such as France, Germany, Italy, and Spain seems less prone to retail discounting than the US (e.g., case discounts, "clearance" sales and closeouts), though it occurs, especially in supermarkets.

If we want to study wine markets, their behavior and dynamics, and the impact of the inordinate level of government intervention in these markets, collecting price and quantity data is obviously necessary since those represent the heart of market outcomes. Neither is readily available, but the difficulty with quantity data is primarily that it is often proprietary. Finding reliable price data—the prices at which transactions actually occur—is likely the greater challenge in testing our ideas about how buyers and sellers actually transact.

## INDUSTRY STRUCTURE AND ITS DETERMINANTS

Our discussion of supply has focused upon the role of the producer's cost in predicting supply behavior as captured in a supply curve, using wine production as the context. But how do market circumstances on the supply side affect industry supply conditions? For example, what difference does it make whether wine is produced by some monolithic organization that has gained control of the world's vineyards—a DeBeers of Wine that is, in effect, a production monopoly—or by thousands of small producers? How do the circumstances of the market affect the tendency toward either one of these market structures or something in between?

Such differences in industrial organization can have a profound effect upon market outcomes like sales and prices. Among the most important differences is the effect upon pricing flexibility. If one firm controls market supply or is so dominant in the industry that it can control supply by representing a mortal threat to any competitor, then it is effectively a monopoly. While it is incorrect, or at least misleading, to assert that a profit-maximizing monopolist can charge "any price it wants"—it might be able to influence demand (e.g., by advertising), but all firms are subject to the discipline of respecting their products' demand curves—it is true that a monopolist is a "price setter" in contrast to a "price taker", that is, a firm that is so constrained by competition that it has essentially no control over the price it charges if it wants to survive.

A price taker behaves as if it faces unlimited demand as long as it charges the current going price—like a farmer selling a globally traded commodity crop (e.g., wheat, corn) on the world market. While a downward sloping demand curve would characterize market-wide demand, the individual producer can act as if she faces a horizontal, infinitely elastic "own demand curve", producing and selling all it wants as long as it sticks to the market price. Since, in effect, the pricing decision is beyond her control—the competitive behavior of the many buyers and many other sellers has set the price in a Walrasian sense—her choice is simply when and how much to sell in a world of constantly changing prices. She produces and sells as long as the available price—her constant (at least for the moment) marginal benefit (or marginal revenue) from selling—meets or beats her marginal cost.

By comparison, a price setter has some flexibility in its pricing: in the extreme case of monopoly, the monopolist firm faces the entire *market* demand curve and can choose the price that is consistent with its goals. This flexibility presents a dilemma for any producer who has it because any pricing choice represents potentially "good news" and "bad news". For example, assuming that buyer behavior is reflected in a typical downward sloping market demand curve (especially not vertical), the good news from choosing a lower price is that one can sell more; the bad news is that one makes less on all the inframarginal units—strictly speaking, all but the last unit sold—than if one had charged a slightly higher price. This means that this producer's marginal revenue—the additional revenue resulting from charging a slightly lower price that increases sales by "one more unit" and, in effect, the "net news" from charging that lower price —is less than her price. Like her perfectly competitive counterpart, she produces up to the quantity where her marginal revenue just covers her marginal cost; but, unlike her counterpart, the corresponding price is higher than her marginal cost since her price exceeds her marginal revenue. The technical proof of this contrast is widely available in textbooks providing a rigorous discussion of the distinction between monopoly and perfect competition (e.g., Mankiw 2015: 303–313): for our purposes, the upshot is that we expect a price-setting monopoly industry to charge a higher price and sell a smaller quantity than an otherwise identical perfectly competitive industry comprised of many price-taking firms.

An important implication is that a monopolist—or any price-setting firm—tends to adjust marginal revenue to equal, but price to exceed, her marginal cost. If we recall our three advantages of the competitive market outcome described earlier in this chapter, one is that it "stops transactions at exactly the right point"—where willingness to pay, or marginal benefit to the buyer, just covers marginal cost. While this is true for price takers—acting as if they face a horizontal own demand curve, price equals marginal revenue—we see that, for price setters, this is not true: the price charged exceeds marginal cost. In effect, production and sales stop prematurely relative to a competitive counterpart. We shall return to this distinction shortly.

By the way, we have seen the good news/bad news distinction before when we discussed the own price elasticity of demand (Ed) in Chapter 4. The point from the example of wine pricing we used there is the same as here: the concept of marginal revenue captures the "net news" about revenue when the producer chooses a different price, assuming she has that option. The value of Ed at which the choice of a (slightly) different price occurs tells us whether the net news will be good.

A close reading of the preceding leads one to see that the "taking versus setting" distinction about the firm's degree of control over price amounts to describing the shape of the demand curve the firm perceives itself to face: setters can act as if they face a downward sloping demand curve— they have some flexibility in pricing and must address good news/bad news—and takers do not. This, in turn, reflects the degree of competition in the market—primarily the availability of close substitutes for the firm's product which can limit its pricing options, potentially to none.

We can understand what constrains a firm that must compete if we think about what intensifies the competition in any market. First, competition intensifies with an increased *number of suppliers* doing virtually the same thing: offering the same or very similar products to buyers at the same place. For example, we see this when we see the patterns of price movement among the numerous gasoline stations in a large city— facing a large number of buyers seeking the same product, many suppliers of virtually identical products whose prices tend to be very similar, especially during periods of stability (e.g., oil prices, driving patterns). One witnesses a similar pattern of similar prices for similar wines in the "value" section of a large wine store or supermarket—what we have characterized as beverage wines. Alternatively, one realizes quickly in such a shopping environment the importance of understanding whether observed price differences say anything about differences in the value— perhaps the quality—of the products. Lacking much information, the buyer's challenge in such circumstances is our focus in a later discussion of asymmetric information.

The requirement of virtually identical products among competing firms is a second feature that intensifies competition. If they cannot distinguish among equally accessible products, then rational buyers will choose the least expensive among equals (the condition of equal access is important: among otherwise identical products like gasoline, we often choose the most convenient). This recognition of the role of *product homogeneity* in intensifying competition begs the question of the definition of the product and, more generally, the definition of the market. What is required to determine that one product is different from another? How much of such a determination is more perceived than real? Unlike gasoline, no two wines seem truly identical, but we can often find a large number of wines that are sufficiently indistinguishable that we have no basis for paying more for one than another. If competing producers agree, they will avoid pricing that differs much from their close competitors.

Producers are probably more aware than buyers of the *threat of entry* from potential competitors as a third condition intensifying competition. Its impact upon the sense of competitiveness is no less real. If we can assume that market intelligence about the profitability of a market (e.g., by location, by varietal) is available, then the threat of potential competition depends primarily upon the cost of entry. The potential of constructing significant new production quickly is limited, given the requirements such as assembling expertise and developing vineyards. However, given enough time, the threat is significant as demonstrated by the emergence of significant new production in areas as different as Australia and the French Midi over the past 20–30 years.

That example reminds us of another form of entry: in what has become the global wine market, import competition from existing producers is likely more of an entry threat than the appearance of new local producers. Given the international character of wine markets, the more immediate threat of entry is from the reallocation of existing production from off-shore where producers re-direct production and branding from one market to another, particularly using international varietals such as cabernet sauvignon and chardonnay. The threat from those sources is more dependent upon access to the market, given the generally protectionist policies of most countries toward imported alcoholic beverages (e.g., tariffs, labeling requirements) and the time needed for consumer acceptance of new, less familiar sources (e.g., New Zealand pinot noir, Uruguayan tannat). Coping with the variety of government policies and processing of information are part of the larger consideration of *transaction costs* which are a fourth condition affecting the competitiveness of a market.

The assumption of knowledge of profitability and its impact upon entry and exit decisions is a significant one in the wine industry since so much of ownership is non-public. That is an example of a fifth contributor to the competitiveness of the market, namely, *the extent of information available and knowledge*. Buyers' search for lower prices and engagement in comparison shopping depends upon information about the number of sources of supply available and knowledge of the substitutability among those products. That also affects sellers' production planning and propensity to adjust prices. As one considers competitive behavior, the central role of information and knowledge is clear.

A thorough discussion of the determinants of competitive behavior could be lengthy; it should also expand to include consideration of the institutions that encourage or impede that behavior—from the content and enforcement of competition policy to the integrity of the judicial system. However, our short list of five market characteristics provides a good basis for what follows.

To an economist, an industry's structure is typically a reflection of its characteristics along dimensions such as the five just discussed. In a *perfectly competitive industry*, many knowledgeable suppliers offer a homogeneous product to knowledgeable buyers. Transactions occur easily (interferences, or costs, are minimal), and the threat of entry by new producers responding to evidence of positive profits is always present (as is the ease of exit in the presence of losses). At the other extreme we find a monopolist who is, strictly speaking, the only supplier in the market.

Not surprisingly, the factors contributing to the intensity of competition suggest the market conditions contributing to monopolization—number of suppliers, product homogeneity, threat of entry, transaction costs, and the extent of information. By definition, the number of suppliers is effectively one—but what leads to that? Sometimes barriers to competition such as property rights—intellectual (e.g., patents, copyrights) or otherwise (e.g., a vineyard of extraordinary quality with a single owner)—protecting some unique product provide a sustained limit on the number of producers. (More transitory uniqueness occurs naturally as entrepreneurs try new, differentiated products and temporarily have monopoly power—a rare occurrence in the modern wine industry.) Such barriers effectively preclude entry, though uniqueness is a matter of both degree—like computer operating systems, no two copyrighted books are the same, but monopoly power is considerably greater for the former than the latter—and disagreement as suggested by active litigation of intellectual property.

Unique natural or cultural endowments can also yield product uniqueness: there is only one Mount Everest and one Mecca, and their uniqueness yields monopoly power to those supplying goods and services attached to them. While many sources of diamonds exist (e.g., mines, secondhand market), DeBeers has attempted to control all of them, either through acquisition or marketing ("a diamond is forever" is another way of saying "it violates the meaning of diamonds not to keep yours forever—do not even consider selling yours on the secondhand market which is our competition"). The rationale for appellation designations in wine regions is the demarcation of areas with unique natural characteristics such as soil and climate which, when planted with certain varietals, can produce unique types of wine such as Margaux in Bordeaux or Chianti Classico in Tuscany. Whether intended or not, these regulations also impart some monopoly power to producers protected in these regions: producers outside those appellations cannot legally label their products with those names, cannot produce that wine, and thus cannot produce a perfect substitute (though they might produce something better).

As a form of transaction cost, transportation costs and costs of market access to both buyer and seller have tended to limit competition historically, especially when the product is not durable over space (e.g., fragile) or time (e.g., perishable). This applies to both supply side competition where price varies inversely with its intensity as more competing producers access the market and to demand-side competition where price varies directly with its intensity as more buyers enter the market. A variety of market developments over the last half century—from more rapid shipping and better packaging, packing, and storage technology (supply side) to the expansion of the internet market (both demand and supply intensifying)—have only increased the competitiveness of wine markets. Some of those same factors have also contributed to the remarkable expansion of New World wine markets such as South America and Australia and New Zealand. To some extent, developments in public policy reflect a reaction to counter those competitive pressures.

One might consider the costs of acquiring and processing information another transaction cost. One aspect of it is so significant in the wine market—the consumer's challenge of knowing what is in the bottle—that it deserves special attention and is the focus of Chapter 7. Incomplete information and difficulty in processing information inhibit competitive pressures in a variety of ways. As with any industry, the cost of learning how it works and what is needed for survival deters participation on the supply side. The consumer's significant challenge of becoming knowledgeable about the product certainly inhibits participation on the demand side. Gaining the technical knowledge needed to grow and process grapes efficiently requires either lengthy experience or formal education or, at its best, a combination of both as does navigating the business of producing wine profitably. However, this knowledge is available easily enough that its cost certainly does not eliminate competition. Because of the breadth of products available due to characteristics such as vintage variation and varieties of grapes and blends and *terroirs* and the cost of learning about them, consumer education is also costly and is more likely to inhibit demand-side competition. It is difficult to know the extent to which consumer ignorance inhibits demand for wine generally, but it is likely that it plays a significant role in the demand for particular products—one reason wine tastings are a prominent though relatively costly marketing tool for wineries. In the largest in-depth study of wine consumer behavior ever undertaken (Veseth 2008), over half of the wine consumers surveyed (57 percent) could be described as either "overwhelmed" by the complexity of wine shopping or only marginally interested in what was actually in the bottle. What we do not know is how many consumers actually avoid the market entirely because of the cost of information and knowledge.

A notable recent example of the impact of information upon competition has been the emergence of New World wine producers such as Australia, New Zealand, and Argentina whose wines were largely unknown to the global market 30 years ago—and whose flagship varietals of shiraz, sauvignon blanc, and malbec were simply obscure except to serious students of wine, largely because they were used in Old World wines that were identified by place and not by varietal. Through both the marketing efforts of these countries' producers and their governments and the consumers' aroused interest in response to appealing, affordable wines, consumers have increased their sense of what wines compete with each other.

So how competitive is the wine market?

## STRUCTURE OF THE WINE INDUSTRY

The wine market actually involves a wide variety of markets—from production to wholesale and retail sales and then all the related markets from land and rootstock and barrels to advertising and expert evaluation. It is relatively safe to assume that some parts of the market are inherently competitive—for example, the demand side of retail—and we must be selective in considering the rest. Therefore, our focus will be the structure of wine production.

Production falls between the two structural extremes we have described. The industry is certainly not a monopoly, and it is not perfectly competitive. In most markets, we find many producers and the barriers to entry to becoming some kind of producer are low, but their products are not homogeneous. At the level of beverage wine, the products are similar and highly competitive, but fine wines are highly differentiated. Comprehensive data on industry structure are not available globally or by country. However, we have some analysis of the US industry. Table 5.1 presents data from WineAmerica, a trade association, on the size distribution of wineries in the United States in 2004, based upon data from the US Alcohol and Tobacco Tax and Trade Bureau (TTB) in the Department of the Treasury (WineAmerica, http://65.36.226.44/newsroom/wine%20 data%20center/2004%20Winery%20Distribution%20by%20Size.pdf).

We see that that almost half of 2,481 wineries were in the smallest production category, and they produced less than half a percent of total

*Table 5.1*   *Distribution of US wineries by production size (based on TTB tax receipt data), 2004*

| Production ('000s gals.) | Number of Wineries | Percent of Wineries | Gallons Produced ('000) | Percent of Production |
|---|---|---|---|---|
| Up to 5 | 1,121 | 45.2 | 1,976 | 0.4 |
| 5 to10 | 277 | 11.2 | 2,006 | 0.4 |
| 10 to 25 | 403 | 16.2 | 6,382 | 1.2 |
| 25 to 50 | 200 | 8.1 | 7,023 | 1.3 |
| 50 to 100 | 155 | 6.2 | 10,946 | 2.0 |
| 100 to 150 | 166 | 6.7 | 19,109 | 3.5 |
| 150 to 250 | 55 | 2.2 | 10,167 | 1.8 |
| 250 to1200 | 55 | 2.2 | 29,017 | 5.2 |
| Over 1200 | 49 | 2.0 | 466,967 | 84.4 |
| Totals | 2,481 | 100.0 | 553,593 | 100.0 |

*Source:*   WineAmerica (2004).

*Table 5.2   Size distribution of US wineries by employment, 2002*

| All establishments | 1,189 |
|---|---|
| 1 to 4 employees | 709 |
| 5 to 9 employees | 104 |
| 10 to 19 employees | 140 |
| 20 to 49 employees | 143 |
| 50 to 99 employees | 49 |
| 100 to 249 employees | 31 |
| 250 to 499 employees | 6 |
| 500 to 999 employees | 5 |
| 1,000 to 2,499 employees | 1 |
| 2,500 employees or more | 1 |

*Source:*   US Department of Commerce (2004).

production in 2004. The category with the largest producers dominates output, producing almost 85 percent of the total—but it still contains 49 wineries. The domestic industry certainly contains many small wineries—but it also contains many large wineries—so it is difficult to conclude that it is anything other than highly competitive with products differentiated to varying degrees depending upon which segment of the market we study.

Corroborating evidence of the size distribution comes from the US 2002 Economic Census which produced a report on US wineries during that calendar year (US Department of Commerce 2004). The data in Table 5.2 show the size distribution of US wineries by employment (size distribution by production is not collected): the general pattern is the same.

In 2002, the two states with the most wineries were, first, California with 666 (187 with 20 employees or more) and, second, Washington with 83 (7 with 20 employees or more) which represent 56.0 percent and 7.0 percent of the total above respectively. We do not have state-level data to compare with the national pattern in Table 5.2 but expect that it would be broadly similar. We cannot know what is behind the likely difference in counting wineries between them in 2004 and the Department of Commerce in 2002—it seems unlikely that the number of US wineries more than doubled in two years—but the pattern is of more interest to us.

Recent research is broadly consistent with these patterns. Cyr, Kushner, and Ogwang (2014) studied the historic pattern of the size distribution of California North Coast wineries which has tended to be right-skewed as both distributions above suggest. However, they find evidence that the distribution is developing a second mode (other than the left tail) consistent with "mid-size wineries being squeezed out" by larger and smaller wineries, suggesting, among other things, that small wineries are still able to enter that market (Cyr, Kushner, and Ogwang 2014: 57–60).

The fact that imported wine also plays a significant role in the US market (e.g., 28 percent of US sales in 2008 (http://www.trade.gov/td/ocg/wine2008.pdf)) only reinforces the impression that the market is highly competitive, though with differentiated products—and the situation is potentially similar, at least among many industrialized countries, around the world. The conclusion is qualified because of the prominent role of government in some countries that, in effect, removes wine sales from freely competitive conditions at least in retail markets.

Thornton (2013) has provided some useful analysis of industry structure around the world. His view of the data is that the global market is certainly competitive: his analysis of concentration ratios (the share of market sales represented by some number of the largest firms in the market) indicates that the share of global sales represented by the largest two to thirty firms averaged 5.5 to 21.1 percent respectively during 2003–2009 (Thornton 2013: 289). Thirty firms are unlikely to avoid competing with each other for long (e.g., through collusion); if they serve only one fifth of the market, one expects that global competition is robust. However, while Old World countries have competitive producers' size distributions (average domestic four-firm concentration ratio of 12.6 percent for France, Germany, Italy, and Spain), the major New World countries have relatively high domestic concentration ratios (the four-firm ratios for Argentina, Australia, Chile, South Africa, and the US are 60.5, 62.3, 80.0+, 37.1, and 56.0 percent respectively). As we suggest above, access by imports increases the competitiveness of the US market (imports are 28 percent of 2008 consumption), but government policies in the other four New World countries listed keep imports around 1 percent of domestic consumption in three of the four other New World countries. Australia is the exception at 12 percent (Thornton 2013: 288–289).

Governments have created many of the barriers to competition in the wine market. One can view the extensive use of geographic delimitation—the AOC system in France, the DOC system in Italy, the DO system in Spain, the AVA system in the US, the VQA system in Canada—as quality control, but it limits the supply of grapes and wine that can bear a certain name; and, as such, it limits the number of suppliers. We discuss this more in Chapter 6.

The size distributions indicated above, especially within the US and the Old World countries, describe firms that, at their largest, produce large quantities of beverage wine that is either bottled or sold in bulk or, toward the left tail, hope to produce fine, or finer, wines that can sell at prices that will cover the relatively high unit costs of small-scale production, marketing, and distribution. Of course, many of the largest producers include divisions that focus upon fine wine which benefit from economies of scale in operations, marketing, and distribution resulting from being part of the larger organization. The evidence from concentration ratios suggests that the beverage wine market is highly competitive in most major wine-producing countries, especially those where imports represent a significant share of sales.

The fine wine market reflects characteristics of both of the structures that we have discussed but is distinctly different. *Monopolistic competition* describes industries that resemble perfectly competitive industries—many producers, easy entry—but with the important exception that their products are perceived to be differentiated so that they are not perfect substitutes for each other. That imperfect substitutability means that producers are more likely price setters, albeit within the narrow range of prices that their close (but not perfect) competitors allow. Many familiar industries seem to fit this structure: examples with many producers and easy entry but somewhat differentiated products include many small businesses such as restaurants, personal service providers (e.g., hair salons, spas), tax preparers—perhaps wine shops. Given evidence of the size distribution of wine producers, they would seem to fit this structure as well.

Monopolistically competitive producers share the characteristic with monopolies that they tend to produce inefficiently low levels of output (recall our earlier observation about monopolies that, at their target production, the benefit to the marginal buyer (i.e., price) exceeds the marginal cost of producing it). However, they do not share another characteristic of monopolies that allows monopolies to thrive—namely, the lack of competition. In contrast, the competitive environment of these firms means that, considering profitability and survival, we expect them to be inefficiently small and have difficulty making and maintaining a profit (e.g., Mankiw 2015: 329–344). The "second wine miracle" of small winery profitability introduced in Chapter 3 comes to mind.

Since they are often sole proprietorships or partnerships, the smaller producers whose focus is fine wine production are not required to report financial performance so it is notoriously difficult to measure the profitability of monopolistically competitive wineries. We also lack data on the profitability of the fine wine operations of larger producers. Stories of success—or how to achieve it (e.g., Pellechia 2008)—and failure (e.g., Stang 2012) are plentiful, but we do not have the data to demonstrate whether the performance of this sector of the industry fits the model of monopolistic competition. The recent research from Cyr et al. on California's North Coast wineries suggests that smaller "new firms can enter and succeed" (Cyr et al. 2014: 60), but these results do not control for two extenuating circumstances. First, they do not control for ownership so it is possible that wineries are persisting, but they are turning over as owners try and fail to make a profit.

Second, survival does not mean profitability because, aside from profitability, owners' behavior may involve utility maximization from the experience of owning a winery. We cannot measure the extent to which owners cover their losses personally because they enjoy the lifestyle, but it would not be surprising to learn that a significant number of small producers report net losses to the tax authorities.

While one can find pockets of monopoly power in wine production, albeit perhaps fleeting in some instances or government protected in others, the overall business climate is competitive. We discussed earlier the theoretical appeal of competitive markets which, at their best, are responsive to buyer preferences, minimize production costs, and thereby generate maximum aggregate benefits from transactions to those able to participate in them. However, we have also emphasized the importance of complete information in achieving that outcome and alluded to the difficulty in achieving that in wine markets. While the idea of wine knowledge is the focus of Chapter 7, we turn now to a more systematic discussion of information imperfections in wine markets.

## THE CHALLENGE OF ASYMMETRIC INFORMATION; LEMONS AND THE WINNER'S CURSE

Asymmetric information (AI) is a pervasive issue in understanding transactions: we often participate in markets where buyers and sellers of a product have significantly different amounts of information about the good being traded so that, under competitive conditions, the asymmetry puts the less informed side at a potential disadvantage in the transaction. Consumers' willingness to pay may be distorted by missing information so that they either overpay for an item that they value less once they know more about it or forgo a transaction that would have been beneficial. Alternatively, producers may either sell too little for too little because they underestimate the market's valuation—*Antiques Roadshow* reminds us that rummage sale shoppers sometimes know more than sellers about value—or they produce too much and ask too much because they misread buyer interest in a product. The model of market operation that yields predictions about minimum cost production of goods that consumers most value assumes costless and perfect information. Consumers know about all products, the benefit they provide, and their prices (so that "bang per buck" is known); and producers know what consumers know as well as all the ways to produce what they want and the related costs of production. We can imagine products that would approach this level of familiarity in the market—everyday items that many consumers have used regularly for generations and that many producers have produced over the centuries. Interestingly, many of these products are foods and beverages such as bread, milk, sugar, and common meats and vegetables. Among wines, this could describe the beverage segment of the industry—perhaps less familiar in North America but familiar in traditional wine-producing countries.

On the other hand, another segment of the wine market is that category of goods in which the asymmetry is so severe that it represents a significant interference with transacting.

Beyond recognizing the role of AI in transacting, it is worth identifying different sources of AI:

1. Technical asymmetry: In these transactions, one party has more technical knowledge of the product than the other where the technical characteristics of the product bear upon the consumer's willingness to pay. For example, buyers and sellers of medical care do not have the same information. Consumers are at an information disadvantage which could and perhaps does lead them to miss beneficial treatments—or to pursue ineffective or harmful ones. Appreciating this risk, most turn to experts who have been certified to have more reliable medical knowledge than they do. Ostensibly one can verify this information advantage through testing, peer review, validating training, and other methods often used to certify professional competence. These experts also know less than their patients about the patients' conditions, but one hopes that knowing how to elicit that information is part of their expertise.

2. Experiential asymmetry: In these transactions, one party has had more experience with the product than the other and thereby knows more about it. However, with more experience, one can learn about the good; this is less likely with technical asymmetry where formal education may represent the information differential. Another distinction is that knowledge gained from experience with a good may be more subjective: the product's characteristics are more difficult to describe in objective terms, and it is more difficult to improve others' decision making. So it tends to be with painting—or wine. One expert's "bold brush strokes" may be another's "amateurish splotches". One's "subtle elegance" may be another's "light, simple, and forgettable". This AI is more difficult to measure objectively than technical asymmetry.

3.  Dynamic experiential asymmetry: Product characteristics can change from time to time so that both parties must refresh their knowledge of the product periodically.

We shall examine the AI problem in a relatively simple and familiar context and then apply the analysis to wine markets.

Akerlof (1970) was among the first to understand and analyze the significance of AI in a pioneering paper on "the market for lemons". The lemons of interest here are automobiles—or any product, often relatively complex technically, where the seller (e.g., owner, producer) knows significantly more about the product's characteristics than the potential buyer. We can imagine a market for a relatively complex product such as automobiles—or, more particularly, used automobiles—which likely have very different histories and performance limitations that are difficult to learn. Imagine that, potentially, the market offers a wide range of quality among used cars. Potential purchasers know much less than the cars' owners about their quality—efficient operation, reliability, flaws and damage, and so forth. In the absence of any observable information about the cars' characteristics, those potential purchasers will tend to assume that a randomly chosen used car will have average quality, and they will form their willingness to pay for such a car accordingly. Perhaps, under current market conditions, the typical consumer would offer $10,000 for a randomly chosen used car expected to have average quality. Anticipating that potential buyers will not recognize above-average quality, owners with above-average quality cars would withhold them from the market, and the actual average quality of available used cars would be lower than the population average quality because the upper end of the quality distribution has been withheld.

Anticipating this—that the best quality cars are missing—potential buyers would lower their estimated average value; and sellers, anticipating that reaction, would withhold more cars and so forth. The hypothesis is that the market shrinks or disappears until or unless enough information emerges to sustain reliable transactions: as buyers lower their quality expectations and WTP and sellers withdraw their products, the number of potential transactions shrinks.

While conceptually, the antidote to this problem is removing the information asymmetry, achieving that may not be straightforward: if, ultimately, the goal is full knowledge of one's choices—so not only having the right information but also being able to process it—then numerous challenges arise from the cost of acquiring and validating the information to processing it correctly. In cases of technical asymmetry, we sometimes have "certification" that allows at least some ability to distinguish quality (e.g., formal degrees and qualities of training (e.g., medical doctors) or objective audits of performance (e.g., audited financial statements)). In cases of experiential asymmetry, which is more applicable to wine, finding the antidote is more elusive. If the costs of "solving" the problem are high enough, it remains unsolved and the market languishes or never emerges.

Winemakers must decide whether to produce wine and, if producing, what quality to offer. The task for producers of beverage wine differs little from that of other processors of fruits and vegetables (e.g., frozen orange juice, canned peas)—or, for that matter, other alcoholic beverages such as mass market beers and spirits: continue to produce the product that customers have come to expect and maintain consistency and adequate supply.

On the other hand, unlike almost all other fruits and vegetables, certain grapes have properties that consumers may value highly if they are processed properly. Consumers who are aware of that potential are prepared to pay generously for those properties—or for the prospect of discovering new ones. But how do they know where to find them?

If winemakers can produce the potentially highest valued wine possible from the resources available, how do they know that it will be recognized if buyers are unable to know the quality? Winemakers might think that they have produced a great wine, but how do buyers know that? This asymmetric information is not an issue for most of the wine consumed globally, but it is an issue for the potentially most highly valued wine. In a sense, the producer's challenge for these wines resembles the challenge of introducing a new product—and, for vintage wines, introducing one every year. Aside from the producer's reputation, which can carry considerable weight, how do buyers know what to expect?

Anticipating our discussions in Chapters 7 and 8, it is worth emphasizing here a characteristic of wine that distinguishes it from most other products—its role as a cultural good. In this chapter, we think of winemaking primarily as a business where long-run profit making is among the goals if not the only goal. If, instead, we think of wine as an expression of creativity like fine art that may or may not be "correctly" valued, then the challenge to transacting knowledgeably moves beyond mere information asymmetry. One might be able to learn enough about used cars to overcome or at least diminish the "lemons" problem. However, the challenge of knowing fine art or fine wine and of understanding the motives for their creation largely moves those markets into a different line of enquiry that those chapters try to capture.

One of the hypotheses from the lemons model is that, to the extent that winemaking is profit oriented—in contrast to, say, a hobbyist's or gifted winemaker's desire to express creativity—AI deters certain kinds of winemaking. Rather than car owners withholding cars, winemakers decide to adjust their production to reflect the difficulty of educating consumers. They may be able to enhance the quality of a wine by acquiring better fruit or owning and harvesting more storied vineyards or using a more severe selection or aging the wine longer or under more costly conditions—all cost-increasing choices—but they cannot know that the consumer will have enough information to value these enhancements adequately. They may invest heavily in education and other signaling to counteract the consumer's lack of information, but buyers may distrust seller-supplied information.

One interpretation of Robert Parker's motivation to produce the *Wine Advocate* was to address the AI problem and to do so without accepting advertising because of the risk or appearance of conflict of interest (McCoy 2005). Following Parker's example, the proliferation of expert opinions such as wine ratings and tasting notes in recent years has perhaps mitigated the AI problem in wine markets. However, once there is a market for such opinion, a nested AI problem arises: the consumer faces a distribution of opinions and imputes only average reliability to a randomly chosen one.

Given the information problem, consumers have tended to adopt three responses to the wine market (we exclude from consideration those who do not participate in the wine market for reasons such as allergies, objections to alcoholic beverages, or dislike of wine). First, they limit wine purchases to products they know that vary little over time. These are likely beverage wines that may not even be distinguished by vintage: they buy what they know, and producers serve that market by continuing to produce consistent products. Second, they largely avoid the market or participate minimally. The quantity of information required to make knowledgeable choices deters participation, and the cost of a mistake can be costly or unpleasant or embarrassing. They are willing to accept wine but see it as simply another beverage among many and see no particular reason to prefer it. Third, they see the thousands of wines available and attempt to sort them by some combination of personal experience and expert guidance—or own experience and the experience of others—and they are prepared to be surprised regularly, both pleasantly and otherwise. These categories correspond approximately to the categories discovered by Constellation Brands' path breaking study of wine consumers (Veseth 2008).

One reaction to the problem of asymmetric information is to claim that consumers can acquire the needed information only by "experiencing" the good. Nelson (1970) discussed the idea of experience goods which are goods whose value the consumer can determine only by experience with them. In this sense, all goods are experience goods at some point in one's life so this illustrates the fluidity of applying this concept to anything in particular that we consume. However, many goods become relatively familiar to us over time so that the combination of our experience with them and their relatively stable characteristics—pieces of furniture, items of clothing, everyday foods, and others—means that we come to "know" them. Some have argued that fine wine is an experience good (e.g., Storchmann 2012; Ashton 2014). We shall assume this for now but question it in Chapter 7.

Many factors challenge the attempt to know fine wines: we can divide them into supply side which arise from the various challenges of getting a wine to market that buyers will know and demand side which arise from what the consumer brings to the market.

Probably the most familiar supply side reason is the variation that arises from a change of vintage. This is primarily and most predictably the weather conditions affecting the vintage, and these influences can be numerous: average temperature, variations in temperature over the year, temperature at critical times in the growing season such as bud break or harvest, similar measures for rainfall and sunlight, presence at critical times of weather events such as hail storms or strong winds, and so forth. Researchers such as Ashenfelter (e.g., *Liquid Assets*, various years) have argued that weather conditions are, with location, essentially the key determinants of wine value and have provided the empirical evidence to support that claim.

Vintage influence can be dramatic. While expert evidence of that might be debatable, economic evidence is relatively straightforward—for example, the difference in value between two reasonably proximate vintages of the same wine. A number of studies have measured the importance of vintage to value (e.g., Marks 2009), but a straightforward examination of auction prices makes the point. Examine the pre-sale estimates for different vintages of the same wine offered at a major wine auction (e.g., http://www.sothebys.com/en/catalogues/ecatalogue.html/2012/finest-and-rarest-wines-featuring-three-superb-continental-cellars#/r=/en/ecat.fhtml.L12706.html+r.m=/en/ecat.list.L12706.html/0/60/lotnum/asc/), and the effect of vintage upon expected willingness to pay becomes apparent.

While vintage influence is one of the most fascinating and challenging characteristics of fine wine, some winemaking traditions suppress its effects by blending vintages in an effort to produce a consistent, non-vintage (NV) product—for example, the primary "brut" bottling of many producers in Champagne and assorted NV bottlings from many Portuguese port houses whose flagship bottlings are vintage port. These are probably the most established examples of vintage suppression, reflecting an industry decision to sacrifice the potential value of interesting differences in vintage for the sake of product consistency. That said, it is noteworthy that many Champagne and port houses "declare vintages" and include vintage products in their product lines which, because they are chosen selectively, are considerably more valuable than their NV products.

Less typical are decisions by producers typically producing vintage wine to suppress vintage for a particular product line presumably because of the opportunity to produce a quality product if freed from the requirement to honor vintage (e.g., Sean Thackrey's Pleiades Old Vine series, Rosenblum's Vintner's Cuvée zinfandels).

However, other production adjustments—perhaps related to weather conditions—might be considered vintage specific such as a change in grape sourcing or a change in the proportions of relevant varietals that has been influenced by weather conditions. Other conditions can also change from year to year but are not particularly related to the annual period of a vintage. For example, changes arising from the appellation allowed to produce the wine could matter. These might be changes in the production requirements in the area (e.g., rules for irrigation or fertilizing, varietals allowed) or changes in the delineation of the area (e.g., soils in an area newly included might be different). A variety of changes in the production process could also affect the product—for example, changes in technology (e.g., switch from tanks to barrels), personnel (e.g., the winemaker, the grape harvesters), techniques related to economic conditions (e.g., more or less selection to affect production levels).

We can imagine other reasons effectively beyond the producer's control when we think of disappointing product characteristics in our food consumption. Do fruit and vegetable growers know exactly what the consumer will purchase from the produce market? Might the apple or orange be mealy? Might the melon never sweeten? Might the potato be rotting from the inside? Conditions within the winemaking environment (e.g., presence of brettanomyces or "brett") or from the packaging (e.g., cork taint or TCA) can frustrate the producer's intentions, although opinions about the undesirability of some of these effects vary (e.g., some consumers enjoy the influence of brett). Pushed far enough, we beg the question of intention: do producers know enough about the winemaking process that they know the outcome they can achieve? Is there not a degree of uncertainty of outcome in every wine produced—some would say even in every bottle of wine produced?

Once the wine is produced, subsequent events can affect it—both its handling at the winery and especially transportation and storage, both conditions (e.g., temperature, moisture) and duration. While technically describing the wine's origins, the set of conditions describing the wine prior to the current sale is called its provenance. For example, if it is in their favor, wine auction houses and some vendors (e.g., Garagiste in Seattle, USA) highlight the importance of the provenance of the wines they sell in an attempt to reassure a buyer that the wine has been handled carefully and is authentic.

Even if all the controllable circumstances on the supply side never changed, vintage will always matter, though a producer may try to suppress its influence in a NV bottling. Moreover, on the demand side, it is still difficult to know a wine because of both our limited ability to identify what we sense from the wine itself in a consistent manner—its intrinsic qualities—and the importance of the environment in which we taste a wine and the objective information (e.g., label, bottle color, price) that we have about it—what the consumer marketing literature calls the extrinsic cues.

Another AI phenomenon seems consistent with consumer behavior toward fine wine, especially at wine auctions or at flash sale sites offering limited quantities but perhaps as well with retail transactions. With AI, the consumer lacking information must estimate what s/he does not know—for example, one unfamiliar with the particular characteristics of a product whose quality is variable so that s/he has, at best, a good sense of the range of characteristics that a product might have, but the range is wide enough that s/he is concerned about regret—from either missing a good value or paying too much.

Imagine that a group of potential bidders is interested in a product whose characteristics are known only as a distribution—that is, the best and worst possibilities with a sense of the relative likelihood of everything in between. Their bids will reflect their relative valuations of the product: skeptical buyers will bid less than hopeful buyers, the more hopeful buyer is likely to bid more, and the sizes of bids are likely to vary directly with the number of bidders (more competition for the product drives bids up). The most hopeful bidder offers the most and emerges the winner. The winner's hopeful valuation may be accurate, but on average the quality of the product will be less than the winner's estimate so that we observe "the winner's curse" (e.g., Thaler 1994).

In the absence of complete information, fine wine buying might resemble this. Abstracting from the complication of different tastes, wine consumers have different levels of knowledge about a given wine. At a given price, some buyers will find the wine unattractive—not enough estimated benefit for the asking price—and they will pass. In an actual auction setting, among the others, the most hopeful buyer will bid the most, *cet. par.*, and is likely to be disappointed. While this has not been tested empirically, one can speculate that we would find similar results with online flash sales: with imperfect information and a lack of close substitutes (assume fine wine), limited quantity (actual or claimed), limited time, and potentially many thousands of buyers, it resembles an auction. The most hopeful participants are likely to be the first buyers and again might tend to be disappointed.

## CONCLUSION

In order to have transactions, we need sellers to join the buyers. This chapter has discussed the supply side of the market as a reflection of suppliers' best decisions in light of the market conditions they face and their objectives. Buyers and sellers engage in transactions, and we have considered the idea of market equilibrium and its appeal as well as alternative market outcomes such as transactions at non-clearing prices and reactions to them. Consumer markets tend to be inherently competitive on the demand side, but industry structure on the supply side can vary from competitive to monopolistic—with monopolistic competition being a blend of the two—with structure having further implications for market outcomes: generally, more competition means lower prices and production costs, though the pursuit of product differentiation among wines complicates this.

We have also discussed how asymmetric information between buyers and sellers can deter transactions and the difficulty of interpreting the prices we observe. We shall return to some of these topics such as incomplete information and knowledge after turning to discussion of the role of the public sector in wine markets.

## NOTES

1.  No two wine producers are alike so this is a strong assumption, but it allows us to illustrate the role of the number of producers in determining the industry supply curve. The number of producers in the industry serving a market depends upon how narrowly or broadly we define the industry—from "wine" to a particular bottling (e.g., vintage, vineyard, format) from a single producer. In the latter case, the producer who controls the entire supply would be a monopolist. If her supply has been distributed to a number of vendors (e.g., wine shops, grocery stores), then the supply becomes more competitive. The discussion of industry structure occurs later in the chapter.
2.  It is convenient to represent a graphic presentation of behavior such as consumer demand and producer supply with linear relationships, in part because we can easily write down equations that represent those relationships (relative to more complex equations that might represent the market more accurately but that could be considerably more difficult to manipulate and understand) and then use those equations to provide further information about the market such as a precise description of its market-clearing conditions. Given the logical relationship one wants to capture with a "formula" representing

demand behavior, one would say that the quantity demanded is determined by own price plus, in a more thorough representation, expressions involving the other key variables such as income, the prices of related goods, and so forth: the quantity demanded is the outcome (a "dependent variable") that reflects the influence of the other variables (the "independent variables" such as income). For example, a generalized linear expression of such a formula would be:

$$Qd = a_0 + a_1P + a_2X$$

where Qd is quantity demanded, P is own price, X is some other key variable, and the $a_i$ terms are coefficients which indicate the impact of a one-unit change in a variable upon the outcome: for example, in this expression, a \$1 increase in P would change Qd by $a_1$ units. The $a_0$ term is a constant indicating how many units would be demanded regardless of the values of the other independent variables (often needed to provide a complete mathematical description (i.e., a non-zero Q-axis intercept) but sometimes logically challenging (e.g., how can consumers buy anything if income is zero?)). A more complete expression would include X-terms for all the key variables expected to influence quantity demanded.

In addition, in a more thorough model, we would recognize that the independent variables might not be truly independent. For example, we would allow a change in the price of substitute good B to affect the demand for good A, but the resulting impact upon the price of A could then feed back into the market for B, affecting B's price, and so forth.

Using the same approach for representing supply behavior, we could write down a generalized linear expression for quantity supplied:

$$Qs = b_0 + b_1P + b_2X$$

with a similar explanation for the terms here—for example, Qs is quantity supplied and X would be a key variable affecting that such as the price of some input (e.g., new vine rootstock).

Because of the economist's tradition of putting own price (P) on the vertical axis (the Y-axis in the Cartesian system) and the more general convention of writing the Y-variable as a function of the X-variable(s), we often write down the demand and supply relationships in *inverse* form—that is, solve the Qd or Qs equation for P.

In the example in Figure 5.5, we are suppressing the explicit presentation of the role of variables other than own price. We are using the following inverse demand equation:

$$P = \$24 - Q$$

where Q is measured in thousands of bottles of wine. We are using the following inverse supply equation:

$$P = \$3 + 1.25Q.$$

Since these are linear relationships with different slopes and intercepts, they can have at most one point in common—the price at which the quantity demanded equals the quantity supplied. For this example, those are P=\$14.67 and Q=9,333 bottles (recall that Q is measured in thousands of bottles).

3. In thinking about a Walrasian auction, one might wonder about the prospect of using price discrimination: if one knows buyers' entire demand curves, one could charge different prices to different buyers depending upon their willingness to pay. Aside from the incentive this would create for buyers to act strategically and distort their willingness to pay, price discrimination would be difficult here because wine can be re-traded. Unlike

airplane seats and medical care—established examples of price discrimination—wine sold to some buyers at a lower price can be re-sold so that those buyers become competitors of the producer by offering to re-trade their purchases.

4. Compared with the US and Canada, the Mexican wine market is small. For example, adult per capita wine consumption in liters in Canada, the US, and Mexico in 2009 were 1.87, 1.30, and 0.10 respectively (Anderson and Nelgen 2014: 53, Table II–21). Retail wine sales are less competitive, and discounting is less common.

# 6. Wine and government

## INTRODUCTION

A discussion of transactions assumes the presence of government. Many of the ideas behind transactions that we have discussed up to now virtually require the existence of some authority that facilitates the making and enforcement of contracts, the accuracy and completeness of information, the definition and enforcement of property rights, the safety and security of everyday life from working and shopping to traveling, the defense of the community which includes the marketplace—and the authority to raise funds through taxation to pay for itself. Beyond these government activities which are, in economic terms, microeconomic, lie all government's macroeconomic activities oriented toward monitoring and managing the aggregate economy—pursuing monetary policy by managing and regulating a central bank and the banking system, stimulating and constraining the economy through fiscal policy, and redistributing resources in pursuit of fairness. All schools of economic thought address the choices and rules that a community must make on behalf of its members—that is, a role for government. They pay considerable attention to the choices that should be made—a normative proposition reflected, for example, in using government instead of markets for authority-based allocation that was introduced in Chapter 2. They also study the choices actually made and try to measure their impacts and understand why they occur. This emphasis on positive analysis—How does the world work?—is distinct from normative analysis which would substitute the word "should" for "does" in that question.

We now turn to the role of government in wine markets in which we shall use this distinction. We ask first what we observe governments actually doing and then discuss how sensible those policies seem.

Beyond the role of government in the lives of consumers and firms generally we can identify a number of areas in which we observe government intervention that is more specific to alcoholic beverages generally and wine in particular such as:

- Regulation of origination: definitions of products containing alcohol for consumption and the specific definition of wine; for wine, the

locations allowed to produce specific wines or, alternatively, regulation of the use of certain terms to describe the wines produced in a given location;
- Regulation of processing: the process of commercial production of wine from the agricultural processes used to grow grapes to the kinds of product manipulation allowed before the product is offered for sale; the labeling allowed and required for wine;
- Regulation of safe commercial shipping and of import, wholesale, and retail sales and the circumstances under which alcoholic beverages can be purchased for home ("off-premises") consumption, including prohibition;
- Regulation of on-premises consumption, including prohibition;
- Regulation of interjurisdictional shipping (e.g., international, intranational); and
- Taxation specific to alcoholic beverages.

We discuss below the special role of government in this market.

## GOVERNMENT'S ROLE: REGULATING NARCOTICS

As the preceding list suggests, governments tend to regulate wine markets more closely than many markets. The literature in economics, law, and politics suggests a number of reasons for this.

Narcotics are substances that induce narcosis—a state of dulled senses, drowsiness, and perhaps unconsciousness. Given that meaning, alcohol is arguably a narcotic, though that designation for alcohol is controversial because of the negative connotation of narcotics in some societies. Some authors actually define narcotics as being illegal (e.g., Hart, Ksir, and Ray 2008: 470). Governments have targeted the production, transaction, and use of narcotics for centuries, though this is not without controversy.

We approach this subject with the assumption that the burden is on government, or those supporting it, to demonstrate its usefulness beyond the basic services described initially. Unless we choose to use government as an employment creation project—perhaps efficient occasionally (e.g., during the Great Depression) but not normally—we look for a benefit to weigh against the direct and indirect costs of using public resources to intervene in transactions.

It is helpful to consider, first, the relevance of alcohol and, second, the specific concerns about wine. Probably the most widely defended normative rationale for regulating narcotics reflects a general concern about the behavioral impact of narcotics and related addictive substances and related spillover effects upon families and communities—concerns such as related healthcare costs that fall upon taxpayers, economic and social hardships on families of addicted individuals (including threats to family members' health), impacts upon the wider community of addictive behavior (e.g., driving while under the influence of a narcotic and similar risks from operating machinery while under the influence, crimes related to addiction such as robbery of both general property and pharmaceuticals). This is largely a spillover, or "externality", argument: among the benefits and costs of the alcohol transaction, the benefits are all fully internalized by the buyer and seller, but the costs are not. By interfering with the transaction in any or all of a variety of ways, the government hopes to discourage the undesirable behavior: raising the overall price of the transaction through taxes, behavioral sanctions, scrutiny by law enforcement, social stigma—any or all of these—reduces the quantity desired. If the consequences of alcohol consumption were limited to the consumer involved in the transaction, then this rationale would weaken. However, these examples suggest that they are not.

Related to this is regulation based primarily upon moral and religious objections (which may flow from behavioral concerns) whose popularity varies widely by community—from places where governments resist adopting any particular moral or religious code of conduct to those where the lines between legal authority and moral and religious authority is virtually nonexistent (e.g., theocracies where government authority is greatly or entirely influenced by some religious authority). For example, governments whose citizens are almost all devout Muslims (Pew Research Center 2011) often prohibit the availability of alcohol with minor exceptions such as tourist hotels and restaurants (e.g., Saudi Arabia, Yemen). This rationale reflects another form of spillover effect where the consequences of a seemingly private transaction go beyond the immediate participants: certain behaviors offend "community standards", and the community has decided that this offense is sufficiently widespread that it will limit or prohibit the transaction—raise its price as high as necessary to discourage it to the extent desired.

We take both of these rationales, arguably and albeit in different measures, to be the normative basis *ab initio* for the extra regulation of narcotics generally and alcohol in particular around the world. The most intrusive public policy response is prohibition of the transaction, and a variety of reactions to that creates an array of related economic incentives such as the stimulation of black markets and the production of counterfeits. It is difficult to see a clear economic incentive for prohibition—in effect, an intention to eliminate a market by outlawing it—unless, perhaps, one hopes to stimulate the demand for close substitutes which seems unlikely in this case. However, as we shall discuss below, economic incentives are more likely present for regulation short of prohibition.

## REGULATING WINE

This chapter's focus is the extent of government intervention in transactions. It is helpful to discuss the nature of intervention by referring to the transactions "landscape" represented by demand and supply conditions in a market such as that depicted in Figure 6.1.[1]

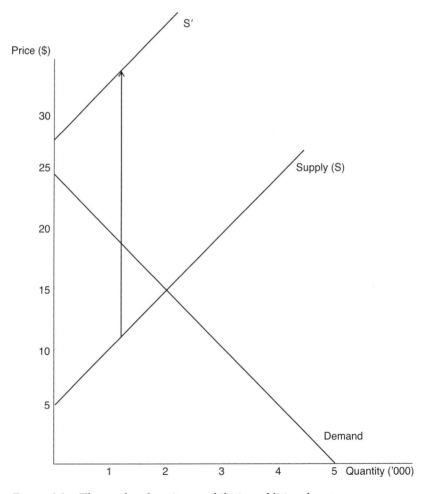

*Figure 6.1    The market for wine: prohibitive additional cost*

Recognizing that the purpose of government intervention in the wine market must be to affect the number of transactions (and/or raise revenue in the process) can guide our understanding of public policy options by considering that landscape. As indicated at the outset, the list of areas of potential intervention is lengthy. We shall focus upon intervention in wine production and consumer markets, including taxation. Because of its history, France has provided a particularly informative example of government intervention in wine production which has gone on to become the basis for European Union (EU) Wine Policy. On the other hand, compared with, say, North America, EU intervention in wholesale and retail trade is more limited, likely reflecting the minimal impact of Prohibition in the US (1920–1933) that has, in contrast, left such an imprint on North American markets.

If left alone, we expect that the market will always be moving toward the maximum number of mutually beneficial transactions at the market-clearing price. However, this assumes that the demand and supply behavior depicted captures all of the costs and benefits of these transactions, and we have just seen the case against that. For example, some communities feel that the costs of these transactions are so much more than those captured by, say, the direct costs of production (the usual meaning of the supply curve) that the lowest cost of a transaction exceeds more than what anyone is willing to pay. In effect, public policy can make supply so costly (as with S' in Figure 6.1) that no mutually beneficial transactions survive. Our focus is a less extreme outcome.

## REGULATING WINE PRODUCTION: THE CASE OF FRANCE AND THE EU

More than any other country, France has arguably had the greatest impact upon the role of wine in the modern world. The quantity, variety, and overall quality of French wine in the world continue to impress. Given its tradition of importance in the global wine market, France has also had a significant effect upon views of the proper role of government in the wine market, particularly production. Meloni and Swinnen (2013) have provided a comprehensive review of the impact of French wine regulations upon EU Wine Policy—the policy governing the world's largest wine region for production, importing, and exporting. They conclude that French policy is likely the single most important influence upon that Policy: "what were initially mainly French and, to a lesser extent, Italian national regulations now apply to approximately 60 percent of the world's wine production" (Meloni and Swinnen 2013: 272). EU Wine Policy now governs production in member states but acts to underpin national wine laws. Thus, French wine law regulates its wine production, and EU laws supplement that.

Because of the asymmetric information problem in wine transactions, producers look for ways to communicate the content of a wine bottle to consumers before they open it. The consumer's ability to evaluate a product and arrive at a willingness to pay for it depends significantly, though by no means entirely, upon that information: if it is established, the producer's reputation plays a significant role in that process (e.g., Landon and Smith 1998; Marks 2009).

One way to communicate product content to consumers is to control what goes into production. French and EU rules govern wine production in myriad ways, but many attempt to reduce uncertainty through a number of restrictions imposed upon production—for example, permissible grapes—with the idea that more restrictions suggest less uncertainty about contents. While the particular restrictions change from time to time, the core concepts have endured.

Probably the strongest motivation for introducing France's regulation of the wine industry—the Appellation d'Origine Contrôlée, or AOC, system—was the wide variation in quality, often involving fraud and adulteration, that resulted from unregulated production prior to its introduction during the 1930s (e.g., Colman 2008: 7–22). In the absence of regulation, both the quantity and quality of wine production could be anything that producers wanted, including production offshore (e.g., French colonies such as Algeria), with the result that consumers had little idea of what they might find in the bottle. Even if a producer worked to produce a consistent product, one had no assurance that adulteration would not occur; and, if a producer established a reputation for consistently good production, it was difficult to protect against counterfeits.

Of course, achieving the benefits of the market system requires a "free market", but that assumes that the participants know what is being transacted.

In this sense, one can understand that both buyers and sellers could support the concept of regulation: for example, if the government could enforce regulations that limited production to only one or a few grapes (e.g., only pinot noir in Burgundy's reds), then consumers know much about the contents of a wine from that region. Producers are free to produce anything they want— interesting new and delicious wines emerge from France regularly—but they cannot label it as a wine of a particular AOC whose requirements it would violate.

AOC regulations govern several components of wine production (Robinson 1994: 40–42): most importantly, production area or location, allowed varietals and allowable proportions for blending, ripeness and alcoholic strength, yield per unit of land and minimum vine age, viticulture (e.g., vine density, pruning, vine training, irrigation), and winemaking and distillation. EU regulations also govern vineyard removal ("grubbing up"). The relevance of each of these components may be self-evident, but they are worth reviewing. While it would be difficult to segregate them on this basis, they seem to represent two broad themes: quality control and supply management. The former seems difficult to oppose, given the difficulties created by asymmetric information: in principle, serving that theme is consistent with efficiency. The legitimacy of the latter likely depends upon one's faith in the efficiency of markets: restricting supply artificially is good for producers (and producer surplus) but perhaps detrimental to overall market benefits (Total Surplus) by restricting supply and raising prices.

It may be futile to try to determine which came first—the value of associating a wine with a place or of associating a place with a wine—but the AOC system embodies a strong connection between wine and place: to be labeled as such legally, the different wine types of France from Aligoté to Vouvray can be produced only in those places. The power of this requirement may not extend far outside of France. Non-French producers have regularly appropriated the French place names over the years as a marketing strategy for their wines, perhaps most visibly in the United States. Over the years, we have seen Almaden Mountain Chablis and Korbel Champagne in North America, neither of which has any legal—or much sensory—connection to their authentic French counterparts. The French concept of *terroir*, signifying a sense of "local-ness", attempts to capture this quality and seems to include everything from the soil characteristics to the weather and climate to the more subtle winemaking techniques— even the yeasts in the air—that influence the wine produced in the locale. This is clearly a claimed characteristic of wine of particular importance to the French, among others, at odds with any movement toward producing "global wine" or serving an "international taste" that would invite competition to decrease production costs and pursue substitutability from anywhere.

In the case of wine, one can acknowledge that, by its agricultural nature, no two locations are alike—no two vines are alike—and therefore one cannot literally produce a Fronsac wine outside of Fronsac or a Fronton wine outside of Fronton (just as one cannot grow a Vidalia onion outside of the 20-county production area around Vidalia, Georgia, USA). As we noted in Chapter 5 in the discussion of asymmetric information as a supply problem, the same can be said of any agricultural product, but the market seems to support the respect for place that is especially important with wine and largely disregarded for almost all other agricultural production.

If it is in the interest of local producers to develop monopoly power, then we can see the appeal of this restriction on location: it limits the allowable production area. After that, it is a matter of convincing consumers that wines from any other place are not substitutable, and a matter of taste and perhaps faith in *terroir* that determines their willingness to do that.

Restriction to place is the first step and delineating that place is the second, bearing in mind that drawing wider boundaries probably increases supply and decreases price. AOCs are not islands so it becomes a matter of judgment where to draw the boundaries of an AOC. AOC designation can have value, and different AOCs have different values: Pauillac northwest of Bordeaux is a more valuable designation than Gaillac to the southeast.

Generally, we expect existing AOC producers to be protective of their boundaries to protect their control of supply—perhaps its quality, probably its quantity and price. However, our discussion of elasticity reminds us that lower prices might actually be desirable as when demand is elastic. Thus, existing producers actually welcomed recent increases in the size of the Champagne AOC (http://www.nytimes.com/2008/06/14/business/worldbusiness/14champagne.html?pagewanted=all). However, we cannot expect this always to be the case. Historically, the French have opposed liberalized planting rights, but the EU has extended them (Meloni and Swinnen 2013: 257).

AOC restrictions which seem aimed at quality control, in contrast to supply management, are grape varieties and blending proportions (including minimum and maximum shares of each permitted variety), vintage requirements (minimum content from a given vintage), ripeness and alcoholic strength, and minimum vine age (since vine age affects grape characteristics) and maximum vine density (since a given volume of earth contains only so much of the elements that affect the quality of the grapes). The latter restriction is related to restrictions on yield—maximum quantities that can be harvested per unit of land area. One can understand that these restrictions on "ingredients" are consistent with ensuring that a '09 Margaux rouge is a '09 Margaux rouge and not a too sweet or too dry, diluted blend of juices from an assortment of varieties and vintages— even if the latter might be preferred by some consumers. In this sense, the restrictions reflect a kind of "take it or leave it" attitude from the local producers, and they must believe enough in the value of their local product to subscribe to that because they cannot legally do otherwise.

Of course, rules to protect the essence of some *terroir* or AOC could, in principle, be site-specific with variations in blending proportions and vine age, for example, to reflect every nuance of location. The actual restrictions are thus necessarily some compromise or limit, perhaps influenced by politics here and there that allow producers some leeway in pursuing their goals.

Unlike other popular wine-producing regions like California's Napa Valley or Australia's Barossa Valley, France virtually prohibits irrigation or any artificial watering of vines once they are producing grapes (usually once they are three years old). This restriction reflects the French judgment that a wine should reflect its place—including that vintage's weather at the place. Not surprisingly, the quantity and timing of access to moisture has a significant impact upon the quality of fruit from a vineyard. For example, if the season is too dry, then yields are smaller, and the flavor components may be unbalanced. If it is too wet—perhaps significant rain before or at harvest fattened the grapes—then production may be high but flavors diluted. But that should be captured in the final product because that is what happened at that place at that time—subject to the winemaker's ability to deal with the challenge. This represents a profoundly different view of the idea of winemaking that allows much less "unnatural" treatment in the production process and challenges both the producer and the consumer—the extent to which production reflects what nature has provided instead of what can be done to make a wine "easy to like". That begs the question of the determination of liking, but liking what nature has provided from a given place would seem to require more cerebral involvement than the more hedonistic test of what tastes good instinctively with no regard for origins.

The AOC production restrictions are clearly intended to restrict the quantity supplied. If one believes that all the rules are required for authenticity and if they are strictly enforced, then one could argue that, theoretically, they allow an appellation to produce all the wine of its type that it is possible to produce. It is a differentiated product so the industry for that appellation has some monopoly power, but it is no more anti-competitive than allowing an inventor to hold a patent or a company to own a trademark. The restrictions are necessary to preserve that product.

We have sketched the French approach to regulating wine production—identifying wines that the global market has come to recognize as eponymous among all wines and naming them for the places in France where they began, defining the places in the country that are best suited to producing those wines, and regulating some of the basic choices involved in their production. The French can produce any wine they want; but, theoretically, it can be sold as one of these eponymous wines only if it has been produced according to the rules.

Before proceeding, we must realize that the effects of the regulatory structure that France has erected depend upon its ability to enforce its rules. To what extent does the French government ensure that a bottle labeled with the name of a French wine has been produced legally? The breadth of enforcement runs from the locations of vineyards and how they are maintained to the various steps in producing a bottle of wine.

One of the most invidious continuing problems is adulteration, especially including ingredients—often from excluded grapes—prohibited by the AOC rules. For example, some vignerons specialize in growing *teinturier*—grapes whose primary function is to darken red wine—which they sell to producers. If allowed at all, their use is highly restricted. Another practice is captured in the phrase "Bergerac dans la nuit, Bordeaux le matin" ("Bergerac in at night, Bordeaux out in the morning"), reflecting an illegal practice of using wine from a neighboring, less valued appellation to boost the quantity or quality of production of a more valued appellation.

The French example illustrates clearly some of the dilemmas of regulation of production. Simply put, we do not know that the French wine industry is more valuable because of the AOC system. Subject to our caveat about enforcement, we might say that the AOC system is best at producing AOC wines—which is not to say that those are the best wines. In their analysis of the relative impacts of endowments (elements of *terroir*) and technology upon wine quality and price, Gergaud and Ginsburgh (2010: 12) remind us that the market values some non-AOC French country wines (*vin de pays*) significantly more than it does other wines produced, perhaps defiantly, in accordance with AOC requirements. We do know that most major wine producing areas have adopted the concept of regulating what domestic producers can say about their wines (e.g., on labels) and have adopted regulations that resemble the broad outline of the AOC system—perhaps defining a wine, identifying where it can be produced, and specifying what must go into a bottle before it can be labeled as one of that country's defined wines. Again, the impact of any such regulations depends upon their enforcement, among other things.

Gergaud and Ginsburgh's analysis of the relative impact of endowments and technology challenges the value of the AOC system. They conclude that "technological choices affect quality much more than natural endowments, the effect of which is negligible" (Gergaud and Ginsburgh 2010: 3), with the latter finding challenging the *terroir*-honoring AOC system. They acknowledge that technology cannot replace *terroir*—that, as of now, it does not allow us to produce the same wine in a different place—but it does allow us to produce comparable quality (as measured by expert ratings or auction prices) in other places.

Relative to AOC rules, EU rules are more clearly aimed at supply management—policies such as subsidies for reducing the size of vineyards ("grubbing up") and for shifting some output from wine to distillation as well as restrictions on new vineyards. This reflects in principle the seemingly universal idea that, left to their own, agricultural markets are inherently too risky to attract an efficient level of resources. One could never demonstrate that agricultural policies like the EU Wine Policy increase the overall efficiency of the market: evidence of that is lacking. Evidence to the contrary is clear and reflects the importance of interest groups shaping policies to their advantage (e.g., Moleni and Swinnen 2013).

## REGULATION BEYOND PRODUCTION: INTERNATIONAL TRADE POLICY

We have sampled from an elaborate and well-established example of government intervention in the wine market that focuses upon production. However, our discussion has not yet touched upon wine transactions involving either intermediate buyers (e.g., distributors) or final consumers. Once the wine has been produced (legally), are producers free to sell to anyone?

Globally, governments can intervene in this part of the market in a variety of ways. For example, producers, or domestic merchants who have bought from them (e.g., negociants in France), might want to export wine to another country. Governments decide to regulate exports for a variety of reasons. They may hope to keep domestic prices artificially low for important domestic consumption (e.g., grains), or they may be concerned about technology transfer, especially if it involves national security. Without addressing the wisdom of such policies, we doubt the relevance of such motivations to wine: governments have shown neither an interest in encouraging domestic wine, or alcohol, consumption by restricting exports nor a concern about the national security impact of sharing its wine or wine technology with the world.

Government policies toward imports are a different story because (a) imported wine often competes with domestic products and (b), regardless of that, import restrictions can increase government revenue. Wine-importing countries often place various trade barriers between exporting countries and their domestic market. These take a variety of forms:

- Because, in effect, they raise the cost of supply, tariffs, or special taxes imposed on imported products, raise import prices relative to those of domestic substitutes to the potential disadvantage of imports and may raise significant revenue for the domestic government (e.g., along with comparable treatment for beer and spirits, the highly lucrative Canadian federal and provincial system of taxes on imported wine that also contributes to remarkably high prices for Canadian wines);

- Quotas, or restrictions on the quantity of a product allowed into the domestic market, tend to raise the relative price of imports by restricting their supply artificially (the supply curve of imports to the domestic market becomes vertical instead of upward sloping at the quota quantity value)—otherwise why bother with them—which favors domestic production and may increase government revenue indirectly (e.g., through increased sales and income taxes from retailers);

- An array of other treatments of imports sometimes called "non-tariff barriers"—such as special labeling and packaging requirements, content requirements (e.g., inclusion or exclusion of certain ingredients), special inspections, quarantines, domestic shipping restrictions—may reflect the legitimate concerns of the domestic community about product quality or safety or may be thinly disguised deterrents to foreign exporters (or both). In effect, they raise the cost of supplying imports to the domestic market.

Beyond protecting domestic firms and raising government revenue, import regulations might create public sector employment and even encourage foreign producers to move production capacity to the importing country to avoid them, thereby increasing foreign direct investment (FDI) in the domestic economy (e.g., Japanese automobile manufacturers investing in domestic production plants in the US in recent decades). Given the location-specific impact on quality, this last outcome is unlikely with wine. Regardless of the motivations of domestic lawmakers, protectionist import regulations almost necessarily disadvantage import sales relative to domestic substitutes.

## REGULATION BEYOND PRODUCTION: VARIETIES OF DOMESTIC REGULATION OF CONSUMPTION

We find a wide range of government regulation of domestic transactions of alcohol—from prohibition in Islamic countries to minimal regulation in countries with a long tradition of consumption (e.g., perhaps some restrictions on hours and locations of sale and minimum age of purchaser). One irony of this kind of regulation is that it can foster the very behavior that it is intended to inhibit. A textbook example is anti-narcotics enforcement (e.g., Mankiw 2015: 105–107). We know from our earlier discussion of supply and demand moving toward equilibrium in a market that one can reduce the number of transactions either by decreasing demand (equilibrium price would decrease) or decreasing supply (equilibrium price would increase) or a combination of both (number of transactions would decrease, but the overall impact on equilibrium price is indeterminate). If the government tackles narcotics abuse by decreasing supply (e.g., intercepting smugglers at borders, arresting dealers), then the price is likely to increase, the total expenditure in the market will increase as well (we assume that demand for such addictive substances is inelastic), and consumers must finance that increased expenditure somehow. Tough enforcement intended to decrease antisocial behavior and related transactions may actually increase it through the increase in crimes associated with the trade.

Reducing transactions through decreased demand—perhaps more difficult since it involves changing preferences—would seem more efficient if it can be achieved.

While contemporary varieties of regulation seem generally accepted around the world (but see Hicken (2012) for a counterexample), the example of Prohibition in the United States (1920–1933) illustrates this phenomenon. From what we have learned about that experience, the amount of illegal activity associated with the alcohol market increased dramatically during Prohibition (e.g., Okrent 2010: 267–288) without a significant decrease in the amount of undesirable behavior related to alcohol, including perhaps alcohol consumption itself (Ashenfelter 2010). Given the widespread, successful, and peaceful prohibition of alcohol in Muslim countries, we know that the popularity and effectiveness of various forms of regulation are sensitive to culture, content, and timing.

The repeal of the National Prohibition (Volstad) Act in 1933 resulted in the primary power to regulate alcohol reverting to the US states. While our focus is not the US, the variety of state reactions to repeal illustrates conveniently the variety of policies that we observe around the world to regulate the distribution and retail sale of alcohol. Thorough discussion of even one state's, or country's, laws would take us too far afield, but we can identify the major provisions adopted by governments that likely affect the number of transactions in the market:

- Sale prohibited below a minimum age (virtually worldwide; limits and enforcement vary);
- Restrictions on the days and times of sale (virtually worldwide; times and enforcement vary);
- Restrictions on the locations of sale, which usually translates into (a) an alcohol licensing system and/or (b) a government monopoly or near-monopoly on retail sales that may allow for "outsourcing"

through private stores (e.g., Pennsylvania, New Hampshire, Sweden, Norway, Canadian provinces).
● Beyond this, jurisdictions regulate advertising, consumption during certain activities (e.g., driving), public consumption, etc.

In addition, the US has a unique system of distribution—the so-called "three-tier system" of producer or importer/distributor/retailer—as well as state-specific interstate shipping laws which can limit the degree of competition for their purchases that state residents enjoy.

Our interest in this variety of regulations is their purpose. One might justify some of the AOC regulation in France on the basis of quality control, though supply control seems not far below the surface. One might justify some of these domestic regulations as efforts to reduce social costs (e.g., prohibiting drunk driving or sale to children). The difficulty is that some of the regulations that begin with a laudable purpose such as circumscribing alcohol consumption might become distorted to benefit certain interest groups such as liquor license owners, government monopolies, or distributors in the US states.

We can illustrate the problem by returning to our competitive market. Figure 6.2 represents the same wine demand curve illustrated in Figure 6.1: assume it aggregates the demand for that wine from 400 identical consumers and is the only demand for alcohol in the jurisdiction. Assume the following:
● The competitive retail price for the wine is $15 (e.g., a number of online retailers out of jurisdiction would be willing to sell it for that price);
● If the government authorized free access to this market by those retailers, then the 400 consumers would realize $10,000 in aggregate consumer surplus (the shaded area between the demand curve and the $15 price)—each one would receive $25 more benefit than they put into purchasing the wine;
● The government controls access to this market because of concern about allowing a "free market" for wine.

If the government wanted to make money from this market, it could become the retailer and require consumers to join the Public Spirits Wine Club (PSWC) in order to purchase the wine at $15/bottle—an example of the two-part pricing model we introduced in Chapter 4. In our simplified market, each of the 400 consumers would be willing to pay up to $25 for the membership. They would prefer not to—they would prefer to buy from the competitive retailers and realize their consumer surplus—but, lacking that alternative, their willingness to pay indicates that they would join the PSWC and pay their full willingness to pay rather than do without.

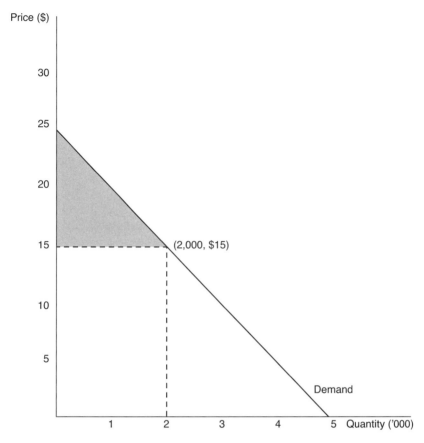

*Figure 6.2    The market for wine: potential rents from regulation*

As an alternative, the government could auction a single license to a retailer to service this market. Seeing the opportunity to require consumers to pay an "access fee" (e.g., the PSWC fee) that would allow them to buy the wine, retailers competing for the license would be willing (perhaps reluctantly) to bid up to $10,000 for the license since the winner could recover that by charging an access fee such as club membership.

We have just told a story about the process of "rent seeking" (e.g., Tullock 1967)—the effort by government or those seeking favorable policies from government to capture wealth from or through the government due to its ability to control access to markets.[2] To the extent that the EU's purpose in restricting grape production is to increase the wealth of farmers from the higher prices they could charge, that is capturing rents for those farmers. To the extent that existing farmers lobby the EU to do that so that they can be more profitable (or to impose other restrictions that limit their exposure to lower cost competition (e.g., Meloni and Swinnen 2013: 261–262)), that is rent seeking.

When one considers the vast array of policies that governments at various levels can use to benefit some special interest group, one realizes how pervasive this behavior can be. Tullock's original examples were tariffs protecting domestic producers and the government's ability to increase monopoly power—for example, by not preventing a merger that would increase the resulting firm's monopoly power. One can see how the US three-tier system that forces wine retailers to buy from in-state distributors reduces the competitiveness of that retail wine market and similarly for restrictions on interstate shipping that restrict or eliminate consumers' access to out-of-state vendors. A check of Google Scholar lists many hundreds of articles on the subject.

The use of a government monopoly to distribute and sell wine deserves special attention. For example, the government monopoly on the distribution of alcohol in the Canadian provinces began, perhaps, as an attempt to regulate behavior—to reduce nominally undesirable behavior in particular. Public support for that rationale has dropped over the years, but the provincial revenue raised from the monopoly power to control distribution and price has become so significant (e.g., about 75 percent of the British Columbia Liquor Distribution Branch's $1.2 billion revenue went to general revenues in 2011 (Hicken 2012)) that it cannot afford to leave the marketplace, even to the limited extent that the alcohol market is a "free market" in the United States to the south.

It is important to look carefully at conditions that are conducive to rent seeking: it is too simple to say that anyone can simply go to the government, ask for a favor, and get it. One influences policy by influencing those who make it—typically legislators. Legislators respond to the needs of those who can help them stay in office. One hopes that these are voters; but, in an era where political campaigns are expensive, financial contributions are attractive to legislators. Pareto tells a story that makes the point:

- Assume a society of 30,000,000 citizens.
- Thirty of them decide they each want $1,000,000 from the government.
- This could be raised by taxing each citizen $1.
- The thirty work hard to influence politicians to pass the tax to fund the allowance—each one has $1,000,000 at stake.

- The cost to each of the remaining citizens is so slight that none bother even to learn the details of the legislation.
- The thirty are well organized and are willing to support the politicians financially; the rest do not bother to organize any opposition "for so small a sum".
- "The spoliators win hands down" (Pareto et al. 2014).

This story of "concentrated benefits/diffused costs"—a relatively small, well-organized group with much at stake per capita to be financed by a much larger, diffuse group (e.g., taxpayers, consumers) with much less at stake per capita—provides a useful example of the configuration of group size and vested interest per capita that can often elevate the special interest over the public interest (Olson 1965).

Rent seeking is also subject to the "transitional gains trap" (Tullock 1975). Imagine that the retailer noted above is granted the privilege of an exclusive license to sell wine. If and when she sells her business with the license, the value of the license will have been capitalized into the value of the business. The government can no longer remove the license without imposing a capital loss on the new owner: policy is trapped with the licensing arrangement.

## A NOTE ON TAXATION OF ALCOHOL AND A PUBLIC SECTOR DILEMMA

Whether or not they are familiar with the concept of elasticity, governments seem to have realized that taxation of alcohol can yield significant revenue (e.g., Canada, Sweden). That idea was not only recognized early in the history of the US but played a significant role in the repeal of Prohibition (Okrent 2010: 53–55, 361–362). Recall from our discussion of the own price elasticity of demand that raising prices when demand is inelastic increases total revenue. In addition to other actual or stated reasons, governments may target markets involving alcohol because the consumers in such markets are easy targets and numerous—consumers find few if any legal close substitutes for alcohol, and, for many, alcohol is an addiction to some extent—and thus the own price elasticity of demand is inelastic. If a government imposes an excise tax upon alcohol and total sales revenue rises, the increased revenue is all tax revenue. This is obvious if demand is completely inelastic. However, in the inelastic range of demand, unit sales will decrease, and the after-tax price to sellers typically decreases (so net revenue to sellers decreases). If total revenue rises, then the increase in total revenue is the minimum amount of the tax revenue gained.

Given the social cost of excessive consumption, the legitimate need to deter consumption among some groups, the political powerlessness of some consumers (e.g., tourists), and the moral color often associated with alcohol consumption, it becomes clear why politicians find significant alcohol taxes not only remunerative but also popular with many voters. However, the public interest in encouraging moderation in alcohol consumption conflicts with its interest in raising revenue, and research has not revealed which of these competing interests is stronger in shaping tax policy toward alcohol. As illustrated by the dramatic example of US Prohibition and its repeal as well as subsequent varieties of regulation and taxation of alcohol, the public sector finds itself simultaneously wanting to encourage and discourage behavior: aside from questions of individual liberty, greater consumption of alcohol is problematic, but the increased revenue is attractive. The comparison with legalized, often government-sponsored gambling (e.g., lotteries) comes to mind as does the larger dilemma of "sin taxes" (e.g., Sandel 2005: 69–73).

## SPECIAL TREATMENT FOR WINE?

Our focus is wine markets, but our discussion of the rationale for, if not the specific content of, government intervention could be applied to the markets for all alcoholic beverages. Our discussion of government's role has been selective, but it is worth noting one topic that might become a more prominent policy focus. As data on consumption patterns grows with the proliferation of social media and the ability of marketers to capture it, one wonders how government policy toward alcoholic beverages might evolve to reflect the different behaviors of consumers of the different types of alcohol. Reflecting perhaps the idea that the extent of regulation should vary directly with the potency of the beverage, it is already the case in many jurisdictions that the beverages containing lower alcohol-by-volume (ABV) levels are more widely available for sale than those with higher ABVs (for example, beer and perhaps wine, but not spirits, available in supermarkets and convenience stores). Also excise tax rates tend to vary directly with ABV levels so that excise taxes on beer and wine are often at lower rates than on spirits. One wonders if, as we learn more about the behavior patterns of different consumer groups, policy might discriminate further to reflect those different patterns (e.g., just as laws toward other narcotics discriminate according to the perceived social cost represented by different narcotics—for example, marijuana compared with heroin). An example of recent research that begs such questions studied the relationship between shares of consumption among beer, wine, and spirits and traffic fatality rates among the US states (Rickard, Costanigro, and Garg 2011) and found an inverse relationship between wine's share of total consumption and the traffic fatality rate: "states with a higher consumption share of wine have lower traffic fatality rates [*cet. par.*]" (Rickard, Costanigro, and Garg 2011: 18).

While the results remain unpublished, they are suggestive of an interesting policy discussion. As a small example, establishing this inverse relationship more robustly might lead to differential treatment of wine sales compared with other alcoholic beverage sales at retail outlets (e.g., available more hours of the day, more days of the week), although this would require evidence of the extent of consumers' willingness to substitute between other beverages and wine. More generally—and acknowledging the importance of evidence of consumer substitution—developing robust evidence of different behavior patterns among different consumer groups might lead to policy treatment that reflects more reasonably the different behaviors associated with different beverages. As another example, one of the primary stated objections to more liberal interstate shipping of wine among the US states has been the risk of minors obtaining alcohol more easily by mail order than through alternative sources. If we learn that minors are highly unlikely to order wine priced above some price (e.g., $50/bottle), then policy makers might be willing to design policies that focus more upon the apparent policy concern and interfere less with reasonable consumer transactions.

The more general idea here is that the policy concern is the relationship between certain types of transactions and socially costly behavior. The experience with Prohibition demonstrated, among other things, that using a blunt instrument to address some specific problems can lead to a variety of undesirable and unintended consequences. To the extent that we can adjust the nuance of policy to the nuance of behavior, we can try to avoid that.

This begs the question of the motivation behind current regulations. For example, if the political basis for restrictions on interstate shipping is limiting the competition faced by intrastate distributors and not protection of minors, then evidence that minors never order fine wine will have little impact on the political decision to maintain that limit, especially since the concentrated interests of a small number of distributors per capita likely far exceeds the diffused costs per capita of the limitation on a larger number of fine wine consumers. However, it will likely sharpen the focus on the basis for the regulation.

## CONCLUSION

For many of us, the concern about government resembles a concern about wine: it is unlikely that the global wine market would have its current size and quality and variety without a significant role for government, but it does not follow from saying that some is good, then more is better. In its role as protector of transactions and monitor of quality and transparency, government is indispensable in the global wine market. However, once government has a seat at the table, then the distinction between government and politics can become blurred, especially given the size of the economic interests. Special interests—especially those with limited membership, each member with much at stake potentially from a wide range of potential changes in public policy—can exploit the politics that accompanies government. One of the two ultimate intended beneficiaries of the global wine market—consumers—are at a serious disadvantage as a special interest because of their size and relatively small interest per capita. This is no different from any other industry except perhaps that government plays a particularly large role in wine markets, and the potential for distortion is perhaps larger.

We turn next to two chapters connected to government's role. Chapter 7 looks more closely at the consumer's challenge of knowing what is in the bottle. While governments can attempt to ensure the provision of complete and truthful information about wine, they cannot protect or guarantee wine knowledge. Chapter 8 questions whether all the value of wine is captured in the private transaction and whether a proper role of government is, like its support for the fine arts, support for the wine industry as a cultural good.

## NOTES

1. The inverse demand equation is $P = 25 - 5Q$ (Q measured in thousands of bottles).
2. Economic rent represents a payment to a resource in excess of what it could earn in its next best use. One of the pioneers in developing the concept of rent seeking, James Buchanan, reminds us that rent seeking is simply what businesses do all the time: seeking profits above and beyond that required for survival (presumably its last best use just short of failure) (Buchanan, Tullock, and Tollison 1980). The concern about rent seeking arises when individuals or groups can influence the community's institutions (esp. governments) to turn public policy governing the marketplace to their advantage but to the detriment of the rest of the community (e.g., protective tariffs, allowing monopolization of an otherwise more competitive market). In effect, they seek profits through distortions in, rather than encouragement of, the competitive marketplace. He identified what might be called "the economics of politics" and something like a market for policy influence and inspired a large literature on those subjects.

    Individuals can also earn employment rents. Some of the more vivid examples are entertainment and sports celebrities who gain some monopoly power (few if any close substitutes) and earn wages in excess of their earnings in their next best employment (e.g., school teacher or coach).

Rent became associated with land (and then housing) because land is available even if it has no use. If its next best use is vacancy—it will be there anyway—then any payment to its productive use is rent.

# 7. A closer look at the transaction: how do we know what is in the bottle?[1]

## INTRODUCTION

A core idea in our understanding of the demand for wine is the consumer's willingness to pay—but what determines one's willingness to pay (WTP)? As we have learned, this question is distinct from what determines the price of a good because it focuses upon the demand side of a transaction, and price—what is offered in exchange for the good—reflects the impact of other influences such as supply and, in the case of wine, various forms of government intervention as well as taxation of alcoholic beverages. The economic theory of the consumer discussed in Chapter 4 recognizes a number of influences upon WTP: our focus in this chapter is the consumer's taste for the good and, implicitly, for related goods. That is, the requirements for a rational determination of WTP would seem to involve knowledge of the product and knowledge of related products, *cet. par.*

We begin this chapter with a discussion of the consumer's problem in knowing a wine as a product and our attempts to capture consumer knowledge as a component of WTP. A primary focus is the interpretation of expert opinions about wines which are often used as a representation of consumer knowledge in empirical studies of the determinants of wine prices, following the assumption that wine is an "experience good". This leads to the larger question of the consumer's ability to know a wine which is distinct from her access to information about it. Note that our reference to consumer ignorance is not a criticism, and it is not the same as stupidity or slow-wittedness or any number of terms that could describe a consumer's mental environment. We treat it simply as lack of knowledge, and it describes all of us.

The question of consumer knowledge is intrinsically interesting but also bears upon a variety of other issues. One of the most important is the impact of consumers' lack of knowledge upon both the size and composition of the demand for wines, especially fine wines, and therefore the market for wine. One expects that a variety of factors affect whether consumers have an interest in wine—location (e.g., country), level of education, economic status, age, gender—but, perhaps surprisingly, there is no comprehensive study of that subject. Moreover, many empirical studies of wine consumer behavior draw upon "convenience samples"—collecting data from anyone who happens to be available at the time one gathers data (e.g., in a store, in a classroom, on the street). Such studies might capture broad patterns of behavior or uncover surprising behavior, but they have little value in providing reliable, robust evidence of consumer buying patterns (Lockshin and Corsi 2012: 19) because they do not collect data from a sample of respondents that are chosen to be representative of the population one is studying (e.g., UK wine consumers, Australian wine retailers).

The complexity of knowing what one is buying—one of the "perceived risks" of wine purchases (e.g., Lockshin and Hall 2003: 8–9)—likely suppresses demand by risk-averse consumers for relatively expensive fine wine and deters many consumers from taking a serious interest in wine or consistently buying any but the most basic wines. Among the six US market segments identified in Constellation Brands' Genome Project study of wine consumer behavior, the largest segment—about one quarter (23 percent)—were described as the "Overwhelmed" (Veseth 2008), and another third (34 percent) had limited knowledge and a limited interest in wine per se: the Image Seekers (20 percent) who see wine as a status symbol and the Satisfied Sippers (14 percent) who are brand loyal and see wine as little more than an everyday beverage. Those who likely have the most serious interest in wine and are perhaps willing to tackle the complexity are a small share of the market. For example, Gallup, Inc., has reported that about two-thirds of Americans acknowledged drinking alcohol in a 2012 poll, averaging about four drinks per week, but only one-third of those (so 22 percent of all consumers) chose wine as their preferred drink. Among those who drink wine, women are 2.5 times as likely (about 16 percent of all consumers) to drink wine relative to men (Saad 2012)—the remaining 6 percent. However, while we know little about gender differences in purchases of "luxury wines" (Lockshin and Corsi 2012: 18)—which would include fine wine—casual observation (e.g., attendance at live wine auctions) and some reporting (e.g., Hanson 2008) indicate that men are much more likely to be wine collectors: that does not mean that men are much more likely to be fine wine drinkers, but it suggests that this small share of the population is the one making the purchase decisions. It might be larger if wine were easier to know.

We cannot know that the fine wine market is smaller because of this component of perceived risk or, if it is, how much; but the resources spent on wine promotion and education and the prominent place of expert opinion in fine wine marketing and the effort to persuade buyers of pedigree, quality, and rarity suggests that sellers want buyers—and potential buyers—to know more or at least think they do. Of course, the risk might attract some buyers, but it is difficult to gauge this market segment, and the Genome Project did not find them.

Our model of consumer behavior developed in Chapter 4 did not allow for a complex set of influences upon the consumer's evaluation of a product, whether wine or anything else. In effect, we assumed that the consumer could arrive at a willingness to pay based upon the intrinsic quality of the product and perhaps some closely related extrinsic qualities such as packaging esthetics and convenience. Of course, the environment in which the product would be consumed matters—willingness to pay for winter coats is greater in Copenhagen than in Cairo—but the role of extrinsic cues seems considerably more complicated here. The apparent role of seemingly psychological influences upon the consumer's decision to transact is far beyond the realm of traditional economic analysis and seems particularly thorny for wine and perhaps related products such as art and so-called experience goods.

Not surprisingly, a considerable amount of research into the determinants of consumer choice and evaluation comes from marketing. The marketing in our model of consumer choice consists of an auctioneer announcing a price to which the consumer responds: that is not much marketing. The model treats the seller as a passive supplier who offers a product and waits for the market response. Granted, she must do all that is involved in choosing products and managing their production, but getting the sale is not part of the model. This reflects the assumption that the buyer has perfect information: if the consumer knows everything, then persuasion and related marketing efforts have no role.

Much of marketing is oriented toward dealing with the absence of information: for example, if consumers have limited information about a product, what do we want to tell them and how do we want to exploit their ignorance and the way they cope with ignorance? Veale and Quester (2008) provide a useful discussion of the relative importance of intrinsic product attributes (e.g., taste or flavor) and extrinsic cues (e.g., price and country of origin (COO)) on consumer evaluation of products. They review the extensive marketing literature that discusses the influence of attributes and cues which shows that (Veale and Quester 2008: 11):

- Consumers use both;
- Reliance varies directly with confidence in their interpretation and predictive reliability;

- Intrinsic attributes get more weight unless they are poorly under-stood or not reliable;
- The most appealing extrinsic cues are brand, price, retailer, and COO; and
- Extrinsic cues gain importance for products associated with self-image, status, or high risk—that is, where others may share the same cues and both evaluate us on our choices and share our same tendencies.

This research posits that, when they lack reliable intrinsic information, consumers can rely heavily upon price cues, apparently invoking a "price-value schema" which reflects a strongly held consumer belief that one gets what one pays for (p. 13).

Of course, this seems to contradict our understanding of consumer surplus whose implication is that we want to maximize the difference between WTP—what we get—and what we pay for. At least a partial reso-lution lies in both the variety of motives for buying and consumer igno-rance. If we allow for the social nature of wine consumption—often not consumed alone but shared with someone "important" and for a special occasion, perhaps given as a gift or otherwise shared with others publicly so that others' impressions matter—it is understandable that price plays a role beyond what our model allows (e.g., we might not know what is in the bottle, but at least we are willing to spend money to please others). If we did not care about others' opinions and satisfaction, we might evaluate differently.

Goldstein (2008a) likens this tendency to a "placebo effect": we think we have been given good wine because it is expensive, and therefore we judge it to be good.

Veale and Quester also review research which they suggest might represent a more significant challenge: in contrast to consumers turning to extrinsic cues when intrinsic attributes are unknown or not under-stood, they wonder whether extrinsic cues can actually overcome product knowledge—for example, failure to identify the flavor of orange juice if it is colored purple (Veale and Quester 2008: 13). However, this raises the question of the meaning of orange juice: the consumer evaluates all of the product's intrinsic properties, and if some of them are inconsistent with the attributes that formed the consumer's opinion (e.g., the color of orange juice), then one could argue that, for that consumer, it is not orange juice. This point might be apparent if, instead of considering all the intrinsic attributes of orange juice and selecting color as the one to alter dramatically, we select flavor instead: when is orange juice not orange juice?

Experiments with product evaluations during wine tastings have yielded some of the most challenging findings. In particular, recall that we have assumed that the consumer responds to price by comparing WTP to asking price to determine if she is prepared to transact and, if so, how much to purchase: price influences only whether to transact and, if chosen, the quantity to purchase. But research challenges that limitation.

Related to the marketing research is the research of Goldstein and his colleagues (2008a, 2008b) that challenges the aforementioned consumers' price-value schema that "you get what you pay for". Rather than study whether price information influenced consumers' opinion of a wine's quality, they explored how judgments about wine quality related to actual prices asking, in effect, whether more expensive wines taste better so that one does indeed get what one pays for. They collected over six thousand observations of consumer ratings in 17 double-blind (neither servers nor tasters knew what was being served) tastings held in a variety of non-laboratory settings and asked their tasters simply to assign a rating (from 1 to 4 with 4 the best) to the wines. When they matched prices to the ratings, the result was that the answer is generally "no"—more expensive wine was not better—for non-expert tasters who are relatively naïve and probably more prone to adopt the schema. Tasters with more expertise were more likely to prefer more expensive wines, but the relationship was neither strong nor sizeable.

The distinction between information and knowledge is important in this chapter. We can relate the two simply by thinking of knowledge as information that the individual has processed, synthesized, and retained as true. The focus of the discussion is the examination of wine as a possible "experience good" and the related question of capturing a measure of consumer product knowledge as a determinant of WTP. This is related to a philosophical question of the identification and measurement of taste, and a brief discussion of this appears toward the end of the chapter. The chapter closes with some suggestions for future directions.

This chapter necessarily draws upon the idea of expertise. Throughout the discussion, use of the term "expert" means nothing more than someone who seems widely known and influential among consumers according to published evidence of popularity (e.g., circulation numbers for a newsletter or magazine, regular appearance over time of citations in widespread advertising).

# WINE AND TYPES OF GOODS

At the heart of any transaction is the good involved (perhaps both goods involved if we allow for barter). What is it that defines the nature of a good beyond the tautological definition of that which is transacted? We have paid little attention to this idea up until now. Because it often helps us understand the qualitative differences among various types of transactions in the marketplace (e.g., role of advertising, nature of those transacting, source of supply), economists have identified different types of goods along a variety of dimensions—for example, their relationship to changes in market parameters (e.g., complements/substitutes, inferior/ normal), to the nature of the parties transacting (final goods, intermediate goods), to the capacity to confine the benefits and costs of a transaction to a single buyer and seller (public/private), and to the transactors' information about and knowledge of the good (experience and credence goods). Moreover, beyond all these categories, goods can fall into more than one—for example, an inferior good that is a substitute for some other good.

Most of the world's wine production falls easily into existing categories because that seems to be the primary goal in its production. Beverage wine is designed to be easily understood and identifiable, much like most of the beverages with which it competes such as mass market beer or soda. While it might potentially reflect some of the variations in characteristics that can contribute to the complexity of wine (e.g., differences in blends, differences reflecting changes in vintage and source), the goal is often consistency and homogeneity so that consumers *know* what they are buying. Some have derisively referred to it as "cola wine" (e.g., Aylward 2008).

At the other extreme of the variety of wines available, a small proportion of global production challenges consumers to *know* what they are buying. As with beverage wines, we have no clear or accepted definition of these wines, but we have been calling these "fine wines", following terminology often used to advertise major wine auctions (e.g., Sotheby's, Christie's) and appearing in some of the academic literature (e.g., Smith 2007c: 48–51). The range of wines available in a large, wine-consuming economy fall all along the spectrum from "beverage" to "fine" so the relevance of the discussion to any particular wine will be a matter of degree.

To some extent, understanding fine wines involves issues of asymmetric information (AI): the producer knows considerably more about a wine's origins, production, and final characteristics than the consumer; and the consumer hopes to learn that. Beyond that, however, some wines challenge the consumer's ability to *know* them and therefore to form a WTP for them based upon personal knowledge. Of course, the role of such personal knowledge depends upon one's motives for purchase. To the extent that WTP is a reflection of what one expects others to pay—that is, the return one expects from an investment rather than the utility one expects from own consumption—then external indicators that correlate highly with past value (e.g., producer, vintage, scarcity, ratings, returns on alternative investments) are perhaps most or all of what one needs to know since they represent most or all of what many others consider in making their purchases. Also, to the extent that one's utility depends upon the opinions of others whose valuation is similarly determined by external indicators rather than direct consumption—that is, Veblen or positional goods—then they (the Image Seekers?) might also affect WTP significantly.

Perhaps most challenging, however, is arriving at WTP based simply upon own consumption, that is, the enjoyment one expects from drinking what is in the bottle, presumably divorced from wine's alcoholic effect (though apparently that is not possible (Postman 2011)).

Recognizing the challenge to the wine consumer's knowledge of what s/he is buying, some of the most careful research on determinants of wine prices has turned to Nelson's (1970) concept of "experience goods"— goods whose characteristics and quality are sufficiently costly to discover or to know through simply searching for normal market information that, in effect, "experiencing" them is the only reasonable way to evaluate them. Purchasing and using them is the cost-effective way to know them: "The consumer has a simple alternative to search: he can use experience, that is, he can determine the quality of brands by purchasing brands and then using them" (Nelson 1970: 327). Nelson uses examples like canned tuna fish and home appliances: "To evaluate brands of tuna fish . . . the consumer would almost certainly purchase cans of tuna fish for consumption . . . [and] determine from several purchases which brand he preferred" (p. 312). He also allows for the importance of accessing expert opinion such as *Consumer Reports*.

Treating wine as an experience good seems well established in the literature (e.g., Ashton 2014). In a prominent survey, one researcher states flatly: "wine is an experience good" (Storchmann 2012: 22). However, for those who have tried a wide variety of fine wines, it seems self-evident that, as a problem in determining WTP, fine wines are considerably more challenging to know than canned tuna fish and refrigerators.

How do we represent that component of WTP that reflects the consumer's innate enjoyment of the wine? A popular answer to that question in the literature discussing determinants of fine wine prices and predicated upon the idea of experience goods is to represent wine quality—or what we assume consumers take to represent wine quality—by chateau reputation or one or more expert opinions of the wine (e.g., Thornton 2013: 250–263; Hadj Ali and Nauges 2007; Hadj Ali, Lecocq, and Visser 2008). Unable to know the wine before buying it (e.g., buying futures for Bordeaux wine), consumers use this external information to guide their WTP with better ratings correlating positively with price. However, while this information may influence WTP, it does little to improve the consumer's knowledge significantly. Moreover, expert opinions likely influence some of the other aforementioned motives for purchase that are not own consumption. Taken with the challenge of interpreting price data that may not reflect actual transactions (cf. Chapter 5), this may help explain why the evidence of the impact of expert opinion upon wine prices is mixed and positive correlations tend to be weak (Storchmann 2012: 24): this information may contribute little to the consumer's *knowledge* of what s/he is buying so its influence upon WTP is direct but small.

One might argue that wine consumers do not buy wines that they do not know, and their WTP reflects what they know: somehow they manage to taste a wine through friends or tastings, and those are the only wines they buy. If we limit our attention to fine wines, the proliferation of ratings, tasting notes, and "shelf talkers" and the dependence upon sales staff suggest that simply is not true. Data on the proportion of fine wine sales by consumers who have never tasted the wine are unavailable, but most—perhaps the large majority—of such transactions likely fall into that category (e.g., Thornton 2013: 241–242). Given the virtually unlimited variety of fine wines and, among them, the further variability due to factors such as vintage and provenance, most purchases reflect use of something other than own knowledge to determine WTP.

With that said, what do consumers know? They may have degrees of experience with a particular producer and thus have a sense of its style, but for most transactions, the information available about what is in the bottle is often nothing more than one or more expert ratings.

Given this challenge to the consumer, perhaps instead of the fine wine transaction being perceived simply as an exchange of goods for money, it either is or should be treated as an example of service-dominant marketing (e.g., Vargo and Lusch 2004): an ongoing relationship between seller and buyer, "collaborating with and learning from consumers and being adaptive to their individual and dynamic needs" (p. 6). At least at the level of the retail transaction, for example, one can certainly see a role for this among novice wine buyers who can benefit from an ongoing relationship with a supplier who both educates the buyer and learns both her particular preferences and her willingness to experiment. Perhaps over time the knowledge exchange from the relationship reduces considerably the buyer's perceived risk of the purchase. However, the degree of collaboration

needed here could be considerable and would be subject to risks and constraints of its own: the departure of the seller from the market, continued
compatibility of seller and buyer, frequent enough transactions that the
knowledge exchange remains fresh, the seller's own ignorance of what is
in any given bottle either at the time of purchase or over time, the seller's
potential conflict of interest in selling her own product.

The service-dominant model also looks toward something closer to the
ultimate goal of a purchase: for example, the consumer wants not a furnace
but toasty comfort during cold weather, and sellers offer the ongoing provision of that environment (Vargo and Lusch 2004: 13). In the case of fine
wine, does one want to drink a glass of red Bordeaux, or does one want to
be transported in one's mind to the vineyards along the Gironde in early
October? It is difficult to fit fine wine into that model where the seller
targets the buyer's near-ultimate goal. Also, if the difficulty were simply
the buyer learning what the seller knows, the service-dominant model
would fit better, but the issue of knowledge—or ignorance—of fine wine
is often shared on both sides of the transaction, and neither knows more
than what the experts say.

## WINE RATINGS AS KNOWLEDGE

Are such ratings a good proxy for own knowledge and, in effect, vicarious experience that drives the consumer's WTP? That seems unlikely for
a number of reasons.

First, all prominent experts who produce ratings insist that one must
consider the non-quantifiable tasting notes (TNs) to begin to understand
the expert opinion. For example, Parker writes: "Scores, however, do
not reveal the important facts about a wine. . .. The written commentary
that accompanies the ratings is a better source of information regarding
the wine's style and personality, its relative quality vis-à-vis its peers,
and its value and aging potential than any score could ever indicate"
(Parker 2013). The lesson is: The TN increases one's knowledge more
than the rating. But quantifying the relationship between TN and WTP
is unlikely.

The way to capture the knowledge content of a TN to identify a
measurable effect upon wine knowledge is not obvious, but a reasonable
approach would seem to be testing whether subjects can match wines
with TNs: does this TN let one know enough about a wine that s/he
knows it when s/he tastes it? The research design for such testing would
be challenging—for example, choosing wines that are different enough
that matching a wine with a TN requires only an average level of sensory

discrimination but similar enough that the matches are not obvious (e.g., not simply matching the red wine with the red TN and white wine with the white TN).

Storchmann (2012) reviews some of this research. As noted, the research design challenge is significant here, but the upshot from published research is that, among non-experts, the ability to identify wines after reading TNs is random (p. 25): the evidence is that they add nothing to our ability to know a wine. He cites the limited evidence for experts using TNs, and their success rate is only slightly better (Lawless 1984). It is important that the research on this subject is not extensive—it is not well established that TNs do not aid identification, perhaps because careful testing is likely complex and expensive—but the existing evidence is not encouraging. Also related to this is (a) the evidence of the notorious difficulty of identifying wines in blind tastings (e.g., Smith 2007c: 69–70; Robinson 2013)—experts are rarely able to identify correctly wines they have tasted before—and (b) Hodgson's extensive research on the widespread inconsistency of judges in wine competitions (e.g., Hodgson 2009), leading to headlines such as "Wine Tasting: It's Junk Science" (Derbyshire 2013).

One of the most vivid illustrations of the problem comes from George Taber's reporting on the celebrated "judgment of Paris" in 1976 (Taber 2005) when the French judges famously got it wrong. In recounting Taber's reporting, *New York Times* wine writer Eric Asimov captured the idea well when he wrote (Asimov 2005): "'Ah, back to France,' one judge famously sighed after tasting a Napa Valley chardonnay, while another, sniffing a Batard-Montrachet, declared: 'That is definitely California. It has no nose.'"

Not surprisingly, skepticism about the reliability of ratings and related TNs does not sit well with the experts. One of the central themes of Ashenfelter's useful wine economics newsletter *Liquid Assets* was skepticism about expert ratings of wines and vintages (especially when new) and the implied existence of a "magic tongue" to which skepticism Robert Parker replied "That's bullxxxx!" (Ashenfelter 1993 (December: cover page)). Ironically, a prominent econometrician used that same term to describe the content of TNs (Quandt 2007).

## THE VARIETY OF RATINGS

Second, the variety of available wine ratings begs the question of their capacity to capture experience. Unlike the measurement of temperature or a characteristic like bottle format (regular, magnum, etc.), the measurement of a wine's quality is not well defined. Consider Table 7.1 which

Table 7.1  *Sources and details of wine ratings*

| Ratings Source | Access(O/P/B) | Range of Ratings | Wines Rated | Circulation (P) and/or Subscribers/ Users (est.) (date) | Comments | Source (as of 3 June 2013) |
|---|---|---|---|---|---|---|
| Cellar Tracker | O | NR; 0 through 100? | All | 268,000 + (3 June 2013) | Consumer-submitted tasting notes, often with rating | http://www.cellartracker.com/default.asp |
| Decanter | B | 10 through 20 | All | 40,000/ mo. + online (CY 2012) | Stable in-house panel | http://www.bordoverview.com/?q=Decanter http://www.ipcadvertising.com/ipc-brands/decanter Website unavailable |
| Gambero Rosso | B? | 0 through 3 | Italian | ? | Territorial panels, final panels | |
| Guide Hachette | P | 0 through 3 | French, some Swiss, Lux. | ? | Local panels | http://www.hachette-vins.com/ |
| International Wine Cellar (S Tanzer) | O | 70 through 100 | All | ? | Author and designated others do all tasting (e.g., Josh Raynolds) | http://www.wineaccess.com/expert/tanzer/newhome.html |

| | | | | | | |
|---|---|---|---|---|---|---|
| Jancis Robinson | O | 10 through 20 | All | ? | Author and designated others do all tasting (e.g., Julia Harding) | http://www.jancisrobinson.com/ |
| Wine Advocate (R Parker) | B | 50 through 100 | All | 50,000/bimo. + online (CY 2012) | Roster of experts, each with region of expertise (e.g., Anthony Galloni) | https://www.erobertparker.com/info/WineAdvocate.asp Storchmann 2012 |
| Wine Enthusiast | B | 80 through 100 | All | 108,299 + online (May 2010) | Tasting panels | http://winemag.com/ PDFs/2011 Media Kit/ 2011 Wine Enthusiast Reader Demographics.pdf |
| Wine Spectator | B | 50 through 100 | All | 391,667/mo. + online (CY 2011) | Tasting panels | http://www.magazine.org/ insights-resources/research-publications/trends-data/ magazine-industry-facts-data/ circulation-trends |

provides some basic information about some of the most prominent sources of wine evaluation. For example, included are popular sources of ratings of wines from the global market for many prominent US "flash sale" retail wine websites (e.g., Wines Til Sold Out (WTSO), Cinderella Wine) as well as two well-known country-oriented (France, Italy) printed wine buying guides. Table 7.1 includes the three most widely circulated publications cited by Storchmann (2012: 22)—the others he cites have much smaller circulation (<25,000) and, for two of the three, are California-centric by comparison—as well as some of the most popular sources that depend much more upon online access (the Access codes are O = online, P = print, and B = both).

All sources in the table have in common that they provide numeric ratings, which allow various logical analyses (e.g., ranking, quantitative quality comparison), and assorted TNs.

Beyond that, however, they vary widely and thereby raise many issues:

- They use different levels of discrimination, ranging from a minimum of 4 quality levels to a "maximum" of 51 (plus, for all, a default category of wines that were either missing or too poor to evaluate further—a blending of reasons that is unfortunate in itself), leading one to wonder whether this is an accurate reflection of differences in ability to judge wine quality;
- The maximum number of quality levels is actually greater than indicated through the use of ranges (e.g., 89–91), plusses and minuses, fractions, and so forth.
- The scores are also subject to revision of any size in either direction (within the limits of the rating system), a weakness emphasized by Ashenfelter in *Liquid Assets* (e.g., September 1990).
- The source of the evaluation varies widely: some depend upon an expert individual, some depend upon a nominally stable "committee" of named experts, some depend upon a nominally stable anonymous committee, some depend upon an anonymous committee that may vary from location to location and vintage to vintage (perhaps even day to day—details are not available). Unless committees are either stable or large enough to represent the population reliably (they are not), then consistency in any committee-based evaluation is unlikely.

The widely varying quality scales demonstrate the level of our ignorance. It seems likely that, given 100 wines of some general type (e.g., red, white, sparkling), most consumers would be able to divide them into 4–5 categories: certainly 2–3—like or dislike or indifferent—and then perhaps

1 more between indifference and each of the endpoints. If we turn to the literature on consumers' ability to discriminate, then the widespread use of the Likert scale suggests 5 or 7 categories and pain research suggests 11 (e.g., Farrar et al. 2001). Almost half of the sources in Table 7.1 limit themselves to 11 or fewer categories.

Adopting a scale of 20 to 100 or more degrees of discrimination may be good for marketing—it suggests a remarkable capacity to discriminate— but there is no evidence validating it, and a lack of replication and valida- tion is a structural weakness for all of these sources. No one from any of these sources has ever been able to replicate consistently and regularly the original scores assigned by tasting blind the same wines again, assigning a rating, and checking the consistency of the latter score with the former. Imagine how persuasive such replication and validation would be; its absence from the marketplace says something about the likelihood of its ever occurring. The notes from some sources such as *Wine Spectator* that a wine was tasted one or more additional times "with consistent notes" represents an implied acknowledgment that such replication and valida- tion would be compelling—but they do not represent replication and validation.

The impression from this is not one of precision and consistency. It is, instead, that the vacuum—the absence of knowledge—attracts attempts both to influence consumers and supply the knowledge that consumers would value and perhaps be willing to purchase (e.g., by subscribing to reports of ratings). Consumers are certainly reluctant to accept the dif- ficulty of knowing what is in the bottle: they want TNs and ratings to be important, especially for more expensive wines, because that is all they have. As with the knowledge itself, we cannot identify some shortfall from a maximum attainable that entrepreneurs will attempt to fill, but the exist- ence of these resources also does not indicate that anyone knows much more with them than without them.

A concern hidden in this information is exactly what lies behind the con- struction of the ratings produced. What is the model that experts follow, or act as if they follow, in producing a wine rating?

## WINE RATINGS AS WEIGHTED AVERAGE SCORES (WAS)

All well-established wine ratings are single numbers. Considering the content of the notes that often accompany them, it would seem that a rating is actually a weighted average of the scores of a wine along a variety of dimensions. It could be used as an index number—"a statistic which assigns a single number to several individual statistics in order to quantify trends" (http://mathworld.wolfram.com/IndexNumber.html)— but that use of ratings has not emerged. To the extent that wine experts explain their methods, very few indicate explicitly that they are providing a weighted average score (WAS), but a model of wine rating would suggest that they almost necessarily are. That an expert is acting as if s/he is evaluating the significant dimensions of a wine—for example, appearance, aroma, flavor, finish, overall impression—seems almost self-evident, even though we typically see a single numeric score and we learn nothing of either the dimensions measured, the scores assigned to each, or the weights assumed.

The wide array of evaluation forms used to score wines at wine tastings provides evidence that this is at least the implied model (http://www.google.com/search?q=wine+scoring+sheet&tbm=isch&tbo=u&source=univ&sa=X&ei=RymxUYPfOeTh4AOytIHwBw&sqi=2&ved=0CCoQsAQ&biw=1173&bih=606). One of the simplest examples of this approach is the rating ("tasting") sheet used by the Oxford University Wine Society ("Bacchus") (http://users.ox.ac.uk/~bacchus/docs/tasting_sheet.pdf) which provides space for a wine description (facts about the wine); notes on appearance, nose, and palate; and "conclusions". It discriminates among the three most general sensory characteristics of the wine itself and says nothing about scoring. On the other hand, the UC-Davis Wine Evaluation Chart, also used by the American Wine Society (AWS)      (http://www.americanwinesociety.org/associations/10474/files/Wine%20Evaluation%20chart%202010.pdf) includes a detailed "Aroma Wheel" with 12 categories of aroma, most with sub-categories and specific aromas with each sub-category; and 5 rating attributes, each with its own allowable points with detailed description of each point value (Appearance (4), Aroma and Bouquet (7), Taste and Texture (7), Aftertaste (4), and Overall Impression (3)). Since each attribute can be scored 0, the maximum possible score is 20.

Of course, such a score represents a form of WAS with implied weights and different degrees of differentiation of the attributes it recognizes: think of the possible points as weights and the impression from that attribute as falling somewhere between 0 and 1—from worst to best. According to the model of wine quality implied by the Davis/AWS chart, appearance and aftertaste are equally important; and bouquet and taste are equally important and 75 percent more important than appearance and aftertaste. One's overall impression can add only as much as 15 percent more to one's rating.

The relevance of a WAS model is highlighted by its use without acknowledgment by the wine critic Robert Parker. His model is illuminating. In his

*Table 7.2　A comparison of two prominent weighted average scoring
　　　　　　(WAS) systems*

| Attribute | Parker (% of total) | UC-Davis/AWS (% of total) |
|---|---|---|
| Appearance | 5 (10%) | 3 (15%) |
| Aroma and Bouquet | 15 (30%) | 6 (30%) |
| Taste and Texture | 20 (40%) with finish | 6 (30%) |
| Aftertaste | | 3 (15%) |
| Overall Impression | 10 (20%) | 2 (10%) |
| Total | 50 (100%) | 20 (100%) |

presentation of the Wine Advocate Rating System (Parker 2013), he provides the weights for his rating index:

> my scoring system gives every wine a base of 50 points. The wine's general color and appearance merit up to 5 points. . ... The aroma and bouquet merit up to 15 points. . ... The flavor and finish merit up to 20 points. . ... Finally, the overall quality level or potential for further evolution and improvement—aging—merits up to 10 points.

That is, bouquet is three times as important as appearance and three-fourths of the importance of flavor and finish. Parker allows 40 percent of his points to go to everything after the bouquet and 20 percent to go to overall impression; while AWS allows 45 percent for everything after bouquet but only 10 percent to overall impression. Table 7.2 above summarizes the different WAS models from these two examples.

A strikingly different rating system is Chlebnikowski "Winespider" (CW) which identifies 16 attributes, each of which can earn a score from 0 to 10 (Cicchetti and Cicchetti 2009). The "spider" is the visual presentation of a wine's ratings as a 16-spoke wheel (so 15 equal sides at its perimeter) with the score of each dimension indicated by a point on a spoke and the points connected by lines, giving the impression of a spider web (all 0s appears as a point at the center of the wheel, all 10s appears as a penta-decagon, and all ratings in between appear as a "thread" weaving its way around the 16 spokes or dimensions). The visual presentation facilitates comparisons among wines since one can see the relative strengths and weaknesses of the wines by seeing where each is inside or outside another along any given dimension.

Comparing a CW rating to either a Parker or a Davis/AWS rating highlights the differences among different ratings. CW uses considerably more disaggregated dimensions, but each has equal weight, and it is not apparent how one would aggregate the 16 CW attributes into the 4 or 5 from

Parker and Davis/AWS. Cicchetti and Cicchetti (2009: 76) explain how one can collapse a CW score into a 100-point scale, but the comparability between a score of 86 between, say, Parker and CW is unknown: they could mean very different evaluations of the wine.

If a consumer does not agree with his priorities, then Parker's ratings will be misleading. Considering only the differences between the AWS weights and the Parker weights given in Table 7.2 above, one can see how the same wine may yield different scores if for no other reason than the different weights. To take an extreme example, if a wine is all color and nose (1,1,0,0,0), Parker gives 40 percent of a perfect score. AWS gives 45 percent. If it is all nose and finish (0,1,0,0,1), Parker awards 50 percent of perfect while AWS awards only 40 percent. These differences in scores are enough to give an impression of a risky wine if one looks for "consistent" ratings before settling upon a purchase.

Thinking of ratings as a WAS, it is perhaps more unsettling that wines with the same scores may mean very different impressions to the different experts. A score of 75 percent of possible points could mean excellent color and oral experience to one and great aroma, color, and potential to the other. On the assumption that experts rate wines independently of each other—perhaps a strong assumption since it is difficult to validate—consumers who are skeptical of ratings but are unfamiliar with a wine may favor wines that have two or more favorable ratings from prominent experts, thinking that they know "enough" about a wine that receives similar ratings from multiple experts (where a greater number of similar ratings is taken to mean more reliable knowledge). Wine advertising regularly responds to this instinct by noting that a wine is a "double 90-point" wine or a wine with "three scores in the 90s". In the same vein, fine wine auction catalogues regularly provide a rating and tasting note if it is complimentary from a prominent expert; subject to space limitations, they add additional ratings as long as they reinforce the positive image.

Rarely does a vendor attempt to provide a comprehensive list of ratings, usually opting for the most favorable ones available from popular experts. One vendor that provided relatively full disclosure for several years is the flash sale site "Cinderella Wine" (http://cinderellawine.com/), sponsored by the Wine Library (Springfield, NJ, USA). It is still unusually thorough in providing a link to consumer comments and ratings on "Cellar Tracker" (http://www.cellartracker.com/default.asp) as well as numerous ratings of wines offered, but it has discontinued providing lower scores at the end of the advertisement. It still provides a complete list of past offers (beginning October 2009). Among major online retailers, this would seem to be one whose marketing has been relatively service dominant, though the elimination of the lower scores weakens this and reminds us of the competitive pressure to suppress full information.

Comparing ratings among experts who use different scales is not straightforward. How to compare a two-star rating (out of three possible) from *Guide Hachette* with a Parker score of 88 points is not clear. More subtle is the likely inconsistency of comparing a Parker 88 with a Stephen Tanzer 88 when, relative to Parker, we know very little about Tanzer's underlying model of rating—or, as noted above, a CW 88 where the rating system, while stated explicitly, is so different.

We must bear in mind that most experts do not disclose such details— either the attributes in their weighting scheme, the weights assigned to each, or the quality level assigned to each attribute to arrive at the single rating. Perhaps one could extract an implied model by analysis of an expert's ratings; but that would require identifying the attributes considered significant by the expert (perhaps by an analysis of accompanying TNs if available) as well as the relative importance of each (implied weights) and the scores assigned to each attribute. This would likely require considerable modeling.

Thinking of a wine rating as a WAS suggests a number of concerns. We shall note at the outset two assumptions. First, one's willingness to assign a numeric rating to a wine suggests that one would also approve of assigning a numeric rating to any sensory component of a wine if one could agree that a given dimension is legitimate (e.g., bouquet). Second, a wine rating is intended as a sensory evaluation of the wine. Its other characteristics such as grape content, alcohol level, age, producer, and packaging format are objectively observable, at least potentially.

If a rating is a WAS across a number of attributes, how do we know the sensory attributes included in the rating and, more fundamentally, the extent of disaggregation of sensory attributes? Do we all know what bouquet means? Does bouquet have an initial impression? A length and a finish (like taste)? Can one distinguish as many degrees of finish as one can distinguish flavor? Is one a 3-point scale and the other a 10-point scale?

Among those who reveal something of their model of tasting, some provide more details than others. Parker identifies the attributes he judges and the points allocated to each. AWS indicates not only the attributes but also the number of points allocated to each and the meaning of each point.

Do the weights and the attributes differ by wine or "peer group" since some are known to be more aromatic than others or have better "prospects" (more ageworthy) than others? Does a Beaujolais Nouveau deserve a less-than-perfect score from Parker on "potential" because it is unlikely to improve? What is the "perfect" color of a red Burgundy? If one observes the varieties of behavior among wine consumers, it seems clear that we care about different dimensions—some look for a long time, some smell for a long time, some savor for a long time, and so forth. How does a rating tell a consumer what s/he wants to know?

## IS "VALUE" AN ATTRIBUTE?

A particular concern is the relevance of price to ratings. If one is "grading" wines, then it seems reasonable to include "value" as one of its attributes: give a higher rating to wines that are better value in the eyes of the expert. In the context of experience goods, it might seem sensible to allow for the idea that the consumer hopes to know that a wine is good value.

None of the experts listed in Table 7.1 state explicitly that they consider price in determining ratings, and some claim that they do not (e.g., Parker, *Wine Spectator*). It seems likely, however, that some do. For example, aside from the default category of wines not listed, the two largely country-specific buying guides *Guide Hachette* (GH) for France and *Gambero Rosso* (GR) for Italy have essentially four or five categories of quality respectively, and they assign each wine to one of a few price categories (e.g., in its 2014 edition, GH has, in euros, <5, 5–8, 8–11, 11–15, 15–20, 20–30, 30–50, 50–75, 75–100, + de 100 (Rosa 2013: 8); GR uses similar categories). It seems unlikely that, among red Bordeaux with a GH review, three-star wines are interchangeable whether they are in the "<5 euro" category or the "+ de 100 euro" category. However, GR clouds the issue by highlighting in red the price category of a wine that is a particularly good value.

But why does attention to value raise a concern? Consistent with our economic concept of maximizing benefit and, for every transaction, maximizing benefit per dollar spent that we discussed in Chapter 4, the idea of ratings—notwithstanding the problems of interpretation discussed earlier—is that they should vary directly with benefit (at least the benefit to the rater) and, by extension, one therefore should maximize "points per dollar" with every wine purchase. Indeed, more than most, many wine consumers seem to have taken the benefit-per-dollar concept seriously by focusing upon the idea of a "quality-to-price ratio", or QPR, which apparently is a widely followed measure of value followed by wine consumers relative to all others because of the widespread availability of wine ratings and prices (http://en.wikipedia.org/wiki/Glossary_of_wine_terms). The value of the wine is, in effect, points per dollar.

It is also relevant that wine ratings are most meaningful relative to other wines that consumers would consider close substitutes: they are shopping for a type of wine, and one potential benefit of ratings is to help the consumer know relative quality among the competing wines. For example, one is unlikely to treat Champagne and a fine Australian shiraz interchangeably, and one would expect to find differences in the list of attributes judged for each (e.g., the quality of effervescence, depth of color). In this sense, if the consumer is considering ratings, then Champagne scores will be largely irrelevant to the consumer's consideration of the shiraz scores s/he finds: again, what matters are the scores of the consumer's perceived close substitutes.

With this said, and assuming that ratings are true and comparable indicators of relative quality among close substitutes—a strong assumption, we know by now—the consumer's strategy seems straightforward: among the close substitutes (call them "peers"), choose the wine with the highest QPR, or points per dollar.

But what if value is already considered as an attribute in the rating—if the rater has somehow allowed for something directly related to her judgment of QPR in assigning the rating? We cannot know how one might allow for price—those who seem to consider it (e.g., GH, GR) do not explain how—but a simple, and oversimplified, assumption illustrates the problem. If the score is an estimate of QPR—pure quality rating $(q)$ divided by estimated price $(p)$ (so $q/p$)—but that is not known by the consumer, then the consumer's own naïve calculation of quality divided by price $((q/p)/p)$ yields, in effect, quality divided by price squared $(q/p^2)$, and the consumer has a deflated estimate of the wine's true QPR. Moreover, the distortion grows exponentially with price. The distortion for a $10 wine is that the QPR is 0.1 of its true value (in our simple example), but it is 0.01 its true value for a $100 wine. Thus, the distortion is relatively greater for the more expensive wine, and the less expensive wine appears to be a relative bargain.

Many who have bought relatively inexpensive wines that seemed comparably rated to more expensive wines have been disappointed (e.g., the example described above of the GH 3-star rating in two extreme price categories), probably because they do not know whether and how price has been considered in the rating and they do not know the peer group.

Consider the following example. Without knowing the meaning of peer group and assuming that price is *not* one of its determinants, one finds from Daniel Bolomey's useful website "BordOverview" that Parker rated both the '08 Ch. Duhart-Milon-Rothschild and the '08 Ch. Margaux at 94 points—two wines that one could infer come from the peer group "'08 red Bordeaux". The futures price of the Duhart was 31 euros while the price for the Margaux was 175 euros (http://www.bordoverview. com/?q=Robert-Parker). Why would anyone pay almost six times as much for a wine that s/he can "know" is the same quality? Yet many choose Margaux over Duhart. Are they crazy?

A first alternative is that they are or, more likely, that they feel that the ratings miss a considerable amount of the quality differential between the two wines. Two additional alternative explanations are, first, that price has been considered in the rating (Parker's stated policy notwithstanding) so that—again, oversimplified—the two wines have perhaps comparable QPRs (strictly speaking, the Margaux is almost six times as good as the Duhart but it is also almost six times as expensive), and the consumer should not make some further adjustment for price. A second alternative is that we have misstated the peer group, and, in particular, peer group definition and average price may not be independent.

Many sources of ratings say something about the role of peer groups:

- Parker: "Scores are important for the reader to gauge a professional critic's overall qualitative placement of a wine vis-à-vis its peer group" (https://www.erobertparker.com/info/legend.asp).
- Tanzer (IWC): "Wines are scored relative to their peer group based on their expected quality during their period of peak drinkability" (http://www.wineaccess.com/expert/tanzer/ratingscale.html).
- *Wine Spectator:* "Our tasting coordinators organize the wines into flights by varietal, appellation or region. . .. The tasters are told only the general type of wine (varietal and/or region) and the vintage. No information about the winery or the price of the wine is available to the tasters while they are tasting" (http://www.winespectator.com/display/show/id/tasting-format).

Of these three rating sources, only Tanzer omits commenting upon the role of price in setting his ratings so it is likely that experts understand the sensitivity of confounding ratings with price. The other two say that price is not considered. However, they are vague about the meaning of "peer group": if their identification of peers is straightforward, then they should be willing to identify them, but they do not.

The idea of providing ratings relative to a peer group seems reasonable and appealing and convenient—like attempting to capture the relative quality of some modal group of close substitutes among which the consumer may want to choose—but the difficulties arise in the implementation. Indeed, a goal-oriented interpretation of peers, or close substitutes, which allows implicitly for price, could boost sales of one or a group of wines considerably.

One can imagine defining peer group so as to distort—for example, inflate—the apparent quality of lower priced wines. For example, if the peer group is '02 Champagne Brut Rosé, then all of the peers in that group are expensive, ranging in price per bottle at the time of this writing from $73 to hundreds of dollars using data from the Professional version of www.wine-searcher.com. Thus, if one of these has a 91 rating for $73, then it is doubtful that one can say a 91-point NV Champagne Brut Rosé—from the peer group NV Champagne Brut Rosé—priced at $12, the bottom of that group's range, is about the same quality. However, if one defines the peer group as "Champagne Brut Rosé", then the NV bottle looks like a considerably better value, even though it could be clearly lower quality than the vintage Champagne.

In this example, one might object that wines from these two groups are unlikely to have comparable quality. However, if the rating allows for value implicitly, then such a comparison would not be unusual (cf. the red Bordeaux example above). One objects because the peer group has been specified, and the distortion is clear: that is rarely the case with the experts.

## OTHER ISSUES COMPLICATING THE USE AND INTERPRETATION OF RATINGS

Aside from the questionable value of TNs and the difficulty of interpreting ratings, a third set of concerns about capturing the consumer's experience with ratings is the share of the content of the expert's tasting experience that can be transferred to the consumer's experience. Think of all the advertised circumstances of the expert tasting and the circumstances of one's actual consumption of a wine—starting with the differences in nose and tongue. Aside from the persistent risk of bottle variation, wine rating emerges from an experience influenced by a dizzying number of factors ranging from observable and measurable differences like ambient temperature, wine temperature, time of day, and glassware to presence of others, mood, and presence of other consumables. Judging that a wine is 92 percent of perfection under one set of circumstances may provide only the most general indication of its relative appeal under different circumstances, especially to a different person.

The influence of glassware has received considerable attention. One of the most tangible indications of the complexity of taste is the emergence of different glasses for different wines. The Austrian glassware company Riedel Glas has made an industry on the basis of the vessel delivering the wine to our mouths affecting its flavor—the "functional wine glass" invented by Claus Riedel who "designed its shape according to the character of the wine" (http://www.riedel.com/). If this is correct, then tasting notes should describe the glassware used. If it is the standard International Organization for Standardization (ISO) tasting glass, that should be stated. Otherwise, Riedel Glas would argue that the specifications of the tasting glass should be reported—and corrected if it is not a Riedel glass.

Even if we assume that all experts use ISO glasses in their tastings, how should one adjust those ratings if one's own tasting is from a wine-appropriate glass?

Fourth, a finding of a positive impact of ratings on price does not tell us that consumers are willing to pay more for wines that they know are better. A significant direct correlation between WTP and ratings could mean that 10 percent of purchasers are buying for investment purposes and assuming that higher ratings yield higher WTP from subsequent buyers; and the other 90 percent are buying for own consumption and essentially disregarding the ratings since they find them worthless in evaluating how much they will enjoy the wine in their circumstances. In order to disentangle the impact of ratings, we would need to know more about motives for purchase and allow for a change of purpose over the life of ownership: for example, some may buy wine for investment and then change to own consumption and vice versa.

The available evidence also does not indicate sustained enhanced returns to higher ratings over time. Greater WTP at the time of release says nothing about the ultimate return to the rating in subsequent sales. If a rating actually captures the quality of the wine, then the return would accrue only to the initial buyer with all subsequent buyers getting only normal returns—but then again, we do not know the motives of subsequent buyers.

Complicating this is, again, revision of ratings—probably a reasonable development but another indication of the uncertainty of knowing what is in the bottle.

## WINE GRADES, STUDENT GRADES, AND TEACHING KNOWLEDGE

Many consider one of Parker's more clever innovations in wine evaluation to be the adoption of a grading scheme for wines that resembled the grading schemes that most had encountered as students (McCoy 2005: 63–64, 131–133). He was incisive in realizing that US consumers—especially the relatively educated consumers that were likely to become the core of the US fine wine market—would understand wine "grades" on a 100-point scale.

Perhaps ironically, Parker's step in that direction can be extended to highlight the often unreliable content or perhaps transitory value of wine ratings. A closer look suggests that wine grades suffer from many of the same difficulties presented by school grades—for example, multidimensional performance usually compressed into a single dimension; selection of evaluation criteria, weighting, and methods based upon the evaluator's personal preference rather than some well-established set of standards (criteria, weights, and methods); a limited opportunity for evaluation of performance relative to the lifetime of performance of the subject being evaluated; and influences upon the grade from circumstances at the time.

For credibility, both require objectivity, transparency, and thoroughness; but neither reflects and communicates a true and enduring knowledge of what is graded. Perhaps, as with student grades, one gains a better sense of overall quality by collecting numerous evaluations from different reliable sources over an extended period (like a Grade Point Average from a university transcript), but this is prohibitively difficult—and one may still be surprised. Moreover, like sorting student quality, it is still likely to yield only a handful of quality categories.

Taking the comparison one step further, the challenge of teaching reminds us of the daunting task of transmitting knowledge, whether in the classroom or with wine ratings. Assuming we are beyond teaching and learning by rote, anyone who has tried teaching an abstract subject (e.g., economic theory, literary or art criticism) or "thinking skills" (e.g., critical thinking, clear writing) appreciates the difficulty of transmitting what one knows, with reasonable certainty, to those who may want to learn and then attempting to assess the extent to which the knowledge has been transmitted (the point about grading discussed earlier). Overall it is a highly imperfect process whose results are highly variable, especially among heterogeneous students. Transmitting "reasonably certain" knowledge of fine wine to heterogeneous consumers through ratings and tasting notes would seem to be at least as daunting.

## THE PHILOSOPHICAL PROBLEM

Most of our focus has been the question of designating fine wine as an experience good, arising from efforts to identify the determinants of wine prices and, in particular, our ability to represent what consumers know or could know about a fine wine in forming their willingness to pay for it by using expert ratings. We have critiqued this most popular source of information about wine quality available to consumers aside from extensive personal tasting experience. Based upon the analysis, the case for expert opinions in their various forms providing a good proxy for a consumer's knowledge of a wine is weak: such information, even if supplemented by personal tasting experience, still leaves most fine wine consumers surprised much of the time and leaves many others on the sidelines "overwhelmed" by the challenge.

From a philosophical perspective, skepticism about the consumer's ability to know what she is purchasing is on an even firmer footing than the preceding discussion suggests. A recent book (Smith 2007a) collects a number of papers which, according to the editor, represent the first "sustained study of the relationship [between philosophy and wine]." In his Introduction (Smith 2007b: xi), Smith wastes no time in questioning what we can know about a fine wine:

- If much of the pleasure of drinking wine is sharing it with others, how can we actually do that if taste is subjective "as we are always told"? Is sharing during tasting truly a shared experience in the sense of having something significant in common and knowing what each other is tasting?
- When we share and reflect upon a bottle of wine, we think we are reflecting upon the same thing—but what are the properties of this so-called shared experience?
- "How accurate or objective is the language we use for describing [the features, qualities, and character of the wines we talk about]?"
- "How much trust should we place in wine connoisseurs or experts" and are they able to communicate effectively with anyone other than perhaps other experts?
- Knowing a wine requires tasting it for oneself, but does our tasting reveal properties of the wine itself or, instead, our subjective responses to the wine?
- Is judgment about wine neither entirely subjective nor objective but perhaps relative—that is, accurate for "a standard or assessment, or set of preferences," that is not shared among experts? (Smith 2007b: xii–xvi)

It is not surprising that the answers to these questions are neither dismissed nor provided definitively. The contributors disagree fundamentally about the existence of objective knowledge of a wine beyond its technical characteristics which, while objective, will make different impressions upon different consumers, depending upon influences such as their own physical characteristics (e.g., genetic differences, "supertasters" versus "medium tasters"), their backgrounds (e.g., amount of "training"), and the circumstances of the tasting (Goode 2007).

As Smith has stated: "Here we have a key philosophical question: how subjective are tastes and tasting, or to put it in ontological terms: what are we tasting?" (Smith 2007b: xiii).

Finally, it is noteworthy that a core concept in economics and in science generally is replication of results: our willingness to believe something depends upon our ability to demonstrate it again. But that seems particularly difficult with wine and represents something of a challenge to our embrace of the scientific method. There are these phenomena that seem not amenable to scientific method which suggests a certain irony in the scientist's love of wine.

## CONCLUSION

After considering the definition, one must question whether fine wine is an experience good—not that it overstates the complexity of the consumer's problem but that it significantly understates it. For example, Nelson's original examples like home appliances are considerably easier to know than these wines. If one has no experience with a refrigerator, then one may have a difficult time arriving at a WTP for a given refrigerator. Once one buys a refrigerator, one understands its basic function and most of its competing brands. Very few competing products represent a significant challenge to understanding all refrigerators—and similarly for the kinds of goods Nelson describes. Because of the flood of new consumer technology in recent years, many of us who experienced much of this only as adults can identify with this difficulty: If one has never used a smartphone, how does one gauge one's WTP for it? The idea that one can know a type of wine by buying one of its representatives in the same sense that one can know a type of refrigerator by buying one of its type seems misplaced. At least as important in considering the determination of WTP is the consideration that comprehensive knowledge of substitutes among refrigerators is at least feasible relative to the prospect of gaining comprehensive knowledge of all the choices available as substitutes for a type of wine.

We have considered wine's status as an experience good primarily through the prospect of the consumer's vicarious familiarity with a wine through access to others' experiences as represented by expert ratings and both expert and amateur tasting notes. They may be the best proxy we have for consumer knowledge of a wine; but, as knowledge, they suffer from a variety of flaws. Our review may provide some support for the apparently weak ability of such data to explain wine prices. Philosophy is not always considered a behavioral science, but the questions philosophers raise about our ability to know a wine contribute further to our understanding of the consumer's challenge in knowing a wine and what it is worth.

The case for fine wine as an experience good is weak. A product that might be a closer match to the good the fine wine consumer purchases is an informed bet on a horse race. By doing one's research, one can increase one's likelihood of choosing a winner—or at least a show—but the purchase inevitably includes a large element of chance. It seems unlikely that gamblers and wine aficionados are cut from the same cloth, but they are not unrelated—and those who are sufficiently risk averse tend to avoid purchasing fine wine. We cannot know the extent to which this shrinks the potential market, but we expect that many acknowledged wine buyers are "overwhelmed" and that many more potential buyers usually stay away.

Considering only one's own consumption, what then is fine wine's attraction? Part of the appeal is the prospect of betting on the right horse and the potential returns to careful research. Also important is the sense that, when one finds a "winner", it is not only a reward for risk taking and an attractive return on investment but also a gift from the winemaker that yields considerable satisfaction.

The philosophical problem presents a challenge to progressing with this. Two promising areas are, first, further exploration of information sources and processing that contribute to the consumer's ability to recognize a wine. The prospect of learning more, perhaps through neuroscience, about how we register and remember experiences like wine tasting is also attractive (Medina 2008).

The next chapter continues the discussion of categorizing wine in the economist's taxonomy of goods. While our discussion of wine in the early chapters postponed addressing this complexity so that we could focus upon the process of getting to the transaction, we are now digging more deeply into the challenges of getting there. In this chapter, we have asked how the parties to the transaction—especially the consumer—know what is being exchanged, given the protean nature and complexity of wine. In the next, we consider a view of wine that says transactions involve more than simply what is in the bottle.

## NOTE

1.  This chapter is taken from my paper: Marks (2013), "'In Vino Veritas'—But What In Truth Is In the Bottle? Experience Goods, Fine Wine Ratings, and Wine Knowledge". Presented at the 7th Annual Conference of the American Association of Wine Economists, Stellenbosch, South Africa, June 2013.

# 8. Wine as a cultural good[1]

## INTRODUCTION

For many, wine is simply a commodity or an agricultural product whose market does not differ in any significant way from other beverages except for its legal treatment as alcohol. However, those who appreciate wine for something more know that the experiences of drinking it can be significantly different from other beverages. Moreover, the primary distinction is not the presence or absence of alcohol's narcotic effect. Wine appreciation has many dimensions—from history, art, and culture to science and management. The market for wine can touch a number of other markets such as tourism and education. For example, Aylward (2008) has argued that wine is essentially a "cultural good" that embodies more than the sensory characteristics of other consumables.

A recent development in economic thinking is the appreciation of "cultural goods" and the distinction between economic value and "cultural value". Up to now in this book, our focus has been economic value that is a foundation of microeconomics—the market-determined value of something as reflected in someone's willingness to pay (WTP) for it. In light of this familiar concept, what can we mean by a distinct cultural value? Why does the distinction matter, especially in our valuation of goods? Why does the standard economic model not allow for proper valuation of cultural goods?

In this chapter, we examine the idea of cultural goods, the challenges they present for market transactions, and the application to wine. We discuss the relevance of wine as a cultural good to the industry in the traditional but still-evolving wine regions of Central and Eastern Europe where wine culture is longstanding but has been developing unevenly in recent years.

## THE CONCEPT OF CULTURAL GOODS

David Throsby has been developing this idea for some time. While a complete discussion of this concept is beyond the scope of this chapter, we can outline the idea. First, Throsby means, by culture, "certain activities that are undertaken by people, and the products of those activities, which have to do with the intellectual, moral and artistic aspects of human life . . . drawing upon the enlightenment and education of the mind rather than the acquisition of purely technical or vocational skills" (Throsby 2001: 4). In concluding his discussion of the meaning of cultural activities, he provides this guidance:

> they involve creativity in their production, they embody some form of intellectual property and they convey symbolic meaning . . . in addition, a designation from the demand side might point to the accumulation of taste and the dependence of present on previous consumption. Finally, a unique characteristic of such goods can be defined in terms of value: cultural goods embody or give rise to both cultural and economic value, 'ordinary' economic goods yield economic value only. (Throsby 2001: 160)

He also addresses the different motivation of those who produce cultural goods:

> the creation of economic value is not their only *raison d'être*. Processes of production and consumption in the arts and culture, and the broader role of culture in articulating essential values by which human beings express their identity and work out ways of living together, have a crucial content of cultural value, defined against different yardsticks from those we use to measure economic success. Any consideration of the cultural industries . . . cannot afford to overlook or downplay this critical dimension. (Throsby 2001: 134)

Throsby's examples may be helpful. Cultural activities would certainly include those that many would expect: music, literature, poetry, visual art. He would also include more plainly commercial activities such as films, journalism, television, radio, and probably graphic art. While it involves creativity and intellectual property, he excludes scientific innovation because it does not seek the communication of meaning. Road signs communicate symbolic meaning but are weak on the other criteria. Organized sports occupy an ambiguous position—in particular, whether it embodies creativity or, instead, technical skill (p. 5). His discussion leaves the clear impression that, like the identification of public goods and "publicness", goods have more or less degrees of culture. Some goods are clearly cultural, and some are clearly not; but many goods contain elements of culture.

Why do we care about the distinction? Essentially, failing to recognize a distinct idea of cultural value distorts our valuation of cultural goods and thereby their production and preservation:

it is in the elaboration of notions of value, and the transformation of value either into economic price or into some assessment of cultural worth, where the two fields diverge. Economists are deluding themselves if they claim that economics can encompass cultural value entirely within its ambit and that the methods of economic assessment are capable of capturing all relevant aspects of cultural value in their net. . ... If we are serious about striving for theoretical completeness, and eventually for operational validity in decision-making, it is essential that cultural value be admitted alongside economic value in the consideration of the overall value of cultural goods and services. (Throsby 2001: 41)

Among other things, a central theme in the discussion is globalization and concerns that dedication to the apparently narrow economic model promoting efficiency, competition, market growth, and consumer sovereignty will undervalue cultural goods so that they are under-produced or lost in competition with mass produced goods responding to "international tastes".

Can economic value encompass cultural value? Throsby argues that it cannot: "willingness to pay is an inadequate or inappropriate indicator of cultural value". To summarize his argument:

1.  Cultural value may exist apart from an individual's valuation of an object or process: even if we cannot find someone willing to pay, does that mean that it has no cultural value, even for future generations?
2.  People may know too little to form a reliable WTP judgment about a cultural good; if this is widespread, then we may doubt the reliability of individual preferences for the good.
3.  For some characteristics, individuals may be unable to express a preference, only acknowledgment of a difference (e.g., style of a painting).
4.  The cultural value of some characteristics may not be measurable in either monetary or relative prices: the individual values them but cannot declare reliably her WTP.
5.  Valuation may be difficult when the value arises because one is a member of a group (e.g., benefits of national identity or membership in a theater audience): the benefit exists only in a collective sense, and aggregated individual WTP understates the aggregate value to the group (Throsby 2001: 31–32).

One can add that WTP reflects the distribution of purchasing power. We may lack a market supporting some good because those who value it lack the purchasing power to support production. However, that does not mean that the good does not deserve to be produced—especially if the good's value is primarily or even entirely cultural. How many cultural goods have been lost because those valuing them could not afford them?

How many have been preserved only because devotees other than private consumers asserted that the community should preserve them—largely through public sector expenditures or charitable donations?

Throsby concludes that, while we may find a direct correlation between economic value and cultural value which might tempt us to use economic value as a proxy (e.g., the Mona Lisa), there are numerous counterexamples where values along the two dimensions vary inversely (Throsby 2001: 34)—for example, a piece of ephemera such as a political poster promoting South Africa's first black president. In a more recent paper (Throsby 2008), he distinguishes cultural value and its measurement: "[that reflects] assessments of the significance or worth of the work judged against aesthetic and other artistic or cultural criteria that may transcend individual valuation and/or may not be expressible in financial terms . . . [I]ndividual judgments . . . cannot be fully reflected in financial assessments and indeed may lie beyond the scope of measurement altogether" (Throsby 2008: 76).

## WINE AS A CULTURAL GOOD

Recently, Hugh Johnson asserted that wine is a cultural good in an essay opposing a recent French anti-drinking movement and a radical revision of EU appellation systems: "its properties, traditions, varieties, and indeed its effects, are a part of European culture and identity as important as any other. It is as much our right to enjoy them as it is to walk our streets or fish our rivers . . . it is our duty to conserve such a cultural asset" (Johnson 2009: 6). A productive approach to applying this concept to wine is by analogy. Is wine closer to a painting or to a screwdriver? For some, the answer may not be obvious, but for many wine consumers, it is. How does wine gain cultural content?

A comparison with food might be illuminating. Cooking and cuisine are the subjects of seemingly endless books, media programs, and classes. For many who wish to nurture the roots of their culture—the one in which they live, the one from which they came if it is different—a reliable and regular means of doing that is in the kitchen and at the table: "As Italians have done forever, we remembered who we were through food" (Esposito 2008: 39). Beyond its role in nutrition, a group's cuisine reflects the natural and economic conditions from which it sprung. Its cuisine is often woven into its religious life and its politics. Most of us would include cuisine in any description of a culture that we could identify. The website for the newsletter "Food History News" provides a directory of over 1,400 food and beverage museums around the world. Books on food and culture abound: a search of the current availability of books from Amazon

(USA) with the words "food" and "culture" in their titles yields 2,418 titles. Removing titles that are off-topic leaves at least hundreds of current titles on the subject (e.g., 826 titles considered "history", 407 considered "cooking, food, and wine", 39 considered "travel", 26 considered "religion and spirituality", etc.). Many books discussing food and culture have neither word in their titles—for example, Visser's anthropological analysis in *Much Depends on Dinner* (1986).

Just as cultures have their cuisines reflecting the climates, natural products, and rituals associated with them, wines reflect the variety of cultures that originated them. Cultural conditions such as climate, terrain, soil, comparative advantage, technology, and spirituality shape the kind—and even the existence—of wine arising from a culture. Among many others, a wine geographer (Sommers 2008) says that "the appreciation and love of wine goes beyond the wine itself. . .. Wine is an expression of places and people" (p. 264). He draws a connection among geography, history, architecture, and art through wine using their convergence in France's southern Rhone Valley where "the wines . . . have a strong connection to the history of the Roman Empire . . . seen in the architectural heritage of the towns . . . you can feel a tangible connection to history. You can easily imagine that two thousand years ago people sat in the same place and drank the same wines" (Sommers 2008: 265–266). Similar connections apply to all of the historic wine regions of the world.

After water, the only beverage that generates as much interest as food is wine—not so much the production as the understanding of it. The comparison is even starker if we limit ourselves to alcoholic beverages (more on the role of alcohol below). Unlike most beverages, a central theme in the wine market is "appreciation". Like food, interest in wine supports wine tasting and appreciation courses, winemaking courses, and thousands of publications. A check of listings with Amazon.com (US) finds more than twice as many "wine books" (68,625) as books on tea, coffee, beer, and alcoholic spirits combined (30,180) with almost 4,000 wine titles involving religion and spirituality, history, and travel.

While the analogy with food is instructive, applying Throsby's criteria for either identification or valuation of cultural goods strengthens the case—in particular, the role of creativity and symbolic meaning in producing wine. It would be appealing to assign enforceable rights—intellectual property as Throsby's second requirement—to the creations of the world's great wineries; but, aside from protecting the brand through trademark law, they could not be recorded and preserved like art or music.

It is self-evident that winemaking involves creativity, especially for wines bearing the winemaker's name. Like chefs creating cuisine from local ingredients, many winemakers want to create a wine that embodies the place where it is made. Our discussions in Chapters 5 and 6 of policies like the AOC system in France emphasized that a sympathetic interpretation for restrictions on farming, processing, and labeling is that producers want the wine to represent the place—limited intervention in growing and producing to preserve the effects of weather and soil, limited or no introduction of foreign substances including non-local grapes, clear indication on the label of the site of production.

Like food, wine also carries meaning like few other goods. Such wines also have symbolic value as they have come to represent the place where they are produced. Many French winemakers want their wines to capture the *terroir*—the overall sense of place—where their wines are made (e.g., Kramer 2008); the same is true in Slovenia (e.g., Esposito 2008: 132–155). The wine becomes a symbol of the place in the eyes of those who know it: when they drink its wine, they can see the place. For most of its history, the lack of effective storage and inexpensive shipping meant that wine was developed to complement the local cuisine, and it was typically consumed close to its home. Many wines are most appreciated with their partner cuisines such as Loire muscadet and Atlantic oysters, wines from southeastern France with Provençal cuisine, and sangiovese-based wines such as Chianti and Brunello di Montalcino with hearty Tuscan sauces. As shipping and storage have developed and producers have appealed to buyers farther afield, we have seen the emergence of more "international" styles of wine that are less tied to a cuisine or to food at all. They are designed to be enjoyed with various cuisines or on their own, but they are less evocative of a culture.

Connecting wine with place, we see the ascent of riesling as a product which arguably reaches its highest expression in relatively cool regions including Germany, Austria, and the Czech Republic. Different conditions led to the tempranillo-based wines of Rioja in Spain. Slovakian frankovka can be delicious but has not thrived in many other cultures. Tannat seemed to be capable of greatness only in some regions of southwestern France (e.g., Madiran and Tursan wines) until Uruguayan vintners tapped their potential. Thus, some grapes are associated with certain parts of the world. Even those grapes that seem viable globally find different expressions from their different locations—for example, the grapefruit and gooseberry character of New Zealand sauvignon blanc compared with the crisp minerality of Loire Valley sauvignon blanc. Similarly, while changing climates could affect this, regions that cannot grow wine grapes commercially have not developed the industry. Their cultures evolve into production more consistent with local conditions (e.g., brandy in Poland, tequila in Mexico).

Wine's ageworthiness has symbolic value. Beaujolais Nouveau is produced to celebrate the French harvest and shares the fresh and transitory character of that annual event. First-growth Bordeaux is designed to reward patience and to embody the rewards of long life. It could be produced to provide immediate gratification as with some New World "Bordeaux blends", but that is not what makes it distinctive: its examples that are most highly valued for their flavor (as opposed to their pure rarity) are decades old.

More generally, we find a close connection between the discussion of wine and the search for meaning and purpose (e.g., Grahm 2008). Once producers started packaging wine rather than selling it only in bulk, it was packaged in containers that were intended for sharing. We lack the data to know, but one expects that wine is most commonly served in a group of at least two. Unlike beer which is commonly packaged in single servings and spirits which are commonly package in reclosable (often screwcap) containers, wine has been packaged in containers for two or more. It seems designed for sharing, for serving in community.

Along with bread, wine is connected intimately to various religions—the vine as a metaphor for the body of believers, wine as a symbol of God's covenant with humankind, wine's central role in sacraments and celebrations in Judeo–Christian tradition. For example, while our title's reference to wine as "the elixir of life" is a mythical concept, it brings to mind the Christian concept of eternal life through belief in Christ which invites drinking "Christ's blood" (wine) during Christian communion (e.g., John 6:54). At least traditionally, the popular name for evaporation of wine from barrels ("the angels' share") evokes the spirit as does the French phrase *nature conciliante* ("when nature is willing to reward man's effort"). Far from being a coincidence or a convenience, wine as a "living thing" reflects the nature of wine which can have a life of its own and can represent life. A wine is born, and the best wines mature and become their best before they start to decline. They benefit from being treated well and reward being well treated—but, as in life, that is not guaranteed. The discussion and description of wine often involves anthropomorphic language (e.g., Suárez-Toste 2007), and numerous authors and artists have attempted to capture the connection between the meaning of wine and the meaning of life (e.g., Lamb and Mittelberger 1974).

Wine's narcotic effect from alcohol also has symbolic value. The alcohol in wine was historically what made it safer to drink (in moderation) than water. However, its popularity obviously continued and expanded after the introduction of safe drinking water systems, depending upon the role of narcotics in the culture. How does the culture evaluate alcohol's "power to banish care"—the title of the first chapter in Johnson's history of wine (Johnson 1989: 10–13)? What does that option mean to a culture?

Will it tolerate such potential abdication of responsibility, and, if so, to what extent, especially in a product which, at its best, is designed to evoke memory of place? How do cultures that avoid or ban narcotics (e.g., Islamic) accommodate the desire to "banish care" if at all? To what extent are religions and narcotics substitute or complementary routes to the same destination—among other aspirations, perhaps to banish care?

Two other characteristics of cultural value also have particular relevance to the role of wine: "accumulation of taste and the dependence of present on previous consumption" and the capacity of the individual "to form a reliable WTP judgment about a cultural good". One's appreciation and valuation of wine depends upon one's experience with it.

The discussion in Chapter 7 addressed the consumer's ability to know a wine: the clearest challenges are fine wines. It is difficult to determine one's WTP, even with considerable research, and one comes to expect surprises. As discussed in the preceding chapter, given the tens of thousands of wines available at any time, one often turns to the impressions from experts and uses their experience vicariously. Like consumers of many cultural goods, those who develop an interest often consult expert opinion about quality and value. If investment is the motive, then that may be a better guide to what others will pay than one's own enjoyment.

Cultural goods are inherently differentiated—perhaps no two units are exactly alike (e.g., performances of a symphony, paintings): consistency and uniformity are not particular virtues of cultural goods. When are differences significant and perhaps valuable? The only differences that amount to product differentiation in the marketplace are those that are valued differently, and buyers are willing to pay for those differences only if they perceive them to be more valuable. How is this established with cultural goods? For even the most obvious examples of cultural goods such as art and music, how do we value them? Laypeople—most of us—often consider "expert" opinions, hoping to find some of them valid and reliable.

The market for critical wine commentary has grown considerably over the last 30 years. As one of its pioneers, Parker (2008) describes its evolution from uncritical promotional descriptions to please the trade to a proliferation of wine criticism, championed by Parker influenced by his fellow crusading lawyer Ralph Nader (McCoy 2005: 23, 56, 66–67): "wine has become so pervasive in so many cultures and the price of top wines so expensive that, combined with the rarity of many top wines, consumers do need respectable sources of information" (Parker 2008: xvii). This role for expert opinion is one of the valuation methods noted by Throsby (2001: 30): "The input of expertise in a variety of disciplines is likely to be an essential component of any cultural value assessment, especially in providing judgments on aesthetic, historical and authenticity value, where particular skills, training and experience can lead to a better informed evaluation." The appetite for such assistance in understanding wine is evident from the abundance of wine buyer's guides (113 titles currently listed with Amazon(US)), the pervasiveness of wine critics and websites, and the inclusion of critics' notes in wine auction catalogs at the world's foremost wine auction houses such as Sotheby's and Christies.

Note, however, that we are not withdrawing our concerns about the value of expert opinion expressed in Chapter 7. We are simply indicating that the appetite for it is consistent with the special importance many give to wine.

Finally, an offhand endorsement comes from Throsby when he illustrates the idea of intrinsic cultural value with a wine analogy: "Those who accept the notion of intrinsic value believe that cultural value is somehow stored in an artwork like wine in a bottle; it may be drunk from time to time but it is also somehow constantly replenished, so that its amount [of intrinsic value] may even increase with age" (Throsby 2001: 39).[2]

If we can agree that wine and winemaking have significant cultural value and that the market tends to undervalue such goods, then we ask how to preserve this cultural good if we cannot assume that the market will—or that the wines preserved by the market are not necessarily the culturally most important ones.[3]

## A NOTE ON CULTURAL GOODS AND PUBLIC GOODS

Questions about the market's ability to elicit honest and informed expressions of willingness to pay such as Throsby's suggest challenges associated with public goods. One may ask reasonably whether cultural goods are simply a form of public good—goods which have the two characteristics of non-rival consumption (consumers can enjoy the same unit of the good simultaneously) and costly or impossible exclusion—the only way to elicit sincere expressions of WTP is to threaten exclusion, which is impossible for pure public goods (the source of "free-riding" where consumers understate WTP because they cannot be excluded from use anyway).

While some cultural goods are public goods—for example, great architecture or public sculpture—the two categories are different. Especially in the present discussion, consumption of a bottle of wine is not non-rival, and exclusion is straightforward. On the other hand, some features of the wine industry exhibit publicness: its meaning to the local community and wider society (e.g., the meaning of riesling to the Mosel and Rhine Valleys), the reputation of particular wines or appellations (e.g., the Bekaa Valley

in Lebanon, the Brda Valley in Slovenia), perhaps the beauty and significance of some vineyard or winery (e.g., Ch. Latour in Pauillac). However,
with either type of good, the market valuation problem is similar: we
cannot rely upon private parties in private transactions to reveal accurately the value of the good. In the case of public goods, the problem is
free-riding from non-exclusion; in the case of cultural goods, the problem
is the failure of the individual to value cultural content reliably—an externality issue. Also, the challenge of identifying cultural goods is akin to that
of identifying public goods: it is difficult to find perfect examples, but we
see many imperfect ones. In either case, we cannot expect efficient allocation from the market; and in both cases, we tend to turn to the community,
usually represented by the government, to represent community valuation,
however imperfectly.

## WHAT IF WE NEGLECT WINE'S CULTURAL CONTENT? THE CASE OF AUSTRALIA

Several years ago, the prominent wine scholar Professor Kym Anderson
(2004) described how the Australian wine industry had begun to realize the
potential that some had foreseen for it throughout the twentieth century,
having grown dramatically since 1990, trebling its share of global vine area
and raising its share of global export sales fivefold. He went on to discuss
how "Australia achieved that take-off" despite flat wine sales nationally
and globally (Anderson 2004: 252). Four years later, Aylward (2008)
struck a different tone, warning about the stagnation of the Australian
industry:

> Its recipe was based on mass production, standardisation and scientific
> imperatives. For a time, it was very successful. Some less sympathetic observers
> labelled it the 'coca-colarisation' of wine, claiming that short-term economic
> thinking had expunged the 'art' of winemaking and reduced the practice to
> little more than formulaic, assembly-line production. Many believe they were
> correct.

> In fact, it is the previous short-term thinking that is now haunting the
> Australian industry. . ... [As of the late 1990s] Markets were reconfiguring
> into new categories where the competition was moving beyond price to focus
> instead on product. The entrance of additional producers on a large scale and
> the increasing influence of wine writers, commentators and consumer expec-
> tations were driving trends. Such trends had originated with simple product
> differentiation but were now developing into a quest for product story, a
> wine experience, and an appreciation for its cultural qualities. (Aylward 2008:
> 373–374)

Aylward identifies several impediments to the adaptability of the Australian industry, including:

1.  Its centralized structure, reflecting the nationalized collection and distribution of a research and development (R&D) levy to a national research institute (Australian Wine Research Institute (AWRI)) which promotes scientific priorities to the detriment of artisanal ones; and using centralized export guidelines, quality assurance, governance, and industry branding;
2.  "Mass plantation and harvesting, multi-region blending, over-filtration, standardized production methods, and ambiguous geographic indicators" (p. 378); and
3.  The dominant influence of Australia's large owners like Constellation, Fosters, and Casella (makers of Yellow Tail) which produced well over half of Australia's wine in 2009 (http://www.winebiz.com.au/statistics/wineries.asp).

His concern is that the industry's focus upon high volume and low margins and producing "coca-cola" wines has been neglecting potential growth and profitability among more artisanal producers. In the beverage wine market, other New World countries (e.g., in Latin America) are viable threats—able to match Australian quality at lower cost. He also argues that individual wine tastes follow a pattern that leads to demand for more varied wines and that the consumers who began drinking wine with the soft and simple flavors of the Australian beverage wines now seek something more interesting and varied: "their consumers' palates have become more educated and more discerning . . . [they] no longer want a mass produced product that lacks *terroir*, character, or distinction in taste" (Aylward 2008: 377). He notes that Australian wines are still enjoying rising value per liter in nontraditional wine markets such as China and India (p. 378) but implies that these markets will also mature with consumers becoming more discriminating.

The evidence supporting his analysis is primarily consumer and producer opinion surveys, and he does not address the role of other recent threats to industry profitability such as weather. The relative strength of his argument is essentially logic, and he does not truly prove his case. However, commentary on the Australian industry by others provides evidence that its performance has weakened in recent years (e.g., Veseth 2009a, 2009b).

The Australian example is illuminating. It had the land and the weather but not the tradition of the Old World stalwarts in Western Europe, and it was not a traditional major wine exporter but became one. Despite its distance from major markets, Australia promoted its wine industry toward the end of the last century. Australian wine has certainly become a popular beverage wine, but that is a highly competitive market with limited profit margins.

## A PROSPECTIVE CASE: CENTRAL AND EASTERN EUROPE

Australia is perhaps the most prominent of the "New World" wine regions whose quality and quantity of production over the last few decades have reshaped the global wine market and moved its center of gravity away from Western Europe. Seemingly left behind has been the traditionally important neighbor of the Western European stalwarts, namely, the primary wine-producing Central and Eastern European countries (CEEC[4])— bounded by Western Europe on the west (specifically, Germany, Austria, and Italy) and Poland, Ukraine, and Turkey on the east. Ironically, that is a birthplace of wine.

Though lacking the history and tradition of European winemaking, the New World has established itself as an important part of the global wine market: one hopes that non-Western Europe can find its way as well. Rather than following the New World strategy of becoming a major supplier of beverage wine whose lack of distinction may threaten the image of New World production, exploiting its winemaking history and diversity could be its entrée into the international market. It also seems natural that this region's wines should have greater prominence in the global market for fine wine which currently seems to stop—unnaturally, like the Cold War split between West and East—at the German, Austrian, and Italian borders. As a cultural good which, historically, has been an important part of the region and whose production at a competitive level requires significant initial investment, the CEEC wine industry may deserve increased public support.

## CULTURAL GOODS AND THE WINE MARKET'S ROLE IN ECONOMIC DEVELOPMENT

The CEEC has a long history of wine production, and the proximity of many of its current viticultural areas to established and distinguished areas outside the CEEC suggests that it has the potential to play a significant role in world wine production. Large parts of the region have the climate and topography for growing a wide variety of grapes (Gunyon

1971)—and the cultural background. Unlike China which has also risen to prominence in the global wine market, this region shares the European tradition of wine appreciation. The very different roles of Western and Eastern Europe in the global wine market do indeed seem unnatural.

Parts of the CEEC have a struggling but continuing tradition of wine-making—in particular, Hungary, Bulgaria, Moldova, Romania, Slovenia, and Croatia. Production from both classic and recent vintages in some of these countries has reminded us of the quality achievable in these historically important areas. Though limited, bottlings from rieslings to Bordeaux blends are competitive with some of the best products from neighboring countries such as Austria, Germany, and Italy. Hungary's Tokaji is among the best known products from the region, and its innovative wine-makers like Ferenc Takler and Attila Gere produce limited quantities of well-crafted wines—often indigenous grapes (e.g., kekfrankos, kadarka) added to traditional blends (e.g., Bordeaux)—that are sought around the world. Slovenian wines from the Brda Valley (e.g., Simčič, Movia) are competitive with some of the best wines from the Friuli–Venezia–Giulia regions of northeastern Italy. Some Czech "archivni vino" from the 1980s and earlier are delicious.

Production of certain products generates a disproportionate status to a region. For example, it is unlikely that consumers in the world care that the cotton in their clothing comes from China or India. However, knowing that fine rugs come from Turkey or interesting wines come from Slovenia attracts consumer interest in the country and promotes related products such as tourism and cultural education (e.g., language, literature, history). Examples such as Chateau Musar and Kefraya from Lebanon's Bekaa Valley remind us that production of exceptional wine—perhaps an eponymous wine that becomes an "icon" (e.g., Penfolds Grange Hermitage in Australia) (Anderson and Wood 2006)—can bring favor and repute out of all proportion to the investment required.

These countries have faced the recent shifts in global wine production with at least two profound disadvantages: (1) exclusion from the global wine market until recently which denied producers access to the rewards for quality winemaking and (2) a guaranteed market for wine within the Soviet sphere which absorbed all production but rewarded quantity and not quality. The incentive to compete and excel was absent. Exceptional winemaking seems to require generations to achieve: Madame Philippine Rothschild noted that it is easy once you know how—"it is just the first 200 years that are difficult" (Anderson 2004: 12). That continuity of tradition has been almost lost in the CEEC; and the transition to market-based wine production, while continuing, has been difficult (e.g., Noev 2006).

Examining the potential role of wine as a cultural good in the CEEC does not guarantee the "second miracle" of potential profitability of the CEEC wine industry relative to other investment opportunities, but it is a perspective that might increase the appeal of state support for it.

## WINE PRODUCTION IN THE CEEC

In an early edition of his *Wine Buyer's Guide* (1989), Parker used 10 of the *Guide*'s 944 pages to cover Argentina, Chile, Greece, Switzerland, the United Kingdom, Lebanon, New Zealand, Bulgaria, and Yugoslavia (which included Slovenia, Croatia, and Macedonia) with the latter two countries receiving less than a page of text combined. In his latest, seventh edition (2008) containing 1513 pages, Argentina (15 pages), Chile (11 pages), and New Zealand (9 pages) have their own chapters; and Greece, Lebanon, and the United Kingdom have dropped from a combined total of two pages in 1989 to none. "Central Europe" now has its own chapter of 11 pages, but eight of those are devoted to Hungary (four pages on Tokaji and three on other wines) and Slovenia (about a page). He opens the chapter with a three-page section entitled "A Sleeping Giant?" in which he discusses wine production in Slovakia and the Czech Republic, Croatia, Macedonia, Romania, Montenegro, Bulgaria, Moldova, and Georgia—their history of wine production, their proximity to some of the best grape growing regions, their considerable productive capacity (for the CEEC, over 9 percent of global production—about two-thirds of the production of Argentina, Chile, Australia, and New Zealand combined in 2008), glimmers of interesting production here and there (e.g., Napa winemaker Mike Grgich's vineyards in Croatia), and a remarkably undistinguished role in today's wine market.

There is a hidden truth in Parker's chapter title: this is not far from the region—west and south of the Black Sea—where grape winemaking probably began (Johnson 1989). This region was a giant in wine production historically (e.g., Romania's industry dates back about 4,000 years and is now one of Europe's largest (Johnson 2009: 218), Bohemia's production dates since the ninth century (Johnson 2003: 205) but has been almost dormant since early in the last century). In acknowledging the importance of the region in the history of wine, Parker states that "a considerable number of important Central European wine-growing countries . . . straddle borders with Austria, Germany, Italy, or one another, in what was once practically a sea of vines running from the Alps and the foothills of the Carpathians to the Black Sea" (Parker 2008: 1421). Moreover, some of the celebrities and pioneers of modern winemaking have come from this region (Napa Valley pioneers Miljenko "Mike" Grgich from Croatia,

Russian André Tchelistcheff trained in Czechoslovakia and France, Curin and Kupljen Jozhe from Slovenia). However, events of the last century effectively shut down the tradition of quality winemaking in much of the CEEC—in particular, the regions that fell under Soviet domination after World War II. This region has traditionally produced a significant share of global wine output; but, with a few exceptions, its distinguished wines are a small share of its total production.

If the CEEC were trapped with its current constraints on, say, wine production and marketing, then it would remain undistinguished as a region and, in the views expressed above, would not warrant further attention. The global supply of undistinguished beverage wine exceeds demand. The current market seems to be chasing an "international taste", but that is an intensely competitive market, and the CEEC lacks some of the advantages such as low labor costs of other regions such as Latin America and even China and scale economies in Australia and Western Europe.

The CEEC's comparative advantage lies in producing the wines that reflect its culture and its indigenous varietals, but those hoping to produce distinguished wines at competitive prices face significant obstacles not found in many other producing areas with such significant potential—for example, difficulties in contract enforcement and the challenge to economies of scale represented by fragmented land ownership (for Bulgaria, Zaharieva, Gorton, and Lingard 2003, 2004, and Noev 2006; for Romania, Noev 2007). Some signs of excellence have emerged, but the record is mixed.

Table 8.1 provides crude but readily available information on the number of noteworthy wine producers in the region as judged by Hugh Johnson who writes regularly on the global wine market and is one of the foremost critics reporting on worldwide market developments. The data indicate the number of wine producers in each of the countries in the CEEC cited by Johnson in his useful annual *Pocket Wine Book* (formerly *Pocket Encyclopedia of Wine*) as well as their quality according to Johnson's four-star rating system, with four being the best. Reflecting information from the year prior to the title year (e.g., 2008–2009 data in the *2010 Pocket Wine Book*), the data are taken from every sixth year, starting with 1990–1991—a time by which almost all former Soviet satellites had established official independence from Soviet control but had not adapted their wine industries to the change in regimes.

Several interesting results emerge. First, while Austria was initially considered among the CEEC and had to overcome its glycol additive scandal in 1985, its industry was prominent enough by 1997 to warrant its own chapter. Second, other CEE countries had noteworthy wine production soon after "the changes" of 1989–1991, but Austria had moved well ahead

*Table 8.1  Noteworthy CEEC wine producers over time*

| Year | Country | Number* | Stars**:0.0 | 1.0 | 1.5 | 2.0 | 2.5 | 3.0 | 3.5 | 4.0 | Cited*** |
|---|---|---|---|---|---|---|---|---|---|---|---|
| 1990/91 | Austria | 9 | 6 | | | | 3 | | | | 25 |
| | Hungary | 5 | 4 | | | 1 | | | | | 0 |
| | Bulgaria | 11 | 11 | | | | | | | | 0 |
| | Czechoslovakia | 0 | 0 | | | | | | | | 7 |
| | Yugoslavia | 5 | 5 | | | | | | | | 0 |
| | Romania | 2 | 2 | | | | | | | | 0 |
| 1996/97 | Austria**** | 35 | 6 | | 2 | 3 | 12 | 5 | 3 | 4 | 75 |
| | Hungary | 19 | 19 | | | | | | | | 1 |
| | Bulgaria | 11 | 11 | | | | | | | | 0 |
| | Slovenia | 8 | 8 | | | | | | | | 2 |
| | Croatia | 6 | 6 | | | | | | | | 2 |
| | Bosnia/Herz. | 0 | 0 | | | | | | | | 2 |
| | Serbia | 1 | 1 | | | | | | | | 0 |
| | Montenegro | 1 | 1 | | | | | | | | 0 |
| | Macedonia | 0 | 0 | | | | | | | | 0 |
| | Czech Republic | 0 | 0 | | | | | | | | 6 |
| | Slovakia | 0 | 0 | | | | | | | | 0 |
| | Romania | 6 | 6 | | | | | | | | 0 |
| 2002/03 | Austria**** | 34 | 3 | | 2 | 2 | 5 | 15 | 2 | 5 | 81 |
| | Hungary | 27 | 26 | | | | 1 | | | | 19 |
| | Bulgaria | 22 | 10 | | | 11 | 1 | | | | 0 |
| | Slovenia | 21 | | | | 10 | 2 | 8 | 1 | | 9 |
| | Croatia | 13 | | 3 | 1 | 4 | | 5 | | | 7 |
| | Bosnia/Herz. | 0 | | | | | | | | | 2 |
| | Serbia | 0 | | | | | | | | | 0 |

Continuation of table (rotated on page):

| Year | Country | | | | | | | Cited |
|---|---|---|---|---|---|---|---|---|
| | Montenegro | 1 | | | | | | 0 |
| | Macedonia | 0 | | | | | | 3 |
| | Czech Republic | 0 | | | | | | 11 |
| | Slovakia | 0 | | | | | | 0 |
| | Romania | 8 | | | | | | 0 |
| 2008/09 | Austria**** | 86 | 23 | 8 | 14 | 3 | 25 | 12 | 78 |
| | Hungary | 36 | 5 | 1 | 2 | 12 | 12 | 1 | 44 |
| | Bulgaria | 29 | 4 | 5 | 10 | 2 | 1 | | 0 |
| | Slovenia | 32 | 1 | 1 | 12 | 4 | 13 | 1 | 13 |
| | Croatia | 13 | | 2 | 3 | 2 | 5 | | 19 |
| | Bosnia/Herz. | 0 | | | | | | | 2 |
| | Serbia | 3 | 3 | | | | | | 0 |
| | Montenegro | 3 | 3 | | | | | | 0 |
| | Macedonia | 7 | | 5 | 1 | | | | 0 |
| | Czech Republic | 0 | | | | | | | 0 |
| | Slovakia | 0 | | | | | | | 20 |
| | Romania | 18 | 7 | 3 | 3 | 3 | | | 7 |

*Notes:*

*Number of producers with their own entries in each country's section of the book. If a country has no such entries, Johnson provides an overview of the country's industry, noting producers, estates, and growers worth watching. The "Cited" column indicates the number of such citations.

**If given a range of stars (e.g., "*–**"), its star designation is the mean of the endpoints.

***The number of market supply participants cited who do not warrant their own entry.

****Austria was formerly included in the chapter "Central and Southeast Europe"; it had its own chapter in the 1998 edition (1996–1997 data) and following.

*Sources:* Johnson, *Pocket Encyclopedia of Wine* (1991, 1997), *Pocket Wine Book* (2003, 2009).

of this peer group in both number and quality of production 20 years later: it had about 60 percent as many producers as the rest of the region combined and considerably more top-rated producers. Moreover, its entries increased over 150 percent between 2003 and 2009 while the rest of the region increased by a little over 50 percent. Third, the other CEE countries have a growing number of important producers, but the development has been uneven and relatively slow. Bulgaria, Croatia, Hungary, and Slovenia have shown steady improvement in the number and quality of producers: their noteworthy production is small, but it leaves behind their CEEC neighbors. Given their historic importance, the lack of noteworthy Czech and Slovak producers is surprising but clear, especially when we see countries like Macedonia and Romania rising to prominence. Finally, the data confirm that the region is capable of world-class wine production and that its industry is growing and improving. However, given its size and history, it seems underdeveloped—a "sleeping giant" indeed.

The contrast in their development between the Austrian industry and the rest of the CEEC reflects, in part, the combined legacy of the years of economic depression, war, and Soviet domination. The Austrian industry has thrived because of the country's relative prosperity over the period as well as its freedom from the institutional upheavals of communism (e.g., land ownership, control of the size and composition of production by a central authority) and the virtual extinction of rewards for quality instead of quantity (e.g., Zaharieva, Gorton, and Lingard (2004) on Bulgaria). Notable CEE producers illustrate what can be accomplished when those burdens are overcome.

## IS THE CHOICE STRAIGHTFORWARD?

Aylward's analysis distinguishes two paths for Australian producers with a clear recommendation to move from a mass-market beverage to an artisanal orientation along with corresponding changes in commercial policy and institutions. The success of such a supply side adjustment depends upon not only the appeal of the argument to suppliers but also demand conditions. An industry dominated by firms which are indifferent between producing wine and cola may not be receptive, but it is likely to be more receptive if the market conditions are appealing.

Australia's reputation includes efficient production and distribution and effective marketing; and the export market has been willing to pay premium prices for premium Australian wines. A primary challenge is re-shaping consumer expectations and nurturing a reputation for "the greatness" of Australian wines in a country whose familiar wines have not been synonymous with that. Fortunately, houses such as Henschke, Penfolds, and Yarra Yering have been producing outstanding wines for decades so there is some record of "iconic" wines.

Similar questions—and more—arise when considering CEE wines as cultural goods. If one looks back far enough, one finds a greater tradition of winemaking in the CEEC than in Australia—but one must look far back. Iconic wines like Tokaji have survived, but that market is limited. The region has a tradition of exporting—primarily to former Soviet and Western European markets—but only for entry-level, beverage wines of undistinguished quality. The best wines from the region represent such a small share of production, have appeared so recently, and generally resemble wines more associated with other places (e.g., northeastern Italy, Austria) that it will take time for them to carry the reputation of the "great wines of Central and Eastern Europe". Moreover, the standard of living in the region is sufficiently low that, with the exception of Tokaji (Szakál 2009) perhaps, local demand may not contribute significantly to sustaining the market.

Robert Parker (2008) speculates that Slovenia may be "on the cusp of reclaiming fame" because "it is turning out the most interesting wines and had advanced farthest in the direction of sophisticated methods of growing, vinification, and marketing" (Parker 2008: 1424). However, he acknowledges that even this most promising industry still carries "the burdensome legacy of political turbulence and four decades of controlled, socialist economy." Gorton, White, and Dumitrashko (2005) report the case of a Moldovan winery that implemented improvements in procurement, technology, and marketing; and increased its exports of premium wines to neighboring (former Soviet) markets significantly, but one cannot extrapolate from its limited experience. The success of a "cultural good" strategy is likely to rely upon support from the public sector.

## A VIABLE WINE INDUSTRY

Challenging European tradition, the New World has found a niche by producing flavorful, approachable, reliable wines that are easy to understand but often undistinguished. Perhaps it is worth competing in that market, but that will not build a reputation that leads to a profitable following where aficionados are willing to pay premium prices for the distinctive products of the region. Aylward's argument suggests two strategies for survival—or, in the case of the CEEC, for emergence. The first is based upon product differentiation and requires that producers have enough monopoly power to sustain profitability. In the sense that they emphasize the differences among wines—for example, their reflection of place—they reduce the substitutability of goods. Goods from different producers are no longer perfect substitutes, demand for them becomes less price elastic, and therefore producers have some ability to choose price. They are not price takers whose only choice is what and when to sell as with beverage wine.

Producers of cultural products have some degree of monopoly power because of the inherent differentiation of their products, but low barriers to entry mean that such industries are typically monopolistically competitive which is problematic because of the persistent challenge to profitability. Neither this market structure nor the highly competitive, large scale production of beverage wine suggests a promising future.

As an alternative strategy, a cultural good can justify public sector support based upon at least two market failures: (1) left to the marketplace, cultural good production is inefficiently low because consumers undervalue it (externality) and (2) the public goods nature of some of the benefits (Towse 2010: 542)—in the case of wine, some of the public benefits of a thriving wine industry. While also intended to encourage rationalization of the industry, EU subsidies to the wine industry—relevant for members Hungary, Bulgaria, Romania, Slovenia, Czech Republic, and Slovakia—make sense in this light (http://ec.europe.eu/agriculture/capreform/wine/index_en.htm). Eventually, EU candidates Croatia, Macedonia, and Montenegro might qualify for such support with membership; but the industries in Bosnia and Herzegovina and Serbia—among the smallest and least distinguished in Table 8.1—must depend upon national resources until or unless they qualify for EU membership.

What is an outline of public sector support? A key to Austria's recovery from the glycol scandal was the implementation of strict government controls over wine production and labeling (http://www.austrianwine.com/facts-figures/wine-law/). In addition, the industry has benefitted from cooperation among area growers, which might include state cooperation, and a strong domestic market of relatively affluent consumers (Parker 2008: 43). Government oversight of the industry is an option in each country, but producer cooperation either with officials or with each other is more difficult to expect. Also, the lower standards of living relative to Western Europe weaken support from the domestic consumer market.

A plan, some of which has been underway for some time, might allow for the following:

1. Many of the distinctive, indigenous grapes are already under cultivation—for example, kekfrankos (esp. Hungary), saperavi

(esp. Georgia, Ukraine, Moldova), St. Laurent, furmint (esp. Hungary, Slovenia), traminer, gruner veltliner, and some varieties of riesling. If they have not been introduced already, other international varietals may warrant cultivation because they are valuable for blending purposes and have proven consistently to be popular and relatively reliable (e.g., riesling, cabernet sauvignon, merlot).

2. Expecting that domestic agricultural expertise exists already, it is worthwhile to import international technical expertise in enology, production, and marketing. The strategies of other recent successful ventures in markets like Australia and—perhaps more enlightening in the region—Austria—should be instructive.

3. As with many consumer goods, the wine market is inherently fickle so one must be prepared for mixed success. No one produced and distributed Marlborough (NZ) sauvignon blanc until New Zealand producers did—and it has been a success that others hope to copy (e.g., Chile, Sicily). However, wines from others' varietals are most likely to be, at best, good copies of others' successes. Improving the quality of production with indigenous varietals—which may be indigenous and successful elsewhere (e.g., riesling in Germany and Austria)—seems like a promising route to a profitable market niche.

4. The industry is particularly susceptible to the significant risks inherent in agriculture—for example, the natural risks of weather and disease, "good news is bad news" (bumper crops move prices downward—though durable crops like ageworthy wine allow producers to manage supply more profitably) which increases the need for public sector support.

5. This industry requires considerable initial outlays for agricultural experimentation, enological consulting, capital investment, and marketing. Given the cultural value of this product, one hopes that the public sector—either domestic or EU—will provide temporary support, realizing that the value in this sector lies not only in production itself but also in the larger cultural contribution and related industries such as tourism.

Perhaps a good example of a productive approach in this market has been the Slovenians. They have shown that they can produce internationally competitive wines from a combination of indigenous and international varietals; their greatest remaining challenge seems to be marketing. While one of the smallest countries in the region, Slovenia has one of the few successful wine industries. It is probably not simply a coincidence that Slovenia shares borders with the two prominent winemaking areas of Austria and northeastern Italy, the Soviet grip on Yugoslavia was relatively light, and Slovenia is among the most affluent countries in the CEEC.

The suggestion of state support may seem facile. Following upon the comparison discussed earlier, the food industry is certainly viable without a call for help as a cultural industry. The global wine industry continues without a designation as a cultural industry.

Several responses come to mind. First, the industry in the CEEC has encountered a remarkable series of challenges over several decades; the data in Table 8.1 indicate its persistent difficulty in keeping up or catching up with its Austrian neighbor during a period when other regions of the world have changed the face of global wine production. Second, while the global wine and food industries do not generally receive special treatment as "cultural industries", they benefit from government support in many countries (e.g., production subsidies, price supports, widespread protection from imports, subsidies for promotion). Moreover, pockets of production protect traditional methods—perhaps for cultural reasons and perhaps with government support—when, arguably, less costly methods are available (e.g., vineyards on the steep slopes of the Mosel, requirement of hand-harvesting in Champagne): the market value of the preservation of such methods has not been demonstrated. Third, programs such as UNESCO's support for World Heritage Sites remind us of the world's recognition of and significant support for such places and activities. Finally, in the presence of a market failure such as externality, the existence of an industry is not synonymous with allocative efficiency: notwithstanding its considerable size, the global food industry may still be inefficiently small relative to its size if its cultural importance were fully acknowledged—and similarly for the CEEC wine industry.

## CONCLUSION

Chapter 7 discussed one of the fundamental difficulties with the nature of fine wine that complicates our ability to treat it simply as another product traded in markets. The focus was primarily a closer examination of the consumer's ability to form a knowledgeable willingness to pay. The emphasis in this chapter is related but specifies a broader context in which the difficulty of knowing and valuing wine occurs. Fine wine is not simply a complicated, ever-changing product potentially. It can also have cultural significance beyond an individual's valuation that risks being diminished or lost if we rely only upon market valuation to determine the size and significance of the industry. We have considered that added significance in the context of both the emergence and changing fortunes of the Australian wine industry and the prospect of encouraging the re-emergence of fine wine production in Central and Eastern Europe.

Recent experience in the global wine industry demonstrates that regions can change their relative importance by identifying and serving new and underserved markets. However, the Australian experience demonstrates the significance of strategies that may be short-sighted in a market where consumer tastes can mature more quickly than an industry's ability to serve it. Its recent history helps one understand the unrealized potential of wines from Central and Eastern Europe, but their continued underperformance leaves one looking for reasons and ways out. It may be tempting to follow the New World example in trying to return the CEEC wine industry to its former prominence, but the beverage wine market seems adequately served by current producers.

Because of its historic role in the world market and the distinctive wines it can produce, the CEEC industry has cultural value that is undervalued but could provide a more enduring basis for its re-emergence. Of course, the case for wine as a cultural good is not limited to this region, but this region stands out as one whose wines are underrepresented in the global market, especially given the comparison with the more successful Austrian industry.

These days, wine production tends to be either large or small scale, and profitability remains a rare achievement: small-scale producers are as often driven by an almost artistic zeal as by a plan for sustained profits. Given the inherent vulnerability of both monopolistic competition and mass market large-scale production, the nature of cultural goods and the public's tendency to undervalue them argues for an increased role of the public sector in subsidizing and promoting the CEEC wine industry. Whether or not one agrees with the prescription of public support—a convenient alternative for an industry that struggles and an alternative that is compelling generally among cultural industries—it is difficult to deny wine's suitability as a cultural good.

# NOTES

1. This chapter has been adapted with the permission of the publisher Taylor & Francis from my paper: Marks (2011), "Competitiveness and the Market for Central and Eastern European Wines: A Cultural Good in the Global Wine Market", *Journal of Wine Research* 22(3) (December, 2011), 245–263. Available at: http://www.tandfonline.com/doi/full/10.1080/09571264.2011.622517.
2. A more explicit endorsement of wine as a cultural good has come from personal correspondence with Professor Throsby: "[Wine] has the hallmark characteristics that have come to be accepted as defining a 'cultural good'" (personal correspondence, May 16, 2011). In particular, he cites three widely accepted characteristics of cultural goods,

namely (1) embody creativity, (2) convey some symbolic meaning, and (3) embody at least potentially some form of intellectual property.

3.  The characterization of wine as a cultural good is distinct from the idea that most or all goods have "cultural content". In this sense, a cultural good is a technical category of goods with defined production and consumption characteristics drawn from economic theory (analogous to the technical definitions of public goods, private goods, durable goods, club goods, etc.): some of these characteristics contribute to market failure and argue for state support as indicated later in the discussion. The cultural role and meaning of consumption is the basis for a large literature drawn from anthropology, sociology, and economics which explores questions of the meaning of consumption (e.g., status, marking, public versus private) (see, for example, Douglas and Isherwood 1996) and, in focusing upon why people buy, is less concerned with market failure. As of now, these two approaches to the relationship between culture and goods seem to have developed largely independently.

4.  In the context of the global wine market, we shall consider the wine-producing CEEC to be the six former Soviet-dominated countries that have joined the European Union (EU) (Bulgaria, Czech Republic, Hungary, Slovakia, Slovenia, and Romania) and five Balkan countries (Bosnia and Herzegovina, Croatia, Macedonia, Serbia, and Montenegro). Excluding Greece, Malta, and Cyprus, these are the countries included in Hugh Johnson's coverage of "Central and Southeast Europe" in his annual *Pocket Wine Book*. In 2008, these countries accounted for about 5 percent of global wine production. However, Bosnia and Herzegovina, Serbia, and Montenegro had very small production; and, of the remaining countries, only Slovenia had increased production (+17.2 percent) over the period 2004–2008 (http://www.wineinstitute.org/resources/worldstatistics/article87).

# 9. Conclusion

It is not unique to our profession, but economists are drawn to anomalies. Anomalies are often in the eye of the beholder—not everyone has the same experience of normalcy and consistency—but we certainly appreciate hearing about them and they often turn into scholarship. The market for lemons is anomalous, and a number of stories in *Freakonomics* are anomalous. A section of one of our most accessible professional journals, the *Journal of Economic Perspectives*, has a section dedicated to anomalies— the site of one of the first appearances of Richard Thaler's discussion of the winner's curse.

Many are initially drawn to an interest in wine in the usual way through social events with peers and elders that show a correlation between wine and interesting and rich experiences. They may decide that the correlation is not simply a result of narcosis: there is something special about wine. With the encouragement of some mentors, I pursued an interest in wine and began to notice some anomalies. For example, relative to any other menu item, wine is a significant part of the interior decoration of a surprising number of better restaurants in North America and Europe—and it has its own menu. Given all that they could choose to highlight about their restaurant, they highlight wine. Beer and spirits are not even close; meat and fish are probably a distant second. Also, as a gift to those of us who must work at small talk, it is difficult to find people who do not have some interest in wine, even teetotalers. Given its cultural content, almost everyone is curious about wine.

Finally, at one of the early conferences of the American Association of Wine Economists (AAWE), Orley Ashenfelter addressed the opening session and said something ironic to the effect that, unlike other academic conferences, we would have a good time at this one. Having attended conferences for many years and having some sense of how many more he had attended, that got my attention, and he was correct: the conference was a highlight. The wine economics community of scholars and its conferences are indeed special—even anomalously good.

The purpose of this book has been to show a strong and compelling connection between two challenging subjects—wine and economics. Knowledge of either is always incomplete but can improve. We have covered some of the fundamental connections with elementary analysis to make the connection accessible. Just as my interest in wine developed as a byproduct of my career-long interest in economics reflecting the influence of a number of memorable teachers, some of my students develop a more serious interest in economics through an initial interest in beverages. Either way, the spillover has been worthwhile. The basics of comparative advantage, demand, supply, and the operation of markets are sound and useful to know beyond the application to wine transactions. The ability of concepts like elasticity and consumer surplus and rent seeking to illuminate the way the world works and better understanding and decision making go beyond the applications we have discussed.

Aside from encouraging analytic skill, the discussion has tried to highlight several ideas:

- The markets connected to wine share many of the characteristics of markets generally;
- Learning economics through studying wine economics exposes one to a wide range of standard economic analysis as well as some specialized subjects;
- The international nature of the wine market adds significant and interesting complications—for example, the importance of exchange rates, currency areas, and various forms of protectionism;
- The information challenge in fine wine markets is substantial, and the robustness of the market despite the risks associated with that challenge says something about the importance of wine;
- Information problems help explain some of the anomalous characteristics of wine markets such as the perception that more expensive wine is better wine;
- Wine markets raise a number of important issues in neuroeconomics such as the challenge of taste memory and the formation of willingness to pay;
- Wine is one of a short list of subjects that draws a particularly close and illuminating connection between economics and culture: it is an appealing topic to introduce one to the world of cultural goods;
- The concept of *terroir* has cultural content and highlights the importance of place in culture: it provides a challenge to the meaning of and support for globalized markets;
- Discussion of wine and philosophy is lively and overlaps with wine economics in areas such as consumer behavior and the challenge of measurement.

This is a sample of themes that have arisen in the preceding chapters.

We have neglected a number of important topics that only enhance the special nature of these markets. For example, fundamental changes in global weather patterns could alter the distribution and quality of wine production in the future (e.g., Ashenfelter and Storchmann 2014). Investments in fine wine can yield respectable returns as an asset class and have been the subject of a sizeable finance-oriented literature (e.g., survey in Storchmann 2012).

The remarkable values for some bottles have stimulated a notorious and interesting market for counterfeit wine (e.g., Wallace 2009) that has become a focus of not only litigation (e.g., Wallace 2009; Hellman 2014) but also research (Holmberg 2010). Aside from its sensational appeal, the topic reminds us of questions of authenticity, legitimacy, and consumer knowledge discussed in Chapters 6 and 7.

In addition, as just one example from the book, the analysis of the impact of government and the proper role of government in wine markets deserves far more attention than we gave it as does the uneasy relationship between alcohol and civic life and responsibility.

This book was written, in part, to convey enthusiasm for this growing field in hopes of convincing some readers to look for wine economics scholarship published through various journals—it sometimes makes it to the popular press (http://www.wine-economics.org/about/in-the-news/)—and to see and learn more about the economics in so many of the stories that come from the world of wine.

# Bibliography

Akerlof, G. (1970), 'The Market for Lemons: Qualitative Uncertainty and the Market Mechanism', *Quarterly Journal of Economics*, **84**(3) (August), 488–500.

Alcock, J. (2009), *Animal Behavior: An Evolutionary Approach*, Sunderland, MA: Sinauer Associates.

Ali, H., S. Lecocq, and M. Visser (2010), 'The Impact of Gurus: Parker Grades and *en primeur* Wine Prices', *Journal of Wine Economics*, **5**(1), 22–39.

Anderson, K. (2004), 'Australia', in K. Anderson (ed.), *The World's Wine Markets: Globalization at Work*, Cheltenham, UK and Northampton, MA, USA: Edward Elgar Publishing, 252–286.

Anderson, K. and S. Nelgen (2014), *Global Wine Markets, 1961–2009: A Statistical Compendium*, Adelaide: University of Adelaide Press.

Anderson, K. and D. Wood (2006), 'What Determines the Future Value of An Icon Wine? New Evidence from Australia', *Journal of Wine Economics*, **1**, 141–161.

Anderson, K., D. Norman, and G. Wittwer (2004), 'The Global Picture', in K. Anderson (ed.), *The World's Wine Markets: Globalization at Work*, Cheltenham, UK and Northampton, MA, USA: Edward Elgar Publishing, 14–58.

Ashenfelter, O. (Various years 1986–95), *Liquid Assets*, Self-published.

Ashenfelter, O. (2010), 'Review of *Last Call: The Rise and Fall of Prohibition* by Daniel Okrent', *Journal of Wine Economics*, **5**(2), 339–341.

Ashenfelter, O. and G. Jones (2013), 'The Demand for Expert Opinion: Bordeaux Wine', *Journal of Wine Economics*, **8**(3) (Winter), 285–293.

Ashenfelter, O. and K. Storchmann (2014), 'Wine and Climate Change', *American Association of Wine Economists Working Paper No. 152* (March), unpublished.

Ashton, R. (2013), 'Is There Consensus Among Wine Quality Ratings of Prominent Critics? An Empirical Analysis of Red Bordeaux, 2004–2010', *Journal of Wine Economics*, **8**(2) (Fall), 225–234.

Ashton, R. (2014), 'Wine as an Experience Good: Price Versus Enjoyment in Blind Tastings of Expensive and Inexpensive Wines', *Journal of Wine Economics*, **9**(2) (August), 171–182.

Asimov, E. (2005), 'The Judgment of Paris, This Time at Home', retrieved from: http://www.nytimes.com/2005/11/23/dining/23pour.html?ref=bordeaux&_r=0 (accessed October 2, 2014).

Aylward, D. (2008), 'Towards a Cultural Economy Paradigm for the Australian Wine Industry', *Prometheus*, **26**(4) (December), 373–385.

Baye, M. (2010), *Managerial Economics and Business Strategy*, Seventh Edition, New York: McGraw-Hill Irwin.

Buchanan, J., G. Tullock, and R. Tollison (1980), *Toward a Theory of the Rent-Seeking Society*, College Station: Texas A & M University Press.

Carvajal, D. (2008), 'France Looks to Expand Champagne Production', *New York Times* (June 13).

Chamovitz, D. (2012), *What A Plant Knows: A Field Guide to the Senses*, New York: Scientific American/Farrar, Straus and Giroux.

Cicchetti, D. and A. Cicchetti (2009), 'Wine Rating Scales: Assessing Their Utility for Producers, Consumers, and Oenologic Researchers', *International Journal of Wine Research*, **1**, 73–83.

Coase, R. (1937), 'The Nature of the Firm', *Economica* (New Series), **4**(16) (November), 386–405.

Colman, T. (2008), *Wine Politics: How Governments, Environmentalists, Mobsters, and Critics Influence the Wines We Drink*, Berkeley, CA: University of California Press.

Cyr, D., J. Kushner, and T. Ogwang (2014), 'The Changing Size Distribution of California's North Coast Wineries', *Journal of Wine Economics*, **9**(1), 51–61.

Darwin, C. (1964), *On the Origin of Species: A Facsimile of the First Edition*, Cambridge: Harvard University Press.

Darwin, C. and F. Darwin (2013), *The Power of Movement in Plants: Primary Source Edition*, Charleston: Nabu Press.

Derbyshire, D. (2013), 'Wine Tasting: It's Junk Science', *The Observer: The New Review* (June 23), 20.

des Gachons, C., C. Leeuwen, T. Tominaga, J. Soyer, J-P Guadillère, and D. Dubourdieu (2005), 'Influence of Water and Nitrogen Deficit on Fruit Ripening and Aroma Potential of Vitis Vinifera L cv Sauvignon Blanc in Field Conditions', *Journal of the Science of Food and Agriculture*, **85**(1), 73–85.

Douglas, M. and B. Isherwood (1996), *The World of Goods: Towards an Anthropology of Consumption*, London: Routledge.

Esposito, S. (2008), *Passion on the Vine*, New York: Broadway Books.

Farrar, J., J. Young Jr., L. Moreaux, J. Werth, and R. Poole (2001), 'Clinical Importance of Changes in Chronic Pain Intensity Measured on an 11-Point Numerical Pain Rating Scale', *Pain*, **94**, 149–158.

Galmarley Ltd. (2014), '*Gold Fix*', retrieved from: http://www. bullionvault.com/guide/gold/Gold-fix#section-Gold-fix-IsTheGoldFix Fair (accessed May 12, 2014).

Gelles, D. (2014), 'An Investment in the Cellar, With a Nice Bouquet', *Special Section: Wealth. New York Times* (February 2011), F3.

Gergaud, O. and V. Ginsburgh (2010), 'Natural Endowments, Production Technologies, and the Quality of Wines in Bordeaux: Does Terroir Matter?', *Journal of Wine Economics*, **5**(1), 3–21.

Gilbey, W. (1869), *Treatise on Wines and Spirits of the Principal Producing Countries*, London: Walter and Alfred Gilbey, retrieved from: www. books.google.com/ (accessed April 26, 2014).

Ginsburgh, V., M. Monzak, and A. Monzak (2013), 'Red Wines of Medoc: What is Wine Tasting Worth?', *Journal of Wine Economics*, **8**(2) (Fall), 159–188.

Goldstein, R. (2008a), *The Wine Trials*, Austin: Fearless Critic Media.

Goldstein, R., J. Almenberg, A. Dreber, J. Emerson, A. Herschkowitsch, and J. Katz (2008b), 'Do More Expensive Wines Taste Better? Evidence from a Large Sample of Blind Tastings', *Journal of Wine Economics*, **3**(1), 1–9.

Goode, J. (2007), 'Wine and the Brain', in B.C. Smith (ed.), *Questions of Taste: The Philosophy of Wine*, Oxford: Oxford University Press, 79–98.

Goodhue, R., D.M. Heien, H. Lee, and D.A. Sumner (2002), 'Contract Use Widespread in Wine Grape Industry', *California Agriculture*, **56**(3) (May–June), 97–102.

Goodhue, R., D.M. Heien, H. Lee, and D.A. Sumner (2003), 'Contracts and Quality in the California Winegrape Industry', *Review of Industrial Organization*, 23(3–4) (December), 267–282.

Gorton, M., J. White, and M. Dumitrashko (2005), 'Applying the Clinical Inquiry Approach to Understand and Facilitate Enterprise Restructuring in Transitional Economies: A Case Study from the Moldovan Wine Industry', *Systematic Practice and Action Research*, **18**, 35–52.

Grahm, R. (2008), 'The Soul of Wine: Digging for Meaning', in F. Allhoff (ed.), *Wine and Philosophy: A Symposium on Thinking and Drinking*, Malden: Blackwell Publishing, 219–224.

Green, W. (2011), *Econometric Analysis*, Seventh Edition, New York: Prentice Hall.

Greenberg, D. and M. Shroder (2004), *The Digest of Social Experiments*, Washington, DC: The Urban Institute Press.

Gruenewald, P., W. Ponicki, H. Holder, and A. Romelsjö (2006), 'Alcohol Prices, Beverage Quality, and the Demand for Alcohol: Quality Substitutions and Price Elasticities', *Alcoholism: Clinical and Experimental Research*, **30**(1) (January), 96–105.

Gunyon, R.E.H. (1971), *The Wines of Central and South-Eastern Europe*, New York: Hippocrene Books.

Hadj Ali, H. and C. Nauges (2007), 'The Pricing of Experience Goods: The Example of en Primeur Wine', *American Journal of Agricultural Economics*, **89**(1) (February), 91–103.

Hadj Ali, H., S. Lecocq, and M. Visser (2008), 'The Impact of Gurus: Parker Grades and en primeur Wine Prices', *Journal of Wine Economics*, **5**(1) (Spring), 22–39.

Handford, M. and M. Srinivasan (2014), 'Sideways Walking: Preferred is Slow, Slow is Optimal, and Optimal is Expensive', *Biology Letters*, **10**(1), 20131006.

Hanson, R. (2008), 'Women Collectors', *Decanter* (June 9), retrieved from: http://www.decanter.com/people-and-places/wine-articles/485744/women-collectors (accessed October 2, 2014).

Hart, C., C. Ksir, and O. Ray (2008), *Drugs, Society, and Human Behavior*, Thirteenth Edition, New York: McGraw-Hill.

Heien, D. and P. Martin (2002), 'Inside the Bottle: The Wine Business', *Choices*, **17**(3), 30–33.

Hellman, P. (2014), 'Wine Counterfeiter Rudy Kurniawan's Sentencing is Delayed', retrieved from: http://www.winespectator.com/webfeature/show/id/50046?utm_source=rss&utm_medium=rss&utm_campaign=wine-counterfeiter-rudy-kurniawans-sentencing-is-delayed-wine-spectator (accessed May 29, 2014).

Hermacinski, U. (2007), *The Wine Lover's Guide to Auctions*, Garden City Park: Square One Publishers.

Heymann, H. and A.C. Noble (1987), 'Descriptive Analysis of Commercial Cabernet Sauvignon Wines from California', *American Journal of Enology and Viticulture*, **38**(1), 41–44.

Hicken, M. (2012), 'BC Liquor Economics and Privatization', retrieved from: http://www.winelaw.ca/cms/index.php/news/1/228-bc-liquor-economics-a-privatization (accessed September 10, 2014).

Hodgson, R. (2009), 'How Expert Are "Expert" Wine Judges?', *Journal of Wine Economics*, **4**(2) (Winter), 233–241.

Holmberg, L. (2010), 'Wine Fraud', *International Journal of Wine Research*, 2 (October 25), 105–113.

Johnson, H. (1989), *Vintage: The Story of Wine*, New York: Simon & Schuster.

Johnson, H. (1991, 1997), *Pocket Encyclopedia of Wine*, New York: Simon & Schuster.

Johnson, H. (2003, 2009), *Pocket Wine Book*, London: Octopus Publishing Group (Hachette Livre UK).

Klimmek, M. (2013), 'On the Information Content of Wine Notes: Some New Algorithms?', *Journal of Wine Economics*, **8**(3) (Winter), 318–334.

Kramer, M. (2008), 'The notion of *terroir*', in F. Allhoff (ed.), *Wine and Philosophy: A Symposium on Thinking and Drinking*, Malden: Blackwell Publishing, 225–234.

Krugman, P.R. (1993), 'The Narrow and Broad Arguments for Free Trade', *American Economic Review*, **83**(2). Papers and Proceedings of the 105th Annual Meeting of the American Economic Association (May, 1993), 362–366.

Krugman, P.R., M. Obstfeld, and M. Melitz (2015), *International Trade: Theory and Policy*, Tenth Edition, Upper Saddle River: Prentice Hall (Pearson).

Lamb, R. and E. Mittelberger (1974), *In Celebration of Wine and Life*, New York: Drake Publishers.

Landon, S. and C.E. Smith (1998), 'Quality Expectations, Reputation, and Price', *Southern Economic Journal*, **64**(3) (January), 628–647.

Lapworth, P. and C. Sills (2011), *An Introduction to Transactional Analysis: Helping People Change*, London: Sage Publications.

Lawless, H. (1984), 'Flavor Description of White Wine by "Expert" and Nonexpert Wine Consumers', *Journal of Food Science*, **49**(1), 120–123.

Lockshin, L. and A. Corsi (2012), 'Consumer Behaviour for Wine 2.0: A Review since 2003 and Future Directions', *Wine Economics and Policy*, **1**(1) (December), 2–23.

Lockshin, L. and J. Hall (2003), 'Consumer Purchasing Behavior for Wine: What We Know and Where We Are Going', *Proceedings of the International Wine Marketing Colloquium*, Adelaide.

Mankiw, G. (2015), *Principles of Economics*, Seventh Edition, Stamford: Cengage.

Mariani, J. (2014), 'What Price Glory? You Don't Always Get What You Pay For', retrieved from: http://www.huffingtonpost.com/john-mariani/what-price-glory-you-dont_b_5605818.html (accessed July 21, 2014).

Marks, D. (2009), 'Who Pays Brokers' Commissions? Evidence from Fine Wine Auctions', *Oxford Economic Papers*, **61** (March), 761–775.

Marks, D. (2011), 'Competitiveness and the Market for Central and Eastern European Wines: A Cultural Good in the Global Wine Market', *Journal of Wine Research*, **22**(3) (December), 245–263.

Marks, D. (2013), '"In Vino Veritas"—But What In Truth Is In the Bottle? Experience Goods, Fine Wine Ratings, and Wine Knowledge'. Presented at the 7th Annual Conference of the American Association of Wine Economists (AAWE), Stellenbosch, South Africa, June 2013.

Marks, D. and D. Welsch (forthcoming), 'Asking Prices, Selling Prices, and Anchoring Effects: The Elusive Relationship of Pre-Sale Estimates to Winning Bids in Fine Wine Auctions', *International Journal of Wine Business Research*.

McCoy, E. (2005), *The Emperor of Wine: The Rise of Robert M. Parker, Jr. and the Reign of American Taste*, New York: Ecco (HarperCollins).

McCoy, E. (2009), 'Cult Wine Crowd Drops off Elite Mailing List with $350 Cabs' (March 30), retrieved from: http://www.bloomberg.com/apps/news?sid=a8JBRGwER1Mo&pid=newsarchive (accessed October 2, 2014).

Medina, J.J. (2008), 'The biology of recognition memory', *Psychiatric Times* (May), 13–16.

Meloni, G. and J. Swinnen (2013), 'The Political Economy of European Wine Regulations', *Journal of Wine Economics*, **8**(3), 244–284.

Mundell, R. (1961), 'A Theory of Optimum Currency Areas', *American Economic Review*, **51** (November), 509–517.

Nelson, J. (2013), 'Robust Demand Elasticities for Wine and Distilled Spirits: Meta-Analysis with Corrections for Outliers and Publication Bias', *Journal of Wine Economics*, **8**(3) (Winter), 294–317.

Nelson, P. (1970), 'Information and Consumer Behavior', *Journal of Political Economy*, **78**(2) (March–April), 311–329.

Noev, N. (2006), 'The Bulgarian Wine Sector: Policy Issues and Implications after 15 Years of Transition', *Journal of Wine Research*, **17**, 73–93.

Noev, N. (2007), 'Land, wine, and trade', *Eastern European Economics*, **45**, 76–114.

Okrent, D. (2010), *Last Call: The Rise and Fall of Prohibition*, New York: Scribners and Sons.

Olson, M. (1965), *The Logic of Collective Action: Public Goods and the Theory of Groups*, Cambridge: Harvard University Press.

O'Rourke, K. and A. Taylor (2013), 'Cross of Euros', *Journal of Economic Perspectives*, **27**(3) (Summer), 167–192.

Pareto, V., A. Montesano, A. Zanni, L. Bruni, J.S. Chipman, and M. McLure (2014), *Manual of Political Economy*, Oxford: Oxford University Press.

Parker Jr., R. (1989), *Parker's Wine Buyer's Guide*, New York: Simon & Schuster.

Parker Jr., R. (1993), *Parker's Wine Buyer's Guide*, Third Edition, New York: Fireside Books/Simon & Schuster.

Parker Jr., R. (2008), *Parker's Wine Buyer's Guide*, Seventh Edition, New York: Simon & Schuster.

Parker Jr., R. (2013), 'The Wine Advocate Rating System', retrieved from: https://www.erobertparker.com/info/legend.asp (accessed October 2, 2014).

Pellechia, T. (2008), *The Complete Idiot's Guide to Starting and Running a Winery*, New York: Alpha Books/Penguin Group.

Pew Research Center (2011), 'Muslim Population by Country', *Religion and Public Life Project* (January 27), Washington DC: Pew Research Center, retrieved from: http://www.pewforum.org/2011/01/27/table-muslim-population-by-country/ (accessed December 22, 2011).

Pitte, J-R. (2008), *Bordeaux/Burgundy: A Vintage Rivalry*, Berkeley: University of California Press.

Postman, J. (2011), 'Letter to the Editors: Alcohol in Wine', *Journal of Wine Economics*, **6**(2) (Autumn), 278–281.

Quandt, R. (2007), 'On Wine Bullshit: Some New Software?' *Journal of Wine Economics*, **2**(2), 129–135.

Rickard, B., M. Costanigro, and T. Garg (2011), 'Regulating the Availability of Beer, Wine, and Spirits in Grocery Stores: Beverage-Specific Effects on Prices, Consumption, and Traffic Fatalities', American Association of Wine Economists Working Paper No. 95 (December). Unpublished.

Robinson, J. (ed.) (1994), *The Oxford Companion to Wine*, Oxford: Oxford University Press.

Robinson, J. (1997), *Tasting Pleasure: Confessions of a Wine Lover*, New York: Viking Penguin.

Robinson, J. (2013), 'Leading the Blind', retrieved from: http://www.jancisrobinson.com/articles/a201303062.html (accessed October 2, 2014).

Rosa, S. (2013), *Le Guide Hachette des Vins 2014*, Paris: Hachette Livre.

Rosen, S. (1974), 'Hedonic Prices and Implicit Markets: Product Differentiation in Pure Competition', *Journal of Political Economy*, **82**(1) (January–February), 34–55.

Saad, L. (2012), 'Majority in US Drink Alcohol, Averaging Four Drinks per Week', retrieved from: http://www.gallup.com/poll/156770/majority-drink-alcohol-averaging-four-drinks-week.aspx (accessed April 21, 2014).

Salanié, B. (2005), *The Theory of Contracts: A Primer*, Second Edition, Cambridge: The MIT Press.

Sandel, M. (2005), *Public Philosophy: Essays on Morality in Politics*, Cambridge: Harvard University Press.

Sayre, C. (2006), 'Could Red Wine Be the Elixir of Life?' *Time* (US Edition), **168**(20) (November 13), 22.

Semba, R., L. Ferrucci, B. Bartali, M. Urpí-Sarda, R. Zamora-Ros, K. Sun, A. Cherubini, S. Bandinelli, and C. Andres-Lacueva (2014), 'Resveratrol Levels and All-Cause Mortality in Older Community-Dwelling Adults', *JAMA (Journal of the American Medical Association) Internal Medicine*. Published online May 12, 2014. doi:10.1001/jamainternmed.2014.158.

Smith, B. (2007a), *Questions of Taste: The Philosophy of Wine*, Oxford: Oxford University Press.

Smith, B. (2007b), 'Introduction', in B.C. Smith (ed.), *Questions of Taste: The Philosophy of Wine*, Oxford: Oxford University Press, xi–xvii.

Smith, B. (2007c), 'The Objectivity of Tastes and Tasting', in B.C. Smith (ed.), *Questions of Taste: The Philosophy of Wine*, Oxford: Oxford University Press, 41–77.

Smith, S. (2014), 'BC Wine Makers Put a Cork in Their Supply to Create Buzz', *Globe and Mail*, retrieved from: http://www.theglobeandmail.com/report-on-business/small-business/sb-money/cash-flow/wine-makers-put-a-cork-in-their-supply-to-create-buzz/article18771332/ (accessed May 21, 2014).

Sommers, B.J. (2008), *The Geography of Wine*, New York: Plume (Penguin).

Spencer, H. (1978), *The Principles of Ethics* (2 volumes), Indianapolis: Liberty Classics.

Stang, J. (2012), 'State's Boom in Small Wineries Is At Risk', *Crosscut.com* (July 16), retrieved from: http://crosscut.com/2012/07/16/food/109510/stang-washington-wine/ (accessed April 10, 2014).

Storchmann, K. (2012), 'Wine Economics', *Journal of Wine Economics*, **7**(1) (Spring), 1–33.

Suárez-Toste, E. (2007), 'Metaphor Inside the Wine Cellar: On the Ubiquity of Personification Schemas' *winespeak*, retrieved from: http://www.metaphorik.de/12/suarez-toste.pdf (accessed October 2, 2014).

Sullivan, P. (2012), 'Winemaking Lures the Wealthy but Not With Profits', *New York Times* (May 26), B6.

Szakál, Z. (2009), 'A Wine Market and Marketing Analysis of Wine Specialties from the Tokaj-Hegyalja Wine District', *Studies in Agricultural Economics*, **109**, 85–102.

Taber, G. (2005), *Judgment of Paris*, New York: Scribner.

Taber, G. (2007), *To Cork or Not to Cork: Tradition, Romance, Science, and the Battle for the Wine Bottle*, New York: Simon & Schuster.

Taylor, R. (2013), 'Who Gives a Flip? When High-Valued Cult Wines Tempt Buyers to Resell for A Profit', (January 10) retrieved from: http://www.winespectator.com/blogs/show/id/47895 (accessed October 2, 2014).

Thaler, R. (1994), *The Winner's Curse: Paradoxes and Anomalies of Economic Life*, Princeton: Princeton University Press.

Thornton, J. (2013), *American Wine Economics*, Berkeley: University of California Press.

Throsby, D. (2001), *Economics and Culture*, Cambridge: Cambridge University Press.

Throsby, D. (2008), 'The Creation of Value by Artists: The Case of Hector Berlioz and the *Symphonie Fantastique*', in M. Hutter and D. Throsby (eds), *Beyond Price*, Cambridge: Cambridge University Press, 75–88.

Towse, R. (2010), *A Textbook of Cultural Economics*, Cambridge: Cambridge University Press.

Tullock, G. (1967), 'The Welfare Costs of Tariffs, Monopolies, and Theft', *Western Economic Journal*, **5**(3) (June), 224–232.

Tullock, G. (1975), 'The Transitional Gains Trap', *Bell Journal of Economics*, **6**(2) (Autumn), 671–678.

US Department of Commerce (2004), *Wineries 2002*, Washington, DC: US Government Printing Office.

Vargo, S. and R. Lusch (2004), 'Evolving to a New Dominant Logic for Marketing', *Journal of Marketing*, **68** (January), 1–17.

Veale, R. and P. Quester (2008), 'Consumer Sensory Evaluations of Wine Quality: The Respective Influence of Price and Country of Origin', *Journal of Wine Economics*, **3**(1), 10–29.

Veseth, M. (2008), 'What Are Wine Enthusiasts Looking For?' *The Wine Economist* (April 5), retrieved from: http://wineeconomist. com/2008/04/05/what-are-wine-enthusiasts-looking-for/ (accessed April 21, 2014).

Veseth, M. (2009a), 'Anatomy of Australia's wine crisis', retrieved from: http://wineeconomist.com/ (accessed October 2, 2014).

Veseth, M. (2009b), 'Australia at the tipping point', retrieved from: http:// wineeconomist.com/ (accessed October 2, 2014).

Veseth, M. (2013), 'Will Imports Take Half the US Wine Market in 2025?', *The Wine Economist*, (February 19).

Visser, M. (1986), *Much Depends on Dinner*, New York: Grove Press.

Volpe, R., R. Green, D. Heien, and R Howitt (2010), 'Estimating the Supply Elasticity of California Wine Grapes Using Regional Systems of Equations', *Journal of Wine Economics*, **5**(2), 219–235.

Wallace, B. (2009), *The Billionaire's Vinegar: The Mystery of the World's Most Expensive Bottle of Wine*, New York: Three Rivers Press (Random House).

Willig, R. (1976), 'Consumer Surplus without Apology', *American Economic Review*, **66**(4), 589–597.

Yakovlev, P. and W. Guessford (2013), 'Alcohol Consumption and Political Ideology: What's Party Got to Do With It?', *Journal of Wine Economics*, **8**(3) (Winter), 335–354.

Zaharieva, E., M. Gorton, and J. Lingard (2003), 'Procurement Mechanisms and the Emergence of New Governance Structures in the CEECs: Evidence from the Bulgarian Wine Industry', *Journal of Purchasing and Supply Management*, **9**, 235–245.

Zaharieva, E., M. Gorton, and J. Lingard (2004), 'An evaluation of marketing practices and market orientation in the Bulgarian wine industry', *Post-Communist Economies*, **16**, 229–243.


## OTHER WEBSITES ACCESSED:

http://www.amazon.com
http://www.americanwinesociety.org/associations/10474/files/Wine%20 Evaluation%20chart%202010.pdf
http://arcserver2.iagt.org/vll/learnmore.aspx
http://www.austrianwine.com/facts-figures/wine-law/
http://www.bordoverview.com/?q=Decanter
http://www.bordoverview.com/?q=Robert-Parker
http://www.cellartracker.com/default.asp
http://www.chemheritage.org/discover/collections/collection-items/rare-books/dell-elixir-vitae.aspx?image=2
http://www.cinderellawine.com/
http://www.ec.europe.eu/agriculture/capreform/wine/index_en.htm
http://www.en.wikipedia.org/wiki/Glossary_of_wine_terms
https://www.erobertparker.com/info/WineAdvocate.asp
https://www.garagiste.com/
http://www.foodhistorynews.com/index.html
http://www.google.com/search?q=wine+scoring+sheet&tbm=isch&tbo =u&source=univ&sa=X&ei=RymxUYPfOeTh4AOytIHwBw&sqi= 2&ved=0CCoQsAQ&biw=1173&bih=606
http://www.hachette-vins.com/
http://www.ipcadvertising.com/ipc-brands/decanter
http://www.jancisrobinson.com/
http://www.magazine.org/insights-resources/research-publications/ trends-data/magazine-industry-facts-data/circulation-trends
http://www.mathworld.wolfram.com/IndexNumber.html
http://www.nasa.gov/mission_pages/noaa-n/climate/climate_weather. html ('What's the Difference between Weather and Climate?')
http://www.riedel.com/
http://www.sothebys.com/en/catalogues/ecatalogue.html/2012/finest-and-rarest-wines-featuring-three-superb-continental-cellars#/r=/en/ecat.fht ml.L12706.html+r.m=/en/ecat.list.L12706.html/0/60/lotnum/asc/
http://www.trade.gov/td/ocg/wine2008.pdf ('US Wine Industry—2008', US Department of Commerce)
http://users.ox.ac.uk/~bacchus/docs/tasting_sheet.pdf
http://vintagetvseries.com/about-vintage

http://www.warpbreach.com/6/6.html ('How to Make Wine from Common Household Items')

http://www.wineaccess.com/expert/tanzer/newhome.html

http://www.wineaccess.com/expert/tanzer/ratingscale.html

http://www.wineamerica.org/newsroom/wine data center/ 2004 Winery Distribution by Size.pdf (also at: http://65.36.226.44/newsroom/wine%20data%20center/2004%20Winery%20Distribution%20by%20Size.pdf, accessed May 7, 2014).

http://www.winebiz.com.au/statistics/wineries.asp

http://www.wineinstitute.org/resources/worldstatistics/article87

http://www.winemag.com/PDFs/2011MediaKit/

http://www.winespectator.com/display/show/id/tasting-format

https://www.wtso.com/content.php?cms_id=2

# Index

# Wine and Economics